AF392878

SKIN

by

Fernando Gamboa

Translated from the Spanish
by Annie Crawford

Prologue

Hello again! It's been more than four years since I published *Redemption*, the first Nuria Badal novel. (Four years? I can't believe it.) After all this time, I could wallpaper my house with the letters I've received from readers asking me to bring Nuria back—most of which I answered with excuses or vague promises that maybe one day I would get around to it. I'd thought of *Redemption* as a stand-alone novel, not as part of a series. Besides (for those of you who remember it), I would have had a hard time coming up with a better ending for the novel—and for Nuria, considering who she was in reality and what she meant to me. If you don't know what I'm talking about, click here for a link to an article I wrote for *Zenda* where I explain it.

Basically, the fact that *Redemption* had such a beautiful ending and was so well received by readers made the idea of writing a sequel seem almost a sacrilege to me. But here we are. After publishing *The Last Revelation* (a gripping thriller featuring Ulysses Vidal) I felt like going in a slightly different direction. So I challenged myself to do something I'd never done before. I wanted to know if I was capable of writing a TRUE crime novel. Yes, in capital letters, just like that.

Obviously, *Redemption* is a crime novel. But as we all know, a leopard doesn't change its spots, and what I began as a crime novel ended up as quite a different animal once I'd infused it with humor, romance, and action. I felt it didn't qualify as a *true* crime novel. That goal still eluded me.

I'm using past tense here because I believe I can say that with *Skin,* I've finally written a book that falls squarely within the genre, a story that measures up in every way to its North American and Scandinavian counterparts.

The thing was that after I'd made up my mind to write a book like this and had the plot firmly fixed in my head, I still had to strike the right tone, choose the time period, the locale, the characters, etc. I was immersed in all this, preparing the auditions for the casting, so to speak—and Nuria Badal kept coming into my head. I kept thinking she would be the perfect protagonist for the story I had in mind.

The problem, of course, was that I didn't want to talk about what happens *after Redemption*—have I mentioned I think the ending is perfect?—so that left me with only one other option: to make my story about something that happened *before* the story I tell in *Redemption.* A long time before, actually, since *Redemption* is set in the year 2028 and the action in *Skin* takes place at the end of 2023, that is, right now as I write these lines.

What I've ended up creating is a prequel to *Redemption. Skin* is the story of a chilling case, apparently impossible to solve, that Nuria must confront shortly after joining the Criminal Investigations Division of the Mossos d'Esquadra. A case that will force her to cross red lines and that will require both you, dear reader, and Nuria herself to question certain convictions and ask yourself more than once *What would I do in her place?*

    Skin is more than a simple crime novel dealing with officers of the law, criminals, moral dilemmas, and an apparently unsolvable mystery. It will also take you to the darkest corners of your own conscience; corners you may never before have peeked into. Perhaps the most important thing once you've reached the last page isn't finding out who the murderer is . . . It's finding out who YOU really are.

    Not bad for a simple crime novel, wouldn't you agree?

    I hope you enjoy it.

The Monster

Julio Alberto Álvarez de Cortázar could feel every pore in his skin, every muscle in his body, every fiber. He sensed his own weight pressing into the comforter, the itch in his nose, the drop of sweat sliding down his forehead.

He felt it all.

But he couldn't move.

Even an involuntary movement was impossible.

He was completely paralyzed, like in those nightmares where a monster is pursuing you and you can't move.

But this was no nightmare. Though he still couldn't force himself to believe it, this was real. And the monster was standing in front of him, still holding the hypodermic syringe, watching him with the indifference of an insect collector examining a new specimen just added to the display case.

He wanted to tell his torturer he would pay whatever was wanted, he would do whatever was necessary. That he would gladly give everything, everything the person standing over him wanted, that he would hand over a blank check if that was what was needed.

All this he wanted to tell the monster in exchange for mercy, but he couldn't. His tongue and his lips were just as paralyzed as the rest of his body and he couldn't speak either. The only thing he could do was lie there as he was: powerless, naked, useless on his own bed, at the mercy of his tormentor.

That was when he saw his persecutor set the hypodermic aside. From a fanny pack the person pulled something he couldn't identify in the semidarkness of his room. A chill ran through him as he suddenly saw a glint of light flash off a sharp steel blade.

The monster's eyes rested on him. His tormentor approached slowly, at a leisurely pace, knowing he was defenseless, totally at the mercy of the other. Alberto, his gaze immovably trained straight ahead, watched from the corner of his eye as the evil creature came close, holding the razor-sharp blade in front of his eyes as if to make sure Alberto could see it clearly.

Then, leaning toward him, as casually as someone passing along a simple recipe, the monster whispered in Alberto's ear, in supreme detail, precisely what would be done to him.

Alberto felt terror engulfing him, a terror he'd never before felt, that perhaps no one else had ever felt. This couldn't be happening. It couldn't be happening to *him.*

He tried to scream, to make his body obey his orders, but not a murmur emerged from his throat. Alberto knew then that he was going to die, mute and paralyzed. He felt the wetness between his thighs, the ultimate indignity, and knew his bladder had betrayed him and he'd urinated on himself from pure fear. He was going to die smelling of piss.

His last thought before he felt the sharp steel slicing into his skin was that he wished he'd had more time to do things right, to correct his many sins; that his tormentor was wrong and that, contrary to the words Alberto had heard whispered in his ear, his destiny was not to burn in hell for all eternity.

The monster leaned over him. Horrified, Alberto felt his blood begin to flow.

1

A dagger pierces Nuria Badal's heart as she remembers the afternoon of August 17, 2017 when, mere feet from where she now sits, she'd witnessed a van driven by a terrorist mow down more than a hundred people on Las Ramblas Boulevard in Barcelona.

It's been six years and four months since, on the same corner of Pelayo Street where she now finds herself, she'd stood unmoving in the crosswalk in front of that accursed white van, suspicious of the driver's attitude. Since the day when, in spite of her instincts screaming at her that something terrible was about to happen, she'd simply stepped aside and let the van pass.

Maybe there was nothing she could have done to avoid what happened next. Maybe she could have remained standing in front of the van and found some way to alert the police. Maybe she would just have been the first to be run down, as the psychiatrist she'd seen for months afterwards had insisted again and again.

There's no way of knowing.

The fact is, she's still alive and fifteen innocent souls are dead, and she can't—nor does she want to—free herself of the guilt that will be with her for the rest of her life, the same guilt that drove her to join the Mossos d'Esquadra police force years later and become part of the Criminal Investigations Division less than two months ago. The same guilt that ultimately led her to the place where she is at this very moment: sitting in the passenger seat of an unmarked police cruiser on a frigid December morning in 2023 in almost the exact spot where she'd been standing on that hot, long-ago August afternoon.

Nuria may never find the absolution she seeks, but at least she'll try to do the right thing whenever she can. Maybe that way the nightmares will finally fade away.

Lost in these thoughts, she stares idly at the vague image reflected in the passenger-side window. A green-eyed woman approaching thirty looks back at her: angular face, blond hair pulled back into a ponytail, a nose that's a bit too large by Instagram standards, and dark circles under her eyes she doesn't even try to hide. She may never win a beauty contest but with her height and athletic build she has a hard time going unnoticed even when she tries.

With a small sigh, she turns her eyes forward again to the sleet drifting down from a leaden sky. The hypnotic oscillation of the windshield wipers from left to right sweeps it away with a plaintive groan.

This cold weather isn't normal for Barcelona, even in December at this early hour. The general consensus is that they skipped fall and went from hot, shirt-sleeve weather in November straight to hats and gloves in the space of a week. One more consequence of climate change, according to the experts. The conspiracy theorists attribute it to a plot masterminded by Bill Gates, George Soros, and the IMF, and Nuria's mother is convinced it's a punishment meted out by God. There's no shortage of theories.

Even with the heat blasting, Nuria's hands are frozen. She rubs them vigorously as the driver's side door opens and Sergeant Marcos Hidalgo climbs into the double-parked black Citroën Cactus holding a small recycled-cardboard tray containing two large white cups emblazoned with the Starbucks logo.

"Fuck, it's cold!" he protests as he slides in, holding out the tray so Nuria can take one of the steaming cups. "Next time you're going."

"Oh, stop whining," Nuria teases, taking her cup and lifting the cap to smell the contents. "Did you add cinnamon and nutmeg?"

Marcos's frown deepens as he turns toward her. Rivulets of melted slush run from his black crewcut, sliding down his face and dripping onto his down jacket. Though Nuria's partner in the CID is undeniably handsome, he looks more like a wet dog at the moment—with a mood to match.

"It's okay, no worries," Nuria hastens to reassure him before he can growl at her. "I like it this way too." Marcos mutters something through clenched teeth that she's grateful she didn't catch as he brings his steaming *café americano* to his lips.

Nuria follows suit, interlacing her long fingers around the cup of chai to warm her hands as the unmarked car's radio suddenly crackles into life. "Unit 317, headquarters here," says a woman's voice. "Do you copy?"

Nuria responds immediately, adjusting her microphone. "317 here. Go ahead, headquarters."

"Local police have reported a possible homicide at Marinada 10. How quickly can you get there?"

Before Marcos can open his mouth, Nuria presses the transmit button again. "10-4," she says, acknowledging the message. "We'll be there in ten minutes."

"Copy that, 317," the woman's voice confirms. "Over and out."

Nuria replaces the microphone on its hook, realizing Marcos is looking at her stonily. "Seriously?" he protests, pointing to the paper cup in his hand. "Ten minutes?"

"Let me drive. That way you can finish your coffee."

"You're a real pain in the ass, do you realize that, Nuria?"

"All part of my charm," she fires back with an innocent grin.

On her first day at CID, Inspector Sánchez had made them partners on the same beat, and Nuria thought they made a good team. The frequent barbs and complaints they traded had paradoxically ended up strengthening the bond of trust that was gradually growing between them.

Marcos takes a quick sip of coffee before unwillingly wedging the cup into the Cactus's cupholder and turning on the engine. "Ten minutes . . ." he grumbles once more before looking in the rearview mirror and easing into traffic.

By the time they reach the address they've been given, however, more than twenty minutes have elapsed, and that's after turning on the siren. The rain and cold have made everyone in the city decide to take the car to work and to drop off the kids at school. Consequently, the traffic in the upscale area of Barcelona in which they find themselves resembles a religious procession during Easter week in which thousands of devout worshipers of St. Mercedes Benz and St. Range Rover are in attendance.

No. 10 Marinada Street turns out to be a luxury residence surrounded by a two-meter-high adobe wall topped by a hedge. Entrance is granted by double garage doors and a smaller door, painted green. Next to the green door a young local officer is leaning against the wall waiting for them, protected from the rain by the brim of his cap and a Day-Glo-yellow slicker, both a healthier color than his face. A small pool of vomit at his feet is dissolving in the rain.

"This guy's breakfast didn't sit well," murmurs Marcos as he kills the engine.

Nuria adjusts her ponytail and pulls her black Tweety-bird baseball cap down over her blond hair. Wrapping her coat more tightly around her, she steps out of the vehicle. The contrast between the heated interior of the Cactus and the cold outside makes her shudder. She raises her eyes to the leaden sky hanging over her head and makes a face, thinking about those people who say they prefer winter to summer. She is most definitely not one of them.

"Good morning, Officer," Marcos greets the cop waiting at the door, pointedly ignoring the vomit at his feet. "CID," he adds, showing his ID badge. "What do we have?"

"Are you from the criminal division?" asks the officer, his voice unsteady.

"Criminal Investigations Division," Marcos confirms. "What happened?"

"I . . ." The officer motions doubtfully at the door. "A neighbor called it in because the dog's been barking since the night before and . . . well, I rang the bell and no one answered but the door was open, so I went in to see."

"You went in to see," Marcos repeats.

"Yes, well . . ." The young officer swallows, failing miserably in his attempt to appear calm. "I thought it might have been a B and E, and then I saw that the house door was open too."

"So you went in."

"I knocked first," the officer says, looking at Nuria in search of support.

As a rookie CID officer, professional etiquette requires Nuria to remain in the background while Marcos is talking but she shoots the distressed local cop an understanding smile.

"Okay." Marcos nods impatiently. "You knocked, you went in . . . and?"

"The poodle's paws and his muzzle were bloody," the cop continues, swallowing again. "The whole floor of the house was covered in bloody pawprints. I followed them to the bedroom and . . ." He closes his eyes and swallows yet again, looking as if he's about to vomit.

"Relax," Nuria says, laying a hand gently on his arm. "What's your name, Officer?"

"Rodríguez. Jordi Rodríguez."

"Calm down, Jordi," Nuria says soothingly. "Take a deep breath and count to five."

"I'm sorry, I . . . I've never seen anything like that." Obedient to Nuria's instructions, the young officer takes a deep breath, then, summoning all the composure and professionalism he can muster, blurts out in a rush, "A body. Male, between fifty and sixty. No one else in the house except the dog. I locked him in the kitchen. I called headquarters and left the house without touching anything. The ambulance and forensics should be on their way," he finishes. "Though with this weather . . ." he adds, pointing at the sky, but referring to the traffic the weather has inevitably caused.

"Are you sure he's dead?" asks Marcos.

The young cop blinks a couple of times before answering, as if unable to comprehend that there can be any doubt. "Jesus, yes. No doubt about it."

"Very good, Jordi," Nuria says, giving his arm a squeeze. "Anything else we should know before we go in?"

Rodríguez looks at his feet. The remains of the vomit have been almost completely washed away by the rain. Raising his eyes again, he shakes his head decisively as if trying to erase an image engraved on his retinas. "It's horrible," he says finally, his face a sudden mask of fear. "I'd never seen anything like that."

Nuria and Marcos cross the lawn under the rain, following the paving stones that lead to the front door. The house is a two-story mansion, built in a modern minimalist style with straight lines. A façade of huge windows overlooks a large square swimming pool surrounded by a manicured lawn that resembles a golf course. Beds of roses dot the huge stretch of green here and there. Also on the lawn is a wooden doghouse with the name *Dina* carved into a bas-relief bone.

"Holy shit," Marcos murmurs, stopping for a moment to admire the surroundings. "Nice digs. How much does a house like this cost?"

"In this part of Barcelona," Nuria says decisively, "not under fifteen or sixteen million."

"How do you know that?"

"I worked for a real estate agency years ago," she says with a shrug.

"I can't see you selling houses."

"I couldn't either." Nuria begins to walk again. "That's why I quit."

The large front door, glass like the rest of the façade, is standing open. Sleet has blown in, leaving a small puddle on the beech parquet of the entryway. From that point on, as the local cop has warned them, bloody pawprints lead into the house like a macabre trail of breadcrumbs.

Partially protected from the rain by the covered entryway, Nuria and Marcos peer through the large windows into the adjoining rooms but, save for the bloody pawprints, everything seems to be in order. Even the red LED lights on the alarm system control panel continue to blink as if nothing has happened.

"The lock's not forced and I don't see any broken windows anywhere," Nuria says.

"Hold on." Marcos stops her when he sees her move toward the door.

"What?"

"Look." He points at the footprints they've left on the front porch. "If we go in there without booties and caps the CSIs are going to kill us."

Nuria puts her hand into her pocket, producing with a flourish worthy of a magician a cap, a pair of latex gloves, and some disposable white cotton booties. "Is this what you're referring to?"

"Just so you know, you're really starting to get on my nerves," Marcos snorts, throwing a glance over his shoulder. "Wait here. I've got to go get mine from the car."

"Sure, I'll wait," Nuria says, crossing her arms.

Turning around, Marcos plunges into the rain again. Before he's disappeared down the walkway, Nuria has already kicked off her shoes and put on the booties over her socks. Winding her ponytail into a bun on top of her head, she slips the thin cotton cap over her hair and pulls on the gloves. Sidestepping the puddle in the entryway, heart pounding, Nuria enters the house, placing her feet carefully to avoid the pawprints. She scrutinizes her surroundings with each step, trying to memorize every detail no matter how insignificant.

The interior of the million-euro dwelling looks like something out of *Architectural Digest*. Designer lamps and chairs flank a dining table the size of a small boat. In the living room a snowy-white U-shaped sofa with gray throw pillows arranged at precise intervals face a television that takes up half the wall. A pile of magazines is arranged on the tree-stump-shaped coffee table in a perfect fan, waiting for the maid to replace them at the end of the month with new issues no one will read either.

Down a hallway on the ground floor, Nuria can hear the poodle's claws scratching at the kitchen door, accompanied by the dog's whines to be let out. She makes a mental note to call the local shelter. Right now she has more urgent matters to attend to.

Her heart knocking against her ribs with each step, almost tiptoeing, Nuria follows the trail of bloody footprints left by the local cop up the stairs. She grimaces involuntarily, thinking she wouldn't want to be in his shoes when Antonia Grau, head of forensics for the Barcelona metropolitan area, lays into him for having contaminated a crime scene. The poor man's day isn't going to be getting any better.

At the top of the stairs, an anteroom overlooking the ground floor leads into the area where the bedrooms are. An odor that makes Nuria wrinkle her nose floats in the air: a mix of urine, feces . . . and something more subtle, like the sweetish smell that emanates from a piece of meat someone has forgotten to put back into the refrigerator.

The trail of paw and footprints left by the dog and the local cop clearly indicate the way. Instinctively, Nuria's hand goes to her waistband at the back of her pants where she carries her six-shot nine millimeter short Walther PPK.

Though the house seems empty and the municipal officer was there only a few moments ago, her survival instinct and every horror movie in film history have taught Nuria that if you're a blond woman entering a dark house with bloodstains on the floor it's best to proceed with caution.

The door to the room is open, the blinds lowered. The only light filtering in comes from the ground floor. Nuria steps over the threshold and into the room.

Directly in front of her, what looks like a body with its arms outstretched is lying on a king-size bed, but with so little light it's impossible to see clearly. The stench is far stronger in the bedroom and Nuria resists the impulse to cover her nose.

Without taking her eyes off the body, she gropes unsuccessfully for a light switch on the wall. Behind her, she hears Marcos entering the house.

"Nuria?" he calls from the floor below.

"Up here!"

"Damn it, I told you to wait for me."

Instead of searching for an excuse, Nuria turns back to the wall where the accursed light switch is supposed to be. Then she sees it: a small phosphorescent square. She presses it and light floods the room. Though every detail is instantly visible, her brain is unable to process the image before her, and it's only after several seconds that the unimaginable scene assembles itself into coherence before her eyes, just as Marcos comes into the room, stopping behind her.

"My God," he mutters, horrified.

Nuria, however, is unable to utter a sound. Her breath deserts her as an uncontrollable wave of nausea rises from her stomach to her throat.

2

Antonia Grau hasn't uttered a single word for five minutes. She stands next to the bed like a statue, arms folded, taking deep drags on a Marlboro menthol she's neglected to light, ignoring the febrile activity of the CSI agents all around her as they bustle around taking samples with tweezers and setting small yellow numbered triangles here and there. Hundreds of photos are snapped, as if this were a photo op at the Oscars.

With her latex gloves, disposable booties, and protective clothing that leaves only her face visible, the head of forensics for the Barcelona metropolitan area looks like a healthcare worker during the time of COVID. Her inquisitive black eyes are fixed on the body as if expecting it to get up and give her an explanation while she drums her fingers on her forearm.

Nuria knows that under the loose protective suit there's a fifty-three-year-old woman, slender and wiry. A woman of strong character and nervous movements, direct in her speech. A good boss, according to her subordinates on the forensic team, who hates Chinese food, incompetence, and people who talk too much.

Finally she says, "Hmm," barely loud enough for Nuria to hear her. Usually, this utterance is followed by a statement, so Nuria waits patiently in silence.

She likes Antonia and Antonia likes her—she's remarked on occasion that Nuria reminds her of her daughter. If it were otherwise, it's very unlikely Nuria would be present during the CSI evidence-gathering procedure. It's a privilege many more senior members of the division haven't achieved. Antonia had often told her that Nuria, being a new hire, hadn't yet acquired the vices her colleagues had and that she was still in time to save her soul, her career, and maybe even her liver.

So there she is, standing next to the head of forensics, both of them contemplating the body that looks exactly the same as it did when Nuria first encountered it an hour before: the body of a naked man, around sixty years old, of stocky build and gray hair. He lies faceup on the bed, arms outstretched horizontally. All the skin from his lower belly to the top of his head has been removed.

Someone has skinned him like a rabbit in a butcher shop, leaving his muscles and entrails on display. The skin on his face has also been flayed, a scream of anguish frozen on his lipless mouth, his lidless eyes protruding from what remains of his face, an image it will be difficult for Nuria to forget.

The skin that's been flayed from the unlucky soul has been carelessly thrown on the foot of the bed like an old blanket, and the made bed is soaked in blood, now dry. It's even dripped onto the floor after soaking through the down comforter and the mattress. It's not hard to imagine that all five liters of blood that belonged to the poor devil are there.

All his blood except for the amount that's been used to write three numbers on the wall, the object of the forensic photographer's attention at the moment. A mark so obvious, so out of place outside of certain films and rituals it seems impossible that it's been found at the scene of a real crime committed in the twenty-first century.

Three numbers, freighted with multiple meanings, none of them good: *666*. The number of the beast.

Other members of CID are searching the house and interrogating the few neighbors. Even the grave and authoritative voice of Inspector Sánchez, head of the unit, can be heard on the ground floor, issuing orders.

As far as Nuria knows, for Sánchez to arrive at the scene of a crime so quickly is not at all usual. In fact, it's something that never happens unless a terrorist attack is suspected—which doesn't appear to be the case here—or the victim is a big fish and there may be repercussions in the media—which does appear to be the case.

"Hmm . . ." Antonia repeats, shifting her weight from one leg to the other.

Nuria had taken photos with her cell phone before the forensic team arrived, and is now going through the images one by one, enlarging them on the screen to scrutinize details that she missed the first time. "He has marks on his wrists," she murmurs, lifting her gaze from the screen to add, "He must have been tied to the headboard."

"He's also got marks on his ankles," Antonia points out in her gravelly voice. "But there's no premortem bruising, no scratches, no marks on the hands or knuckles."

"There wasn't a struggle."

"Exactly. The poor bastard had no idea what was about to happen to him. Maybe he took advantage of the fact that his wife wasn't at home to have a little party and things didn't turn out quite the way he expected them to."

Nuria turns to the other woman, surprised. "You already know who he is and that he was married?"

"The ring." Antonia points to the victim's left hand. "He took off his Rolex—it's on the night table—but not his ring. So he didn't care whether his guest, male or female, knew that he was married. What's your take?" She lifts her eyes to Nuria's.

Nuria feels as if she's back in the Mossos police academy, presenting an oral exam before the teacher. Taking a deep breath, she considers for a few seconds, then shakes her head. "I don't know," she ventures. "This doesn't feel improvised. It all seems so, I don't know . . . structured?"

"Structured?"

"There are no signs of a struggle, it wasn't a robbery, and this"—she waves her arm to take in the room—"to me looks more like a stage set than a murder scene."

The forensic pathologist observes her with interest. "Explain yourself."

Nuria takes a breath, trying to put her thoughts in order. "I have the odd impression that the murderer—or murderers—wanted to leave a message. Directed to someone."

"Do you mean because of the *666*?"

"All of it. If you want to kill or torture someone, there are certainly simpler ways to do it. This seems to me . . . I don't know. Like an act of exhibitionism."

"Interesting," Antonia muses. Nuria feels as if she's passed the exam.

"Like something staged for someone else to see," Nuria goes on. "They tied him up, they gagged him, and once he couldn't move or scream, they waited for him to bleed out and then skinned him," she concludes.

This time Antonia shakes her head. "No," she corrects her. "They tied him up, they gagged him, and then once he couldn't scream, they flayed him."

"He was alive?"

"And kicking," the other woman affirms with certainty. "There's no doubt about it based on the scarring process. During the autopsy I'll look for traces of drugs or sedatives in the organism. That could explain the fact that he allowed himself to be bound and gagged without resisting. Later they woke him up to torture him."

"They wanted him to suffer."

"Not just that," Antonia adds. "The expression on his face doesn't just indicate pain. It's one of . . ."

"Pure terror," Nuria finishes for her.

"Right," confirms the forensic pathologist. "He was so terrified he literally shit himself."

"Poor man," Nuria mutters, swallowing hard. "It must have been horrible."

"Worse than that," Antonia corrects her. "See the edges?" she asks, using a ball point pen to signal the places where the skin still clings to the body. "They tore the skin off in strips. They made subcutaneous cuts here and here"—she indicates the chest and shoulders—"and then pulled on the skin to rip it off. On the face it must have been even worse," she continues, bending down and bringing her eyes close to the mask of horror worn by the skinless apparition before her. "They did the same here, but there are ten times more nerve endings in the face than in the rest of the body, so the pain had to be indescribable. Perhaps the worst pain a human being can experience."

The bloody mask of muscle and bone that represents what's left of the face seems to confirm Antonia's words. It's impossible for Nuria to imagine the suffering implied in that monstrous torture.

"Mm-hmm," she says, trying to breathe normally.

"Come closer," Antonia urges her. "You can't see properly from there."

Nuria, aware of the privilege of receiving a master class in forensic analysis, takes a deep breath and comes cautiously closer, trying to conceal her apprehension. As she inhales, the sweetish odor of blood and dead meat that hangs heavy in the room fills her nostrils.

"Look," Antonia says, oblivious of the smell. She lifts an edge of the skin. "Here they've made a clean cut through the dermis and the subcutaneous layer of fat as if it were butter. Take a closer look," she continues, like a proud butcher showing off a cut of beef he's just received. "Whoever did this knew what he was doing."

Nuria feels the chai from earlier that morning rising rapidly up her throat. She can barely speak. "How . . ." she manages to get out, swallowing hard, "how could he have experience in doing *this*?"

"Maybe it's someone who's worked in the fur industry, or a taxidermist, or maybe a trapper from Alaska."

"A trapper from Alaska?" Nuria repeats, disconcerted.

"God only knows," Antonia says, throwing her a quick glance, a wry smile on her lips. "That's up to you to find out. I'm just the medical examiner."

As badly as she would like to, Nuria can't drag her gaze away from those lidless eyes that seem to stare at the ceiling beseeching help or the open mouth showing every tooth in a silent scream of agony.

3

The Egara Complex, headquarters of the Mossos d'Esquadra, is a collection of rectangular buildings fronted with tinted glass, arranged around a central patio the size of a soccer field. It rises soberly over the highway that runs between Sabadell and Terrassa. Anyone who misses the discreet logo—four small red squares—on the corner of one of the buildings could easily mistake it for the headquarters of some multinational tech firm.

The CID conference room is located in the southeast corner of the fourth floor of Building D, a nondescript, functional space featuring naked white walls, a drywall ceiling, and fluorescent overhead lighting. Its only concession to decor is a Catalan flag standing in one corner, a topographical map of Catalonia measuring a meter square, and an official photograph of the president of the Generalitat grinning out at the camera from his office in Sant Jaume Plaza.

Seated next to Marcos in the last row of white plastic chairs, Nuria can hear the muted murmur of the nighttime rain behind her as it drums monotonously against the large window of the conference room. The body was discovered a little over twelve hours ago, and since then, she's barely had time to eat or go to the bathroom, much less take a shower. She has to repress her desire to sniff herself, but she's quite sure she smells no better than her partner.

Also in the conference room are most of the other members of the Criminal Investigations Division. From Nuria's position she has a panoramic view of all the coiffures, differing haircuts, and varying degrees of baldness of her colleagues.

The Financial Crimes team, grouped around Deputy Inspector Martos, a small woman with a shrill voice and teeth yellowed by nicotine, occupies the first rows on the right. On her left, the members of the Property Crimes unit are clustered around Deputy Inspector Collbany with his walrus mustache, comb-over, and the cloud of cheap cologne that surrounds him like a force field.

The rest of the personnel occupying the conference room consists of a couple of bewildered-looking agents from Organized Crime and, at the back of the room, the three Personal Investigations teams, specialized in crimes against life and health. One of them is Team C, made up of Inspector Sánchez and four agents who are divided into two pairs of partners: Carla and Raúl, and Marcos and Nuria.

Nuria has never seen so many members of the division together at the same time during her short tenure in the Criminal Investigations Division, nor has she ever seen Superintendent Moncada present at the morning briefing, gravely listening to Inspector Sánchez's words.

Standing in front of the seventy-five inch TV that's currently displaying an ID-card photo of the victim, the head of the CID for the Barcelona metropolitan area is reciting in rapid-fire fashion the initial report elaborated by all the divisions.

"Julio Alberto Álvarez de Cortázar y Luengo. Sixty-seven years of age. Wife and two children. CEO of Nostrum Investment Bank."

Nuria keeps her gaze fixed on the face of the man she found lifeless hours ago, a photo that shows him with his skin still in place. It's not easy for her to reconcile the victim's terrified eyes and gaping mouth frozen in a scream of agony with the air of smug arrogance exuded by the guy on the screen: blue eyes, chiseled jawline, preternaturally smooth skin with a permanent tan from winters spent skiing in Switzerland and summers in the Maldives. His shoulder-length hair has been carefully styled by a salon charging a hundred euros an hour and his disdainful smile reveals an even row of very white teeth. In the photo, he wears a neon-bright tie over a pink shirt.

As she studies the picture, Nuria figures that the list of enemies Julio Alberto Álvarez de Cortázar y Luengo had must have been quite long. And if you included those who simply disliked him, it had to have been very, very long indeed.

"Son of Luis Alberto Álvarez, also a banker, Julio Álvarez inherited the Mediterranean Savings Bank founded by his father in 1963. The bank went under in 2010 after suspicions arose concerning questionable loans made to political parties. At the same time, tens of thousands of elderly clients were ruined by the preferred stock fraud."

Nuria recalls now how, fifteen years ago, her grandfather lost all his savings thanks to that banking fraud case and how, indirectly, the greed of bankers like Julio Álvarez had led to her father's suicide. Biting her lip, she realizes she's just joined the list of people who had a motive to desire the death of the man on the screen.

"Julio Álvarez was accused by the National High Court of misappropriation of forty-seven million euros and unfair management practices," the inspector continued reading. "For this he was condemned to five years in prison. However, after an appeal was made to the Supreme Court, his sentence was reduced to two years. Due to having no priors, he didn't serve the full two years. A year later," the inspector adds with a subtle sniff of disapproval, "he founded the Nostrum Investment Bank, which has also come under scrutiny for irregular management and money laundering."

Sánchez lifts his gaze from the text, giving them all a few seconds to process this information before continuing. "I know what many of you are thinking," he adds, his gaze traveling from face to face, "but get that out of your heads right now. We're police officers and our job is to catch the murderer, not judge the victim. Understood?" A murmur of dubious approbation was heard from the audience. "For the moment," Sánchez continued, "the initial interrogations haven't yielded much. The housekeeper had been given the day off the day before, no neighbor saw or heard anything out of the ordinary, no alarm went off, and there are no indications that the house was broken into."

Nuria raised her hand. "What about the CCTV cameras? I remember there were several in the house and garden."

"They were turned off."

"All of them?"

"Every one," Sánchez confirms. "So our first hypothesis is that the intruder was someone whose presence the victim didn't want a record of. His wife and daughter were in New York visiting the older son who lives and studies there."

"Alone at home, he turns off the cameras and gives the staff the day off . . ." someone from Property Crimes comments acidly. "To me that smells like an out-of-control party complete with hookers."

"Or a meeting he didn't want any record of," points out another officer from Financial Crimes.

"We can't rule anything out," agreed the inspector. "So, Raúl and Carla, when his wife and kids get home this afternoon," he goes on, looking at them, "you're going to go see them and find out what person they trust might have some sort of grudge against the victim. Joan and Josep," he adds, "you two go to the bank offices and talk to the people there. Let's see what they have to say. Marcos and Nuria," he finishes up, "you two look into the numbers."

It takes Nuria a second to understand that he's referring to the graffiti left at the crime scene, the three sixes painted in blood. That means finding and researching those satanist groups that are radical enough and sufficiently well-organized to commit a crime of this type—or as Marcos, at her side, in a barely audible whisper, sums it up perfectly: "We're looking for the nutjobs."

"Did you say something, Corporal?"

Marcos gives a start. Apparently his whisper had been more audible than he thought. "Nothing, Inspector," he says immediately, clearing his throat. "I was saying I was pleased with the assignment."

"I hope that's true," Sánchez grunts. "I want preliminary results this afternoon," he concludes emphatically. Beckoning toward Antonia Grau, he turns the floor over to her. "Deputy Inspector, your turn."

"Thank you, Inspector," she says formally, getting to her feet and replacing Sánchez in front of the screen. "Of the five different sets of fingerprints we found in the house," she begins without preamble, "we've identified three: one belongs to the victim, one to his young son, and the other to the housekeeper. The wife confirms that a few days earlier her sister came to visit, so it may be that one of the two remaining sets of prints we have yet to identify and which are all over the living room are hers. That leaves us with one last set to ID." She presses a key on the laptop sitting by her side on the table and a digital image of a fingerprint fills the large screen behind her. "A partial print found on the doorframe of the bedroom that doesn't appear in our database. Whoever this print belongs to is someone without a police record and, as you already know, without the first and last names of a suspect, we can't access the fingerprint records in the National Police database."

"Are there no other prints in the house?" asks Sergeant Raúl Navarro, nonplussed. "Footprints? Hairs? Fibers? Organic remains? Apparently a municipal cop, a dog, and even some CID agents accessed the crime scene before you guys arrived."

Raúl and Carla are the other set of partners in Team C. Raúl is the officer with the most seniority taking orders from Inspector Sánchez, and by far the biggest jerk, especially when it comes to Nuria, who he thinks isn't ready to be in the CID.

The fact that he'd needed to walk a beat four times as long as she had before his application to the CID was accepted he'd taken as a personal affront, and he never missed a chance to try to show her up or spread false rumors such as that she'd only been accepted into the division after granting sexual favors to some higher-up.

As her friend Susana had once told her, being the brunt of those rumors was the price she had to pay for being tall, blond, green-eyed, and attractive. The men would hate her because they couldn't sleep with her, and the women because the men wanted to sleep with her.

Antonia nods briefly at Raúl's question as if she's been expecting it. "Effectively, there were more prints in the house that we're presently comparing, and we're also screening and analyzing the fibers and DNA from the organic remains we've collected. As soon as we have the results and we've done the comparative study, very likely this afternoon, we'll get them to you," she clarifies, then adds, "What's more, the muddy footprints left by the local cop were easily excluded, and Officer Badal, whom you're obviously referring to though you didn't mention her name"—she shoots him a quick glance—"proceeded with due precautions, so the crime scene wasn't contaminated. Unless, of course, you're considering the dog as a possible homicide suspect? Is that what you meant, Sergeant Navarro?"

Nuria can't keep a small smile from appearing on her lips. Apparently she's not the only one who thinks Raúl is a dickhead.

"Anything further, Deputy Inspector?" asks Inspector Sánchez from the table. "What do we have as a cause of death?"

"Death was due to the removal of the epidermis and the ensuing loss of blood. There can be no doubt of that," Grau confirms. "But what we did find," she goes on, "was a tiny puncture wound on the victim's neck, barely visible, that caused us to broaden the focus of the blood analysis in search of drugs or medications."

Another click on the keyboard of her laptop produces an enlarged image of a lab report with two items on the list underlined in red. "This here," Antonia goes on, pointing to one of them, "indicates traces of a non-depolarizing neuromuscular blocker. Possibly vecuronium or atracurium, both derived from curare."

"Curare?" repeats Inspector Sánchez as if unsure of having heard right.

"Synthetic derivatives of curare, in effect," Antonia confirms. "They're depolarizing agents that act by blocking the ionotropic activity of the cholinergic receptors of—"

"Excuse me, doctor," Sánchez interrupts her, blinking in incredulity. "Are you telling us that a derivative of curare was injected into the victim before his skin was removed?"

"That's right."

"Couldn't that have been the cause of death?" Carla, sitting two seats away from Nuria, asks. "Isn't that what the indigenous people of the Amazon put on the tips of their arrows?"

"Actually, what they use curare for are blowgun darts," Antonia corrects her. "But in this case, the amount found in the blood was so small that no doubt it was used as a paralyzing agent to keep the subject from moving while the skin was being removed. Synthetic derivates of curare are routinely used during surgical interventions to avoid involuntary spasms on the part of the patient."

"So then, you're saying . . . they anesthetized him before flaying him?"

Antonia Grau shakes her head. "They paralyzed him," she specifies. "The subject wasn't unconscious. Actually, I would say he was totally conscious and lucid during the process."

"Holy fuck," says someone from Financial Crimes.

"Because of the adrenaline?" suggests Nuria, pointing to the screen. The number indicating the percentage of adrenaline in the blood is underlined in red.

This time Antonia nods affirmatively. "The adrenaline indicators in the sample are far higher than those that would be naturally generated, even in situations involving maximum stress. My assumption is that he was also injected with an elevated dose of adrenaline to assure that he continued to be awake during the entire procedure. They wanted him to be conscious while they tore the skin off him," Antonia concludes, addressing her remarks to Inspector Sánchez and Superintendent Moncada, "but not to be able to do anything to avoid it."

A somber silence spreads through the audience as the brutality of the act sinks in. "What absolute motherfuckers," someone a few rows in front of Nuria murmurs.

"Do we know anything about the weapon used in the crime?" asks Sánchez.

"We've analyzed the edges of some of the cuts under the microscope and confirmed that an extremely sharp instrument was used. Possibly a scalpel."

"I see . . ." conjectures the inspector. "So, we have someone who knows how to use a scalpel," he sums up after looking through his notes, "and who has access to paralyzing substances and adrenaline." Lifting his gaze to the forensic expert, he asks, "How easy is it to obtain those things outside of a hospital?"

Antonia grimaces wryly before answering. "Easier than it should be," she confirms. "You can buy all those things on the medical and pharmacological web on the Internet with no problem. In fact, obtaining those substances on the Internet would leave less of a trail than taking them from a hospital."

"But to administer them would require a certain level of medical knowledge, wouldn't it?"

"Nothing you couldn't learn from a YouTube tutorial," Antonia says. "If you're thinking the murderer was a medical student, I'm telling you that doesn't necessarily have to be the case."

"Not even to flay someone without killing him?"

"They just yanked it off," Antonia clarifies. "All they did was make incisions and pull the skin up. The agony could have lasted for hours. I can assure you it wasn't pretty."

Inspector Sánchez closes his eyes and takes a deep breath. From the face he makes, Nuria hypothesizes that he's suffering from a stomach ulcer.

"Anything else, Deputy Inspector?" inquires Superintendent Moncada, taking over. The dark circles under his eyes rival Sánchez's.

"That's all for now, Superintendent."

"Very well. Thank you very much, Antonia." The forensic pathologist takes her seat as Moncada stands. Directing himself to Deputy Inspector Collbany, he says, "I want everyone from Property Crimes that's available to compile a list of properties, heirs, life insurance policies, and beneficiaries. Turning to Deputy Inspector Martos, he goes on. "Financial Crimes, I want you investigating his accounts and transactions for the last six months. Organized Crime," he concludes, "look for any skeletons in the closet and their potential links to the money-laundering networks, in case he'd decided to continue in the business. I want to know if he had an unpaid traffic ticket, if he was having it off with the maid, if he recycled his trash. Have I made myself clear?"

Superintendent Moncada, a hard-bitten former member of the Civil Guard, was old-school, with his mustache that had gone gray and one foot already in retirement. He surveys the conference room, scrutinizing the faces of the CID team, his gaze lingering a second longer on Nuria's. For a moment she's seized by the fear that he might make her go to the blackboard to explain the lesson like when she was at the police academy.

Obviously, no one makes a peep.

"Great. I want a detailed report including everything we've got by noon tomorrow," he orders. "And by six tomorrow evening, a list of possible suspects. You need to explore all the possibilities, from a simple robbery to a settling of scores. A financial crime, a crime of passion, even something that might be related to the three sixes. Leave no stone unturned and no loose ends—but do it with tact and discretion." Moncada's eyes come to rest again on Nuria's in what seems to her like a subtle warning. "As soon as details of this start to leak to the press this is going to turn into a media circus. That means I'm going to be getting a lot of pressure from the higher-ups, which means I'll be pressuring Inspector Sánchez, who will in turn be pressuring all of you." He pauses before repeating his question. "Am I making myself clear?"

Nuria knows perfectly well that the word *pressuring* is a euphemism for grabbing them by the balls or the ovaries, depending on the case, and squeezing harder and harder until the case is solved.

A wave of more-or-less convincing nods runs through the room.

"Very well," affirms the superintendent with a decisive clap of his hands. "Go home now and get some sleep—and take a shower. God knows you all need one." A guilty titter runs through the room. "I want the murderer in front of a judge in under seventy-two hours, and since you're the best in the business, I know we can do it," he asserts, sweeping the room with his gaze one more time. "Don't let me down."

After this last pronouncement, he turns and walks out of the conference room with Inspector Sánchez at his heels.

Nuria may still be a rookie in the CID, but even with her limited experience, it's very clear to her that unless the killer decides to turn himself in, there's not a snowball's chance in hell they're going to catch him in under three days.

4

The headlights of the red Volkswagen Polo blink when Nuria presses the button on her key fob. She's left her umbrella in the car, so by the time she's run the hundred meters from the main building to her parking place, she's soaked from head to toe.

Opening the door, she tosses her backpack into the passenger seat and drops into the driver's seat with a sigh of relief. It's been a tough, endless day, but finally her work is done, at least until eight the next morning. She turns the key in the ignition and cranks up the heater, her thoughts automatically going to the long shower she's going to luxuriate in, the pad thai she's going to order in for dinner, the glass of wine she's—

A knock at her window yanks her rudely out of her daydream. Peering out the window, she sees Marcos on the other side of the glass, revolving his finger as a sign that she should roll it down. Restraining a grimace of irritation, she reluctantly leaves her fantasy behind and opens the window.

"One for the road?" asks her partner, seemingly oblivious of the freezing rain that's drenching him.

"I'm dead," Nuria protests.

"I know, I am too, but I thought maybe it wasn't a good idea for you to go to sleep with everything that went down today still running through your head."

"I'm fine, thanks."

"You say that now, but when you get home—"

"Seriously, I'm fine. All I want is to take a shower and pass out in my bed."

Marcos ruminates over this response, wondering if he should keep pressing the point. Finally he sighs. "Okay, fine. I'm just warning you from my own experience. A couple of beers with friends can save you a bundle on sessions with a shrink in the long run."

"I know. Thanks. Another day."

"Sure." He slaps the roof of the car and gives her a smile that's a little forced. "Get some rest. See you tomorrow."

"Tomorrow," Nuria says, starting to roll the window up before Marcos has even had time to turn around. She sits for a moment watching her partner's retreating back, wondering if she should have accepted his offer. Nuria knows, though, that it wouldn't just be a beer and that one way or another, they would end up sleeping together again.

It had happened two weeks ago, after the going-away party of a deputy inspector at which she'd consumed more alcohol than she could remember ever having drunk before. Work relationships were frowned on in the division and they

26

usually ended with a transfer or, if you were lucky, a new partner. Neither of them wants either of these outcomes, each for their own reasons: Nuria because she's a total newbie at the CID and it wouldn't exactly make a good first impression, and Marcos because he's in the middle of a nasty divorce and doesn't want to give his ex's lawyer any more ammunition, especially since her main accusation is serial infidelity on his part. For this reason, they've already agreed not to revisit what happened or give it any more importance than a sort of on-the-job accident fueled by alcohol.

Although if she's going to be honest, she did enjoy it.

The general consensus among the occupants of the women's locker room is that Marcos is hot, and even though her memories of that night are a bit fuzzy, she does remember that she had a couple of good orgasms that, taking the necessary precautions, she wouldn't mind repeating sometime.

But not today. Nor anytime soon.

Should anyone find out, the label of "easy" would be engraved indelibly on the collective imagination of the team and, from that day on, she knew she would lose at least part of her colleagues' and superiors' respect, even if she were to move to another department or even out of the area. A stigma that Marcos, naturally, wouldn't suffer—quite the contrary, he would become the object of complicit winks and pats on the back.

It's fucked up. Unjust, chauvinistic, and antiquated. But for the moment, the only thing she can do is accept it and adapt to her circumstances. There will be time to fight it, when the right moment comes.

But now is not that moment. Now all she wants is to get home as soon as possible.

Thanks to the lateness of the hour and the inclement weather, the traffic heading into Barcelona is moving quickly enough, in spite of the rain, that she'll be able to make it home in under half an hour. The clock on her dash reads *23:21* and Nuria sends up a silent prayer that the restaurant kitchen is open until midnight. Her plan, which consists of a shower, pad thai, wine, and Netflix won't be nearly as pleasant if she's reduced to opening a can of beans from the supermarket.

On the radio, the usual late-night talk-show hosts are chattering on about the ten million sub-Saharan immigrants advancing in caravans from Mali and Mauritania to Morocco; the nth clash between the Russians and the Ukrainians, and the latest virus that's popped up in China because someone again put some questionable critter in his soup.

Same old, same old. Nothing new under the sun.

The 2020s were turning out to be quite entertaining, Nuria had to admit. As her grandpa Pepe had said to her a few days ago, "All that's missing for bingo is an invasion of aliens from outer space and a meteorite." All Nuria's hoping is that she won't have to start wearing a fucking mask again because some Chinese person feels like eating bats.

The infotainment screen in her car lights up, announcing a call. *Mom*, reads the screen. Nuria's index finger hovers between the red circle and the green until, with a brief sigh, she presses the one she would prefer not to but knows she should.

"Hi, Mom."

"Hi sweetie. How are you? I hope I didn't wake you," her mother says.

"No, no worries, I'm driving home."

"This late?"

"Today has been a very long day," Nuria retorts.

"Is it because of that banker who was murdered? Have they assigned that case to you?"

"You know I can't talk about that, Mom."

"Okay, okay . . . Sorry. It's just that I haven't seen you for so long and since you haven't been returning my calls I got a little worried. Knowing the kind of people you deal with . . ."

"I'm fine, Mom. Don't worry, it's just because I'm so busy."

Even though it's true, Nuria feels guilty for the excuse. She's had plenty of opportunities to talk to her mother if she'd wanted to.

"Of course, I know." There's a pause. Nuria knows exactly what her mother is going to say before her voice sounds over the speaker again. "When are you coming to see me?"

There's the guilt, coming at her again.

"I don't know, Mom," she says, barely able to disguise the annoyance she feels. "I just told you I'm really busy. Maybe next week."

"That's what you said last week. You haven't come by for over a month."

Shit, has it really been a month? "Work, you know," she babbles unconvincingly.

"If the rest of the police worked as hard as you do, there would be no criminals left in Barcelona, Nurieta."

"And if there were no criminals left, I wouldn't have a job," Nuria snaps. "Are you doing okay?" she adds in an attempt to change the subject.

"Fine," her mother says, her tone adding *more or less.* "I went to the oncologist for a checkup on Tuesday and this afternoon a friend and I went to a meeting of our Christian support group."

Nuria counts to three under her breath before responding. "Okay . . . Be careful with those people, you know."

"They're good people," her mother immediately replies. "The Reborn are only looking to help. They're not one of those weird sects, they're just good Christians. You really should come with me one day so you can meet them."

"You already know my opinion about religion, Mom."

"That doesn't matter. I'm sure it would do you good, even if it just gives you the chance to disconnect from that world of yours, all police and criminals. So you can see that good people who help others without self-interest do exist."

"I'm surrounded every day by people who are *actually* helping others." Nuria emphasizes her words a little more than necessary. "It's the healthcare workers, the cops, the firemen who are really helping others, not a bunch of fanatics praying and lighting candles." She realizes instantly that she's venting to her mother again.

The death of her father had sent the two of them in opposite directions in many ways, especially those related to religious beliefs. While her mom had thrown herself into the arms of religion in search of answers and relief from her pain, Nuria had turned her back on her mother's god and his earthly representatives. Every time one of the two came up in conversation, she had to bite her tongue to keep from expressing her disdain for a being who was supposedly loving and all-powerful but who had failed her in such a terrible way.

Even so, she shouldn't take it out on her mother. It's totally unfair. "I'm sorry, Mom," she apologizes. "It's been a really tough day and I'm worn out."

Her mother's response is a few seconds in coming. "Don't worry, Nurieta . . . It's okay."

"I promise I'll come by the house next week."

"Okay, just let me know when you can come. I won't bother you any more."

"You're not bothering me, Mom. It's just that—" She has no idea what to say except to excuse herself again. "I'll see you next week."

"Okay, fine. Good night, dear."

"Good night, Mom."

The call signal on the screen goes out, leaving her once more with the familiar feeling of guilt.

In the end it takes her fewer than thirty minutes to reach Gracia, leave the car in the parking lot, and make it to the Thai restaurant before they close the kitchen.

The Christmas lights that decorate the narrow walking streets of the neighborhood are reflected in the puddles on the ground, and the driving rain has given way to a thin drizzle that makes her umbrella unnecessary. So in spite of the cold, her exhaustion, and her mood, the flashes of vivid color, the fragrance of cilantro wafting from the pad thai she's carrying, and the prospect of a long, hot shower bring a happy smile to her lips.

No sooner has she opened the door to her flat on Verdi Street than Melón appears, meowing and rubbing against her leg, loudly demanding his dinner.

"It's coming . . . it's coming," Nuria assures him as she enters the apartment and deposits the Thai food, her keys, and her bag on the coffee table. "Sorry, the day got a little complicated," she apologizes to the feline as she takes a can of chicken-flavored cat food from the pantry and dumps it into Melón's plastic bowl.

The cat doesn't stop yowling until Nuria sets the bowl with its gelatinous contents down in front of him. Wrinkling her nose, she wonders what that mess actually has in it instead of chicken. She strokes his black-and-white fur, bringing a purr of pleasure from him while he wolfs down his dinner, barely stopping to chew.

"You're going to get indigestion if you eat that fast," she chides him, but Melón pays no attention. "Anyway, I'm going to take a shower. Meanwhile, be thinking about what you feel like watching on TV."

Nuria begins to shed her clothes as she walks toward the shower. By the time she closes the bathroom door behind her all she's got on is her black sports bra and a pair of large white underwear that look like they were passed down to her by her grandmother but which nonetheless are extremely comfortable. One of the advantages of winter.

"What a babe," she tells herself with a wry smile as she glances in the mirror. Bringing her face closer to her reflection, she observes her bloodshot eyes and look of weariness. Her hair's a mess when she pulls the elastic band from her ponytail and her cheekbones seem more prominent than usual.

Doubtless she's lost some weight lately, basically by eating little and not very well. She makes a mental note to improve her diet while she pulls off her underwear. Turning on the hot water full force, she climbs into the shower and closes her eyes while she enjoys the light sting of the water against her skin and the steam that envelops her like a Turkish sauna.

"Fuck, this feels good." Right now she's glad she turned down Marcos's invitation. Alcohol and sex are fine, but on days like this, the combination of a hot shower, cozy blankets, and Netflix is unbeatable. The thought amuses her and she wonders for a moment whether if George Clooney were to appear at her door wearing a smoking jacket and holding a cup of Nespresso in his hand she would ask him to come back some other day.

Loving the delicious sensation of the rivulets of water coursing down her skin, Nuria imagines them carrying with them all the awfulness she's seen, touched, and smelled that day. She visualizes every single molecule of the horror she witnessed going down the drain, never to return.

Despite her efforts, the image of the wretched man mired in his own blood, stinking of feces, urine, and the beginnings of decomposition force their way into her memory. Worse yet, the image of the flayed body and those imploring eyes is one that will take her a very long time to forget.

Nodding decisively, Nuria congratulates herself for having held up under the horrific sight. She summons to her mind the words of her more seasoned colleagues who have assured her that witnessing a scene as brutal as that is something that at most only happens once during a cop's career. So, statistically speaking, she thinks with relief, it's extremely unlikely she'll be subjected to a scene like that again in her lifetime.

Unfortunately, it won't take long for her to discover just how wrong she is.

5

At the same precise instant that Nuria is thinking these thoughts, an adolescent girl with long, jet-black hair framing jade-green eyes inherited from her grandmother contemplates her slender body in the full-length mirror, clad only in her underwear. She poses, imitating the models she's seen so many times on TV and in magazines.

Cupping her hands under her breasts, Laura's expression reflects dissatisfaction when they refuse to stand out quite as pertly as she'd like them to. Not that they're bad at all, according to Paula. But then Paula's already a thirty-eight B at fourteen, and it's easy to console someone else when that's the case.

She could buy a Wonderbra and solve the problem, at least when it came to the upcoming end-of-term party—but those bras are super pricy and with her allowance she wouldn't even be able to pay for one on time.

If only she had a job, even just a weekend job. But her mom is immovable on that score: right now she needs to focus exclusively on her studies and not waste time working or dating. This isn't easy, since the number of guys that invite her out is surprisingly large. She's even been asked out by some really hot twenty-somethings with motorcycles and everything. No, it's definitely not easy to resist, not at all.

She has time, so she opens the drawer of her bedside table and takes out the Canon camera she received as a gift a while ago. After checking to see that the battery's still good, she starts to assume various poses and take pictures. First with her underwear on and then trying on several outfits and dresses, including the red satin she's thinking of wearing to graduation. She's not going to fill it out, though, unless her boobs start growing, like, yesterday.

After a long hour trying on clothes, she connects the camera to her computer and downloads the photos so she can see them on a bigger screen. There are a few really tacky ones where she looks like a cheap whore, she thinks, making a face. Especially the ones where she's half-dressed and wearing too much lipstick. But there are others where she looks like a sophisticated woman, several years older than she is, posing at some photo op at an awards ceremony or something. Studying herself on the screen, she thinks that with the right lighting and a professional makeup job, she wouldn't look out of place at all on the cover of *Elle* or *Vogue*.

Some of them, the best ones, she texts to Paula, who instantly responds admiringly in all caps: OMG, YOU LOOK SUPER HOT!! THE RED ONE LOOKS AMAZING! MARIO'S GOING TO HAVE A FUCKING HEART ATTACK WHEN HE SEES YOU!

Mario Rochina was probably the hottest boy she'd ever seen He looked like an actor from Hollywood with his shoulder-length hair, his chiseled jaw, and the black leather jacket he wore when he was riding his motorcycle. He was twenty-one, and when he wasn't working out at the gym he was studying to be a plastic surgeon, which in Paula's eyes, made him the most ideal catch any woman could possibly want.

I told you Mario's not my type, Laura texts her back.

Well, Alberto told me Mario told him he wants to hit on you.

For a second Laura doesn't know what to say. Finally she types, *Did he seriously say that?*

I swear, Paula assures her. *You should fuck him.*

Get out. You're such a dumbass, Laura texts back as a smile curves her lips.

Come on. Don't try to play the virginal little princess with me. I know what happened between you and Óscar at his birthday party.

I was drunk that day, you already know that.

Still counts, Paula texts back with a winky-face. *Are you going to post those pics or not?*

I wasn't planning to.

Do it. You look super hot.

My parents wouldn't exactly appreciate it, Laura objects.

Who's gonna tell them?

I don't know . . . I'm kind of embarrassed.

Embarrassed? What are you talking about? Why should you be embarrassed if you look so gorgeous in those pics?

You really think so?

If you don't upload them, I will.

Okay, okay . . . I'll post a few of them, though I'm not sure it's a good idea.

It is, you'll see. Maybe you'll even be discovered by a modeling agency.

Shut up, Laura types back, though she's secretly thinking the same thing.

Gotta go, my folks just got home, Paula texts abruptly. *See you in class tomorrow.*

See ya!

Laura signs off and, after briefly debating with herself, posts the least explicit of the photos. She just hopes her parents don't somehow find out because she would have a lot of explaining to do.

6

It's not even seven-fifteen the next morning when Nuria gets out of her car after parking in the Egara Central Complex lot and heads for the CID offices. Though the sky is beginning to lighten in the east, it's still nowhere near sunrise. With this interminable storm, the sun won't be peeking through the dense gray clouds any time today either.

She hadn't slept well. In spite of the shower, the couch, and the sleep-inducing show she'd watched, she'd finally been forced to take a Valium to fall asleep. The app on her phone told her she'd only slept a little more than four hours and had only gotten twenty minutes of deep sleep. Even so, when the alarm had gone off, she'd jumped out of bed like a spring. After a double espresso that made her miss Clooney and his Nespresso and an invigorating shower, she'd left the house with her toast still clenched between her teeth. Melón had shot her a warning look, seemingly reminding her telepathically that his dinnertime was at five p.m.

As she strides through the corridors of Building D, Nuria greets the agents who are finishing their night shifts and are no longer surprised to see her arriving so early. From her very first day, she'd made it a habit to be the first of the team to arrive and the last to leave. Nuria told herself it was a healthy habit that gave her a jump on the others when starting the day and made a good impression on her superiors and colleagues into the bargain, especially since she was the rookie on the team. In her heart of hearts, though, she knows the real reason is that she has nothing better to do. Everyone else in the CID has a partner, a lover, or at least a hobby that impels them to take advantage of every possible second somewhere else that isn't work. She has nothing like that.

This is the sad truth that makes her arrive a half-hour before her workday is supposed to start, and though she's aware of this somewhere deep inside her, she prefers to attribute her eager-beaver behavior to her devotion to the job and her true professionalism.

We all have the right to lie a little to ourselves in our efforts to be happy.

"Good morning, Officer Badal."

Used to not finding anyone from her team on the premises at this hour, Nuria jumps when she opens the door and runs into a greeting. Even more so, since this greeting comes from the mouth of Inspector Sánchez, who is sitting at his desk studying the screen of his laptop, his face grave.

"Uh . . . Good morning, Inspector."

"How are you?" he asks, looking at her over his reading glasses as his somber expression relaxes a little. "Did you sleep well?"

"Um . . . Yes, very well, thank you," she lies, hoping her makeup covers the dark circles she woke up with this morning.

Sánchez studies her in silence for a couple of seconds. "We've all been through it at some point, Nuria," he says finally, his tone verging on the paternal. "Don't forget we have a psychological support team. You won't get a demerit if you decide to pay them a visit."

So the makeup hasn't worked. "I'm fine. Thank you, Inspector."

Sánchez pauses briefly again, evaluating her. Then he asks, "Do you know anything about this?" He turns the laptop around.

On the screen, beneath a headline that screams *EXCLUSIVE!! Satanic sect murders banker!* in enormous italic type appears a photo taken at the scene of the crime of the three sixes carved into the dead man's forehead.

"Shit," she murmurs, moving her eyes closer to the screen in incredulity. "But how—"

"That's what I'd like to know," Sánchez grunts. "Whenever I catch whoever leaked that photo to those vultures over at the *Daily Extra,* he's going to wish he'd never joined the force."

"So you think it was one of ours?"

Sánchez blinks a couple of times, confused. "Who else? No one else was allowed into the crime scene except for us and the coroner to remove the body."

"Well . . . actually, there was someone else."

It takes the inspector a moment to understand what she's saying. "Are you suggesting the murderer himself took the photo and later sold it to the paper?"

"Why not?"

Sánchez shakes his head as if trying to drive the possibility from his brain. "Because we'd better just hope that's not the case," he says. "I don't even want to imagine the consequences." He exhales noisily, turning the screen around to face him again. "You and Marcos, prepare yourselves for the shit show that's about to rain down on you," he adds, gesturing toward the corner where she and her partner have their desks. "Every nutjob in the country's going to be on the phone to you denouncing all the Satanic sects that eat children for breakfast."

Nuria turns to look at her desk, eyeing the phone like a poisonous toad. "Oh, damn," she says suddenly, only then remembering that she and Marcos have been assigned to investigate those three legendary numbers.

Several hours later, Nuria peeks at Marcos from the corner of her eye. He's sitting at his desk doodling in his notebook while attending to the thousandth call he's received this morning.

"No, ma'am . . . Yes, of course . . ." Her CID partner adds the finishing touches to a devil with horns and a trident he's just drawn with his ballpoint pen. "Uh-huh, yes, ma'am, I'm taking it down. The neighbor across the street . . . yes, he has a black cat . . . oh, two black cats . . . I see." He sighs quietly, closing his eyes. "Thank you very much, ma'am. We'll be in contact if we need any additional information. Have a good day." Nuria can still hear the tinny voice of the woman coming through the receiver as Marcos replaces it in its cradle.

"Sixteen," he announces, drawing a new line in the corner of his notebook.

"I've got twenty-two so far," Nuria says, showing him her own row of vertical marks. "Stop whining."

"Yes, but you're the new girl," Marcos challenges her with a wink. "You should be doing all this by yourself."

"And deprive you of the pleasure of socializing with random loonytunes? Besides, that wouldn't have left me time to—" Nuria breaks off to stare at her computer screen where a new message has just arrived in her inbox. "Whoa. What's this?"

"What is it?"

"Did you give my email to anyone?"

"Of course not," Marcos said. "Why? Did someone write you?"

"To my personal email," Nuria clarifies, shaken. She turns her screen around to show Marcos. It's an email with *666* in the subject line.

"Does the sender sound familiar to you?" he asks.

"It's one of those temporary accounts that disappear in ten minutes," Nuria says, pointing to the line of senseless letters at the top of the email: *qjoahezmjbjusxxaoh@tmmbt.net*. "But how could he have found out my personal email address?"

"Surfing the web you can find out anything and everything. You know that." Marcos waves a hand, dismissing her concern. "Open it. Let's see what it says."

Still puzzling over the fact that some stranger knows her personal email address, Nuria clicks on the icon. The message consists of one simple line of text: *If you're looking for the devil, find the Sons of Lucifer.*

"Another fucking nutjob," Marcos says with a dismissive snort. He turns back to his work.

Nuria, nonetheless, can't shake the unsettled feeling the fact that a stranger has her personal email, knows she's a member of the CID, and knows she's participating in the investigation has given her. Of course the number of agents assigned to the division is small, and when she'd joined it had been announced in the Mossos official newsletter, that was true. Even so, seeing her name on the email sends a chill of anxiety through her.

She slides the cursor toward the trash can icon, but as she's hovering over it, something tells her not to erase it. Instead, she opens Google and types in *Sons of Lucifer*.

Skimming over the responses from Wikipedia, Amazon, Facebook, and a TV series, she sees at the bottom of the page an entry for a non-profit located in Barcelona with the very same name: *Sons of Lucifer*.

"Hmm," she murmurs, clicking on the link. It takes her to an austere page topped by a symbol that reminds her of a chalice with an *X* in the middle of it. That's all, no angels in flames, no horned demons—nothing even remotely satanic.

Of course, with that name, it's unlikely this could be a charity collecting children's toys, so Nuria begins to read. Clicking on the corporate name, she sees that the organization is registered as a cultural association, which is why it didn't appear in the list of religious entities and sects they'd downloaded.

This isn't exactly a clue but she has to admit that, aside from this, all they've come up with so far has been gossip, fake news, or simple exaggerations in attention-seeking blogs of dubious credibility.

The reality is that during the last decade there's been no evidence in Barcelona or even Spain as a whole of ritual assassinations related to satanic or other similar sects. Beyond the occasional chicken decapitated in a cemetery or pot being substituted for incense in censers—she'd had to admit that was funny—or the theft of consecrated wine from some parish or other, satanic activity in Spain has tended to run more along philosophical or even playful lines. There have even been parties organized in clubs where people dressed in costume and the venues were full of candles. Certainly nothing that could lead to the flaying of a banker.

The site informs Nuria that the head office of the Sons of Lucifer is located on Montcada de Barcelona Street, in the Borne neighborhood, very close to the Picasso Museum.

They could be there in under thirty minutes.

Anything's preferable to continuing to sit there taking calls from the current shift of wackos.

7

One of the perks of being a cop is that you can park pretty much anywhere you feel like it, so Nuria and Marcos are able to drive right into the heart of the Borne neighborhood with its narrow medieval streets and leave their cruiser in a no-parking zone. From there they walk the twenty meters that separate them from the address Nuria's taken from the group's website.

"This is it," she says, stopping in front of an enormous set of wooden double doors at least four meters high.

The narrow walking street, still damp from last night's downpour, is practically deserted and looks very different than it does in the summer when it's thronged with cruise passengers lining up outside the Picasso Museum and crowding into the fashionable restaurants. Truth be told, the entire city is different when it's not tourist season, much quieter, more serene, a bit melancholy.

Lifting her gaze, Nuria sees that they're standing in front of what must have been an ancient three-story medieval palazzo. Some of its original painted designs are still well preserved and can be seen on the façade. There are many buildings like this in the historical center of Barcelona, their worn gray stone camouflaged among a multitude of other more modest dwellings erected later in the narrow lanes of the Borne or Gothic districts.

"Are you sure?" asks Marcos, studying the façade. "I don't see any satanic symbols or anything like that."

"You mean like a plaque saying *Welcome to hell* or something along those lines?"

"Yeah," admits Marcos. "Well, let's see if anyone in hell keeps regular office hours." There's no bell in evidence, so he lifts the heavy iron knocker and knocks loudly a couple of times. In the silence of the street it sounds like the tolling of a bell.

After thirty seconds with no response, he knocks again. This time a distant voice answers almost immediately, "Just a minute, please!"

Moments later, they hear the sound of a bolt being drawn back and then the scraping of metal as a small door at eye level is opened. Nuria sees a man's face with thick eyebrows and an inquisitive expression.

"Good morning, how can I help you?"

"Police," Marcos announces without preamble, holding his badge up to the small window. "May we come in?"

"Police?" repeats the man, his incredulous gaze going from Nuria's face to Marcos's. "What's going on?"

"We'd like to ask you some questions."

"Questions?" the man repeats, more confused than ever. "About what? What's happened?"

"If you'll allow us to come in, we can explain the matter to you without the rest of the neighborhood listening in on our business," Nuria intervenes.

The man hesitates for a moment. When he abruptly closes the peephole door without a word, Nuria thinks he's slammed the door in their faces, but almost immediately they hear more bolts being drawn back. This time, without sound effects, a human-size door opens in the giant double doors of the entrance. Nuria can't help thinking that this is like the matryoshka of doors: doors within doors within a much bigger door.

To her surprise, the man who stands before them in the middle of an elegant patio filled with rosebushes is impeccably turned out in a black morning coat over a white shirt complete with bowtie, gray slacks, and white gloves: a textbook example of a butler.

"How may I help you?"

Marcos, who's as surprised as Nuria, takes a couple of seconds to respond. "Could we please speak to your . . ."—for an instant Nuria's afraid he might say "master"—"boss?"

"Mr. Monells? May I ask why? He's busy at the moment."

"According to our information," Nuria cuts in, bored with all the preamble, "this is the main office of a sect called the Sons of Lucifer. Is that correct?"

"Cultural association," the butler corrects her.

"Whatever. Given that this is the headquarters, do I assume correctly that Mr. Monells is a member of this organization?"

The butler appears to be ruminating a reply that's on the tip of his tongue, but finally gives in. Pointing to the floor to avoid any misunderstandings, he says, "Wait here, please. I will inform Mr. Monells that you are here."

"Thank you." Nuria flashes him a theatrical grin, not sure what's more irritating: the snooty, recalcitrant attitude of the butler or confirming with her own eyes that butlers in the service of people with too much money still exist.

The man disappears up a flight of stairs, walking with a measured pace, leaving them standing inside the door with plenty of time to admire the patio, which is draped with curtains of bougainvillea and around which the palazzo rises. Nuria knows nothing about ancient architectural styles, but the place shouts money. The kind of people who have coffee with the mayor in the morning and smoke cigars in the afternoon with the president of the Generalitat. People, in other words, with whom you need to tread carefully if you don't want to end up directing traffic in some underground parking lot.

"Careful," Marcos, whose thoughts have surely been running along the same lines, cautions her.

Nuria nods. The warning is clear.

Almost five minutes later, about the time that Nuria's begun to think they've been left standing there like idiots, the butler reappears on the stairs and motions to the door he's just emerged from.

"Mr. Monells will see you in the library," he informs them as if announcing their audience with the Pope in Rome.

"Well, isn't that nice," Marcos murmurs, making a face in Nuria's direction. "He'll see us in the library."

After mounting the stairs, they follow the supercilious butler down a wide hallway lined with windows that give onto the central patio. The hardwood floors are carpeted with rugs and on the pistachio-green walls paintings of landscapes and ships that Nuria calculates must be worth more than her yearly salary hang indifferently. She feels as out of place as if they'd been walking through the International Space Station.

At last the butler stops in front of a door and motions for them to enter. "Mr. Monells will be with you shortly," he says before closing the door behind him. The message is clear: there will be no wandering around the house on their own. All that's lacking is for him to bolt the door from the outside.

The ceilings in the library are carved, four or five meters high, and the walls, also painted a pistachio green, are almost invisible behind the proliferation of tapestries, paintings of arrogant-looking ancestors, and of course, books: hundreds of them, bound in leather with gold lettering on their spines, arranged in glass-fronted cases and bookshelves that reach to the ceiling.

In the middle of the room, resting on a Persian rug—Nuria doesn't have a clue when it comes to rugs, but she would bet it had belonged to the shah of Persia himself—a box of cigars sits on a small, round, mother-of-pearl-incrusted table flanked by a couple of wing chairs upholstered in deep red velvet and a Louis who-knows-what-number sofa that looked as uncomfortable as it was undoubtedly expensive. One of those that immediately lose half their value when you plant your proletarian ass on them.

Nuria hasn't finished taking it all in when a door at the other end of the room opens, admitting the person who is indubitably the lord and master of this palazzo. "Good morning, Officers," he greets them in a deep voice. The guy was obviously born with an easy and open smile. His hair is graying and he has just enough wrinkles to denote the dignity merited by his sixty-something years. Nothing is over the top, though. His blue eyes sparkle with an intelligence that harmonizes perfectly with his gentleman-from-another-era look. This is set off by the filigreed blue silk robe he wears that Nuria again calculates probably cost more than her entire wardrobe put together.

"I'm Jordi Monells," he introduces himself. He extends his right hand, revealing a shiny gold Rolex in the process. "Welcome to my house. How may I help you?"

"Good morning, Mr. Monells," Marcos says, shaking the hand Monells has held out to him. "I'm Sergeant Marcos Hidalgo and this is Officer Nuria Badal. We'd like to ask you some questions about the . . . association called the Sons of Lucifer. You are a member, I believe?"

"Founding member," Monells emphasizes proudly. "But please, take a seat." He indicates the two armchairs as he sits down on the small sofa. "What is it exactly you'd like to know?"

"Well . . ." Marcos begins, taking a small notebook from his pocket, "we'd like to know what you do here. What types of activities you engage in and whether you practice any sort of satanic ritual."

Nuria is disconcerted when Monells's response to this question is a brief laugh. Nodding to himself, he says, "Now I understand. You're here because of the man who was murdered yesterday, am I right?"

Well, that eliminates the surprise factor. Evidently the news has traveled like wildfire. "Did you know him?"

"The victim? No, I don't know who he was. A banker, right?"

"Julio Alberto Álvarez de Cortázar y Luengo," Marcos recites, showing him a picture of the dead man while his organs were still inside his body. "CEO of Nostrum Investment Bank."

Jordi Monells studies the photo with the pious, sorrowful look one reserves for such occasions, as if to say *What can we poor mortals do against the designs of God?* "Is it true what they're saying in the papers about his death?"

"I'm sorry," Marcos says. "We can't reveal any details about the investigation."

"Yes, yes, of course." Monells leans forward on the sofa as if his interest has suddenly been piqued by all this. "In regard to the name of the organization . . . I knew that choosing that name for it was going to result in one headache or another, but I never imagined I'd be interrogated about a murder. Forgive me," he adds, "but all of this appears to me to be a fascinating misunderstanding. In reality, though the name may seem satanic or diabolical to you, it actually has nothing to do with that— or at least very little. The Sons of Lucifer is a nonprofit organization dedicated to the diffusion of knowledge, culture, and the highest ethical values of society."

"Culture and ethical values?" Nuria intervenes with a look of puzzlement. "What does that have to do with Lucifer?"

"It's a very common misunderstanding, Officer Badal. In Latin, *Lucifer* literally means *the bringer of light.* It's the name the Romans gave to the planet Venus and it denoted wisdom. He was a god taken from the Greek god Phosphorus, son of Aurora and Cephalus. He was the bringer of a wisdom that was transmitted from the gods to the humans," he goes on, "but the first Christians with their selective fanaticism distorted the meaning of the name, identifying everything that was culture and knowledge as the work of Satan against their rigid and intolerant image of God."

"So, something like today's Islamic fundamentalists."

"Something like that," he agrees. "The early Christians adopted the name Lucifer to baptize one of their demons, and two thousand years later we're still talking about the fallen angel and all that other simplemindedness when in reality he should be remembered as the god of wisdom. That was why we chose that name for our organization, knowing there would be misunderstandings—but never imagining that one day the police would be knocking at my door."

"And in this association of yours," Marcos questions, "if it's not too much to ask, what is it that you do exactly? Read books and smoke cigars?"

A brief smile curves Jordi Monells's lips. "We also organize musical and literary evenings, we sponsor scientific investigations and talks . . . and even organize parties once in a while to shake the dust off a little. We're not quite as boring as we look."

"And rituals?" Nuria inquires. "Is there some sort of initiation rite or do you just sign up like you do at the gym?"

"It's a little more complicated than that, Officer Badal. All the members must demonstrate that they've made a contribution to humanity in some way, whether it's culturally, scientifically, or socially. Then they must pass a little exam and . . . well, participate in a short ritual, effectively."

"What sort of ritual?" Marcos asks with interest. "Like the Masons? You're Masons, right?"

"Some of our members are, Sergeant. And no, our ritual is much less pompous than the Masons'. A few candles, a couple of oaths, that's it. No sabers, compasses, or hoods in evidence."

"What about sacrifices? Do you carry out any blood rituals?"

"My God, no," replies Monells, horrified. "Most of our members are animal-rights activists and many are vegetarian. We would never kill a living being for such a purpose."

"Where is this ritual celebrated?" Nuria asks the question this time, making Monells's head swivel toward her again as if he's at a tennis match. "Here? In this house?"

"Indeed." He nods. "We've fitted out a modest space for the purpose. Would you like to see it?"

"Of course," Nuria accepts, shooting a sidelong glance at Marcos. "Why not?"

8

Jordi Monells leads the small procession, turning on the lights as he goes. They go down a set of narrow stairs off the kitchen.

"Are we going to the cellar?" Nuria asks as they continue to descend.

"It's actually the old larder that we've fitted out as the ceremony room."

"Larder?" Marcos repeats, turning to Nuria.

"Pantry," she clarifies.

"Oh, okay."

" . . . anyway," Monells continues to talk as he leads the way, "who stores food nowadays? We didn't even use it during the pandemic."

Finally they stop before an old wooden door. Monells takes an enormous iron key from the pocket of his dressing gown and opens the lock, which creaks in a way that would have been the envy of Count Dracula.

He stands to one side and turns on the light. Before the eyes of the two cops, a space of about sixty meters squared is illuminated. The walls are bare rock and a couple dozen antique chairs are arrayed in front of a large table of worm-eaten wood that looks like it serves as an altar. At the far end of the room, surrounded by unlit torches, they see the same strange symbol they've seen on the group's web page, painted in red on a wooden panel.

The room's furnishings are a bit underwhelming, reminding Nuria of the time her father took her as a child to see some movie sets. What on the screen had awed her as impressive backdrops turned out by the light of day to be made of papier-mâché held together with boards and scaffolding.

"In the dark, with the candles and torches lit, it looks better," Monells, who has seen Nuria's expression, offers. "I must admit that we add a bit of theater and suggestiveness to the ceremony, but the novices like a bit of mysticism. It makes the ceremony more stimulating."

"It looks like some AA meeting room to me," Marcos whispers to Nuria.

"What does the symbol mean?" she asks, pointing to the far wall.

"It's a magic symbol that represents Lucifer," Monells explains. "Its origin is unclear, but it appears to be from the fifteenth century. They say that the *V* represents the male/female duality, the *X,* power, and the inverted triangle the maternal uterus, but well,"—he waves a hand—"those are only theories and I'm no expert. For us it's more a decorative element than anything else."

"You don't use *666* for anything?" Marcos asks directly.

Jordi Monells smiles patiently. "I've already explained to you that we are not satanists. The *666* appears in a Christian interpretation of the *Book of Revelations,* and this association is cultural and intrinsically secular. So *no,*" he concludes emphatically, seeming mildly annoyed at Marcos's insistence, "we don't use the *666* for anything. May I help you with anything else?"

"Would you mind if I take a quick look?" asks Nuria, motioning toward the room. "It will just be a minute."

"Of course," Monells assents. His tone implies that the limit of his patience is now appearing on the horizon. Before that can happen and he asks them to leave— without a search warrant, of course, they can only remain at Monells's invitation— Nuria walks briskly into the room and begins to go over it methodically, looking for anything that might seem out of the ordinary to her. She doesn't actually expect to find anything, but since they're there, she prefers to waste a little time now rather than regret not having done it later.

She runs her gaze over the chairs, the table, and the low dais on which it rests. As she finishes her brief inspection, a small brown stain in the shape of a teardrop on one of the table legs catches her attention.

Turning her back to Monells and Marcos, who are talking about the increasing numbers of tourists infesting the neighborhood, Nuria extracts a pair of fingernail clippers from a small manicure kit she carries in her coat pocket. Opening the tiny knife attachment, she scratches the surface of the stain until she's obtained a sample, then stealthily puts the kit back into her pocket. To disguise her movements, she runs a hand over the surface of the table as though appreciating the fine woodwork, then stands.

"Well, that's it," she says, apparently satisfied. "Thank you very much, Mr. Monells. We appreciate your cooperation."

"My pleasure," he says with a small bow. "Did you find anything interesting?"

"Everything in this place is interesting," Nuria counters. "But not for our investigation."

"Thanks a lot," Marcos adds. "We apologize for the bother."

"I'm happy to have been able to help, it's been a pleasure." Monells gestures toward the stairs. "Ambrosio will see you out. Feel free to return whenever you wish," he says mendaciously as he takes his leave.

Nuria suspects that this isn't the only lie he's told them.

"Ambrosio," Marcos grumbles as he guides the Cactus along the C-58 on their way back to headquarters at Egara. "Bloody hell."

The sun has peeked through the clouds, illuminating with pitiless clarity the buildings of the Singerlín neighborhood, clustered along the denuded hills of Santa Coloma and overlooking the highway and the power lines. Nuria gazes out the window, waiting for Marcos to finish his rant about the privileged lives enjoyed by millionaires.

"Well," he snorts at last. "At least we got out of the office for a while. Even if we are coming back empty-handed."

"Not entirely," Nuria says, pulling the manicure kit from her pocket.

"What's that? Are you going to cut your nails now? Don't you dare leave nail clippings in my c—"

"Look," she interrupts him, showing him the brown substance clinging to the blade of the small knife along with a few shreds of wood.

"What the fuck is that?"

"I have no idea, but it was on the table in the basement. It looks like dried blood, doesn't it?"

"But . . . when did you take— Anyway, that doesn't matter. You do know that even if it is blood, without a search warrant it's not procedurally valid, right?"

"I know. But it might help us to investigate him further, no?"

Marcos takes his eyes off the highway to glance at her. "You really think that guy might have something to do with it?"

"Not really," Nuria admits. "But I don't trust people that are that squeaky clean. Don't you agree? The cleaner they seem, the better they've hidden the garbage, that's all."

Marcos looks as if he's pondering her response for a few seconds. "Could be," he says finally, evidently seduced by the idea of bedeviling Monells's perfect life a little. "Are you going to get it analyzed? Give it to Antonia and ask her to do it off the record. Then, depending on the results, we can decide how to proceed."

"Exactly what I was thinking."

Marcos glances at Nuria again and smiles.

"What?" she demands.

"Nothing. It's just that . . . you're a smart kid. I'm glad you're my partner."

Nuria tries hard to keep her expression neutral but can't keep the corners of her mouth from curling up in a smile of satisfaction. It's not every day she gets a compliment like that.

Half an hour later, Nuria dangles a small transparent plastic bag holding her nail clippers before the eyes of the forensic pathologist.

"And you say you scraped this from a table leg in a satanist ceremonial room?"

"Yes. Well . . . no. Actually, the guy says it's a cultural association. I just want to make sure he's not pulling our leg."

Antonia nods, doubtful. "Even if it is blood, the DNA might not be recognizable. It might be contaminated."

"Yes, I know. I don't care. I just want to know whether it's blood, which would mean that he lied to our faces about doing animal sacrifices."

Antonia shrugs. "That's easy enough." She takes the small bag and drops it into the pocket of her lab coat. "As you can imagine, we're up to our ears right now, but I'll pass it on to the intern. I'll do my best to have it ready for you this afternoon."

"Thanks very much, Antonia. By the way, have you guys found anything new on the body or the house?"

Antonia's expression registers annoyance. "Nothing new. Whoever did it was very careful not to leave any sort of prints. Undoubtedly he was wearing gloves. That partial print we took off the faucet in the adjoining bathroom is the only one we've got. But until you bring me some suspects to compare it to, it's useless."

"Yeah . . . of course. We're doing what we can, but we don't have anything either."

"No, Nuria," Antonia hastens to reassure her with a frown. "I wasn't insinuating anything, not at all. These things take time. I'm sure you guys are going to end up catching him."

"Let's hope so." Nuria releases a long breath. "Hopefully the other teams had better luck than we did. Thanks for everything and let me know when that's ready." She motions toward the pocket of Antonia's lab coat.

"No worries," Antonia says, turning and walking back down the corridor toward her lab.

Nuria stands motionless for a moment until a ping from the phone in her pocket startles her. It's a brief message from Marcos: *Get up here. Now.*

When she arrives at the second-floor wing of the building that houses CID, she finds Sánchez sitting on the edge of his desk, his face grave, the rest of the team huddled around him. A glimpse at the faces and body language of her colleagues is enough to tell Nuria that things aren't going well at all.

"Sorry," she apologizes in a low voice, entering the room and positioning herself as far as she can from Sánchez and his funereal expression.

"Financial and Organized Crime came up with squat," the inspector proceeds. "Tell me you guys have something. Did you talk to the family?"

"Nothing there, boss. No known enemies, no unsettled vendettas, nothing," Raúl says, consulting a small notebook. "According to his wife, the guy had reformed. Didn't even drink alcohol anymore. Listening to her, it was like she was talking about St. Paul after he fell off his horse."

"Did they say anything was missing in the house?"

"Everything was in its place . . . Well, except for, you know."

"Don't be an idiot, Raúl."

"Yes, sir." He swallows.

Carla continues. "Nothing was stolen, boss. The safe was intact. The victim's Rolex and the jewelry on the night table were still there. Nada, zip," she repeats.

"Well, it's clear this wasn't done for money," states Sánchez. "That leaves us with a score to be settled, revenge, and the nutjobs." He directs the last words of his sentence to Nuria and Marcos.

"We're following up on a clue," Nuria says hastily before Marcos can confess the crude reality. "We could have something more by this afternoon."

"Let's be sure that 'could' becomes a 'we've got it,'" he says warningly. "Understood?"

Nuria swallows and nods.

"Right. Well, I need you all to give me something by seven tonight, whatever it is as long as it's got some meat to it, that I can take to the superintendent. Got it?"

An off-key chorus of *yes sirs* and *right aways* is heard in unison and they all return to their desks with the air of having an important mission to complete.

It's just as well they don't have to learn their living as actors.

"The fingernail-clipper thing isn't a clue, for fuck's sake," Marcos whispers in Nuria's ear as they walk back to their desks. "Now we're going to have to give him something for sure."

"Well, I thought that—"

"Learn this now, Nuria," Marcos interrupts. "This is like the army: it's best to keep your head down and stay at the back of the squad. Those are the people who live to a ripe old age. Do you get me?"

"Yes, but . . ."

Marcos cuts her off again, but in a more conciliatory tone. "It's okay. Let's keep googling sects. With a bit of luck maybe we can duck out of here before seven and avoid another tirade from Sánchez."

Nuria gives in. Sitting down again, she googles *Jordi Monells.* "We'll see," she mutters under her breath.

9

It turns out that in spite of living in a palazzo in the Borne neighborhood and having a butler named Ambrosio, there isn't much information available on the Internet about Jordi Monells. The fact that he's not on social media and comes from a minuscule village in Girona rather than from a blue-blooded Barcelona family makes him almost invisible to the Google feelers. The only exception is the infrequent activities of the Sons of Lucifer, and those aren't exactly making headlines on Facebook.

All Nuria's been able to glean is that his family comes from Catalonian peasant-farmer stock whose status rose in the Baix Empordà region and that his grandfather had been drinking buddies with Salvador Dalí, no less. His mother, after divorcing his father and receiving half the family fortune, had come to Barcelona and bought the palazzo as a fixer-upper decades ago when the Borne district was still a marginal neighborhood where it was risky to venture out at night.

There's no record of the heir to the small Monells fortune engaging in any professional activity whatsoever. From this tidbit, Nuria deduces that in order to maintain the lifestyle he obviously enjoys without running through his entire inheritance, Monells must have some other unknown source of income, possibly real estate or investments. She makes a note to ask someone from Financial Crimes to sniff around a little in the Ministry of Finance.

On the Sons of Lucifer, there is nothing at all. That simple. No member list, no known social activities . . . nothing. They may not be a satanic sect, but so much secrecy raises Nuria's hackles. She can't imagine how they're able to assist in the progress of humanity and all that other bullshit Monells had spouted when almost no one is even aware of their existence. *Although*—she thinks—*that is precisely what defines a secret society, right? Everything for the people, but without taking their opinions or interests into account,* Nuria remembers from high school. She doesn't recall what it was supposed to illustrate, but she has the distinct impression that it pretty well sums up the elitist world view held by people like Monells.

The phone on her desk rings. "Yes?" she answers, wedging the receiver between her ear and her shoulder and returning her hands to the keyboard.

"Officer Badal? Campos here, from Forensics. Antonia told me to call you when I had the results for the sample."

It takes Nuria a second to remember what sample the person is talking about. "Oh, yes," she says. "What did it turn out to be?"

"Positive for hemoglobin."

"Fuck, yes! I knew it!" she exclaims, slapping the desk. "Were you able to determine what kind of animal it came from?"

"Of course," Campos responds. "The kind that has two feet and drinks coffee in the morning."

"Human? It's human blood?" asks Nuria.

"With 99.9% certainty. It could also be from an orangutan, but I don't think that's the case. Would you like a DNA study?"

"Yes!" Nuria's so excited she's almost shouting into the receiver. "Of course! I thought it was impossible. Antonia told me—"

"The blood is relatively fresh and the cell walls still haven't broken down," the forensic tech clarifies, "so we can do a pretty decent analysis for you."

"Fantastic. How long will it take?"

The tech hesitates and Nuria can almost see him checking the clock. It's already after six. "Is tomorrow okay?"

"Perfect." Nuria grins into the phone, excited by this unexpected stroke of luck. "Thanks!"

"You're welcome," Campos says in a considerably less excited tone and hangs up. Bobbing up from her chair like a jack-in-the-box, Nuria goes to talk to Marcos, who's fighting with the vending machine.

Inspector Sánchez takes off his reading glasses and waits for the pair of detectives to finish their presentation before speaking. "That doesn't mean anything. The blood could be anybody's," is his response to Nuria's enthusiasm. "Besides, taking the sample without a search warrant means we can't use it as evidence before a judge to *get* a search warrant."

"It's useful because it means Monells lied to us," Marcos claims in support of his partner's theory.

"Not really. He could have cut himself slicing ham."

"I think he's a vegetarian," Nuria blurts out before she can stop herself.

Sánchez's look eloquently expresses the sentiment that good girls should be seen and not heard.

"Boss, it's worth it to insist with that guy. He lied to us. Let us put the squeeze on him a little more."

"Don't fuck with me, Marcos. You guys don't have shit. If I go to your house with luminol and a black light, I'm sure it would look like a painting by Jackson Pollock."

"Who?" Marcos says.

"I mean you can't search a house or interrogate someone just because you found a bloodstain, for fuck's sake."

"Well, that's all we have," Nuria confesses, spreading her hands. Now it's Marcos who throws her a sidelong dirty look.

"That's not my problem. Keep on looking, damn it all. There has to be something. No one takes the time to leave the number of the beast at the scene of the crime if it's not for a reason. Find out if the victim was connected to the Sons of Lucifer or some other satanic sect."

"According to his wife," Marcos recalls, "It seems like it was just the opposite. He even went to mass on Sundays. He'd suddenly become a believer."

"Maybe he did it just for show," Nuria considers, turning to Marcos. "So that no one would suspect him—or maybe to gain access to consecrated objects. You know, sometimes two different extremes meet."

"That makes sense. If he was a satanist, what better way to disguise it than by looking like a devout Christian?"

"All right, then, see if you can follow up on that," Sánchez says, dismissing them with a wave toward their desks. "Let's see if you can get me something solid before my meeting with the superintendent." He looks at the wall clock. "You've got less than an hour."

Obviously they fail in this assignment. Nuria's glad she doesn't have to be at the meeting of Sánchez and Moncada later in the afternoon. For her and Marcos the shit won't hit the fan, at least until the next morning. But tomorrow's another day.

Right now she's at home with Melón purring in her lap and a bowl of granola with fruit and yogurt on it in her hand. In a departure from her normal routine, Nuria's watching the evening news, and the top headline on every channel is the murder of Álvarez de Cortázar. They've managed to lay their hands on half a dozen photos and there can be no doubt any longer that this was the work of the murderer, who had plenty of time to snap away after finishing his handiwork. It's clear he took his time.

Between spoonfuls, Nuria considers the implications of this fact. Why the photos? Is the guy an exhibitionist? Are they a warning? A twisted way to achieve fame? Was this the work of A) a psychopath, B) a rational and detail-oriented mind, C) a professional, or D) all of the above?

At the end of the day, though, the upshot of all those questions is the same: they're fucked. Even more fucked than they were before, if such a thing is possible. If they fielded more than a hundred calls today, tomorrow it will be a thousand.

Remembering the message in her email, Nuria checks her phone. Nothing else has arrived. Just then, her iPhone starts to vibrate in her hand, startling her, the call icon blinking with urgency. It's Marcos.

"What?" she answers, hoping he's not calling to propose going out for a drink again.

"Are you at home?"

"Yes, in my pajamas and about to go to bed," she says warningly.

"Well, get your clothes on and go to the address I'm going to send you on WhatsApp."

"Listen, Marcos. Thanks, but it's almost midnight. I don't—"

"There's another body."

"What?"

"We have another victim."

"Another victim," she repeats stupidly, trying to get her neurons to work again. "Do you mean . . . related to the other murder?"

"Looks that way."

"But how do you know—"

"I don't have any answers, Nuria. I'm on my way. I'll see you there in a half hour."

10

By the time Nuria parks on the sidewalk on Sant Antoni Abad Street, close to the Raval Theater, the entire street is choked with ambulances, police vehicles with their sirens blaring, a couple of cars with decals saying TV3 and 8TV on their sides, a dozen reporters, and a small band of looky-loos rubbernecking behind the police tape.

At the same moment she arrives, the bells in the nearby San Lázaro church ring, announcing one in the morning. Considering that it's a weekday with temperatures hovering around zero, there are more people than usual out strolling the streets and crowding the balconies. Nuria thinks that what's happening just below their windows must be much more entertaining than climbing back into bed or watching TV.

As she's showing her ID to a local cop, Nuria spies the white Mercedes Vito belonging to the forensic department among the clutter of vehicles jamming the street. Either the forensic techs made it over here in double time or Nuria was the last one to be called.

In the lobby of the theater she shows her ID again, this time to a Mosso d'Esquadra officer who looks like he's taking tickets. Glimpsing herself in the mirrored entryway to the lobby, she almost gives a start of fright when she sees her unbrushed hair pulled back with an elastic band into an improvised bun. She should have looked in the mirror before leaving the house.

Luckily, from that point on, she's required to have a cap on, so she pulls it out of her pocket together with her gloves and disposable booties. Putting on the gear, she goes through the main door into the theater.

For the second time in two days she's rooted to the spot, paralyzed, unable to fully grasp what she's seeing in front of her. From where she stands at the back of the theater, next to the last row of seats upholstered in red fabric, her bewildered gaze contemplates what seems to be a scene from a bizarre play.

In front of the red velvet curtain, a dozen forensic techs in protective jumpsuits and several CID officers are swarming around on the stage, giving nervous orders between camera flashes going off. It's like one of those surrealist plays that even the guy who wrote it doesn't understand.

Above them all, illuminated by the stage lights as if representing an alternative version of the passion of Christ, a flayed man hangs head down, suspended by his feet. His hands and head hang inertly a couple of meters above the surface of the stage, bringing the vivid image into Nuria's mind of a skinned cow hanging from the ceiling of a slaughterhouse. In addition to this, without skin or muscles to hold them in place, several meters of intestines have fallen out of the body and lie in a heap on the floor beneath.

If at the house of the first victim Nuria had felt paralyzed by nausea and surprise, here she's frozen in place by the careful staging of the murder and its obvious brutality. Only in a certain type of film would one ever see something like this, and it was certainly not something she'd expected to see that night while sitting at home eating her bowl of yogurt and fruit, that right now is trying to make its way back up her esophagus.

"Nuria!" A tall, slender figure encased in a protective jumpsuit calls to her from the stage, beckoning her nearer. She recognizes Assistant Inspector Antonia Grau.

Awakening from her trance, she begins to walk toward the scene of the crime, her steps halting. It's hard for her to take in the brutality of the scene. As hard as it is to countenance the apparent indifference of the officers who move around the scene, leaving small yellow triangles here and there, taking photos and picking up samples from the floor like conscientious mushroom pickers.

It's not until that moment that she makes out Superintendent Moncada and Inspector Sánchez huddled together in a remote corner of the stage, talking. From the looks on their faces, they appear to be attempting to digest a very large toad.

Nuria's the last to arrive. As she climbs the small steps at the side of the stage, she begins to recognize her colleagues and the utter barbarity of the crime before her. The pool of blood extends below the body of the victim like a black hole that everyone attempts to avoid. Like the other time, she smells blood, urine, and feces. It smells like death, and Nuria asks herself if all murder scenes smell the same.

"What do you think?" Antonia asks, lowering her mask to place a cigarette she's not going to light between her lips.

It still surprises Nuria that, being the least important monkey in this circus, the forensic pathologist asks her opinion. She tries to choose her words well, trying not to say something too obvious or sound like a know-it-all, or communicate that she would much prefer to be at home sleeping peacefully in her bed.

She lifts her gaze to the man's body. This time the skin on his back has been torn off as well as on his face and torso. "Well, I would say he's not going to recover from this."

Antonia lets out a dry bark of laughter, almost losing her cigarette in the process. Everyone turns to her for a second, surprised by this unusual behavior on the part of their boss.

"Do they know who it is yet?" Nuria asks next.

"It's Arturo Galán," Antonia informs her. "An actor who played the heartthrob in films during the eighties and more recently had worked in theater. I even came to see him act once, years ago. Did you ever see *Love and Glory* or *Midnight Passion*?"

"I'm afraid not."

"Well, you weren't missing much, though back then our friend here was a real studmuf—"

"Assistant Inspector," a member of her team interrupts, "we've finished taking the prints. Should we take him down?"

"Yes, but carefully. Also take prints and fibers from the body and the rope," she adds. "Before it touches the floor."

"Yes, ma'am."

"Well?" Antonia persists, returning her attention to Nuria. "What do you see?"

"Another staged crime." Nuria's had time to think about her answer. "Like the one from day before yesterday, but even more exaggerated. The killer, if it's the same guy, wants to get our attention."

"That's clear. Tell me something I don't know."

"To be able to raise the body that high with ropes he's got to be very strong. Either that or there are more than one."

"Not necessarily," Antonia objects. "The stagehands in a theater use pulleys. A ten-year-old kid could have pulled him up."

"Okay . . . well, ruling out the possibility that the murderer is a ten-year-old boy, I would say that if this was the same person who murdered Alberto Álvarez, he's obsessed with skinning people."

"What else?"

"Well, the way I see it, two murders this . . . bloody in the space of forty-eight hours points to a hitman who's been paid not just to take out two people but also to send a message, Mexican drug-dealer style. That, or we've got ourselves an extremely creative nutcase who's loose in the city and has a serious issue with sexagenarians." She pauses to see if Antonia's heard enough, but the pathologist keeps on looking at her as if she hasn't said anything. "Maybe Mr. Galán could be the clue," she goes on. "Once we establish the connection between him and Álvarez, it's sure to clarify a lot of things."

While Nuria's been speaking, the forensic techs have finished up taking samples from the body and lowered it to the floor. Now they place Arturo Galán and his guts into a black bag and zip it up with a ragged sound before lifting it onto a stretcher.

The stage is now painted in multiple red footprints that extend like rays from the puddle of blood. "Five liters of blood is a lot of blood when you look at it like this," says a voice behind her.

It's Marcos. Nuria didn't see him arrive.

"Approximate time of death?" he asks Antonia.

"Around eight or eight-thirty." Narrowing her eyes at the stage, she says, "It hasn't even been four hours, given the consistency of the blood."

"Who found him?" Nuria asks.

"The cleaning lady," Marcos answers. "As soon as she's recuperated the power of speech, Raúl and Carla will question her. Though I don't think we'll get much from that quarter."

Sánchez is walking across the stage toward them. "Found anything?" Moncada's disappeared, no doubt on his way to the Ministry of Home Affairs of the Generalitat, a few minutes away.

"A million prints, a kilo of fibers, and a fuckload of sleep deprivation," replies Antonia, the only one with the authority to answer the inspector that way.

"How long will your team take to analyze the evidence?"

"If they stay up all night, I could have a preliminary report by noon tomorrow. But if I don't let them sleep, it's more likely they'll make a mistake or miss something important."

"We'll have to take that risk," Sánchez retorts. "I want that report and the autopsy on my desk by nine in the morning."

Antonia inhales deeply on her unlit cigarette. "I'll do what I can."

Sánchez takes a deep breath, seemingly biting back another comment, then adds, "We can't lose a minute." He directs his words to Nuria and Marcos, but they're mainly meant for the forensic pathologist. "Even if it means no sleep for a week, we've got to catch this asshole before he does it again or manages to escape. Everybody will be on us before you can blink. If the killer took photos and sends them to the press again, the mayor, the minister of home affairs, and the honorable president will string us up by our balls in the middle of Sant Jaume Plaza. "*All* of us," he underlines, just so there's no doubt that nobody will escape this fate, not even the rookie.

"We're on it," Marcos says immediately, coming perilously close to being an ass-kisser.

"I hope so."

"Inspector," Nuria puts in. "I suppose that, in view of this"—she motions toward the puddle of blood—"it doesn't really make sense to keep following up on the satanic angle and the same old *666* stuff, right?"

Sánchez studies her for an instant before turning to Marcos and Antonia. "Haven't you told her?"

"Told me?" Nuria inquires, looking at her two colleagues. "Told me what?"

Sánchez grasps the small radio he wears clipped to his belt and speaks into it. "Turn out the lights in the theater for a moment," he orders.

For a few seconds nothing happens. Then, one by one, the lights go out until they're left in total darkness. The inspector shines a black-light flashlight at the velvet curtain . . . and there it is.

Standing out vividly from the luminol is a triple six painted with brush strokes in the blood of an actor.

The week at school had passed with the usual monotony, broken only by the comments she'd gotten on her photos that had gone viral. Most were positive with a few predictable negative ones from the usual jealous types. Plus two or three comments from the hottest guys of the moment that were quite interesting. Mauro hadn't been one of them, but Paula insisted that he'd seen the pics and that any day now he was going to ask her out.

What she really didn't expect was to find a message in her inbox from the Pygmalion Photo Agency when she got home that Friday:

Dear Laura:

We are writing to invite you to participate in a photo shoot and the creation of a professional portfolio at no cost to you. We saw your photos on the Internet and were impressed.

We believe you have great potential in the world of professional modeling and we'd like to help you get started on a promising career as a model.

If this sounds like something that might interest you, please contact us at this email address and provide us with your personal information.

Sincerely,

PYGMALION PHOTO AGENCY

Laura has to read the message three times and verify the email to be sure it's not a scam. *Is it possible?* she wonders. It hasn't even been five days since she posted the photos and Paula's prediction has come true. Laura had thought things like this only happened in the movies and were certainly never going to happen to her.

Her first thought is to call her mom to tell her, but immediately realizes that, with a hundred ten percent certainty, her mother will say no, that what she needs to do right now is study and that if she wants to be a model she can do it once she's graduated from the university.

The email's still on her screen, beckoning to her like an invitation to a parallel world she'd only dreamed about being able to access. High school wasn't going anywhere, but this could be a once-in-a-lifetime opportunity. She thinks about calling Paula and asking her advice, but she also knows what her friend will say. Taking a deep breath and mustering her resolve, Laura begins to write a response.

At dinnertime, Laura's small family sits down around the dining table with the TV news on in the background. It's not until she's eaten her last bit of flan for dessert that Laura clears her throat. Wiping her mouth with her napkin, she dares to ask, "Mom, Dad . . . Would you like it if I were a model?"

Her father raises his eyebrows in surprise and blinks a few times before responding, "Well, if that's what you want—"

"Are you crazy?" her mother cuts in. "You want your daughter to be a model? To end up anorexic and addicted to drugs?"

"Mom," Laura protests. "It's not like that."

"I didn't say I wanted it," her husband protests, raising his hands. "It's just that—"

Her mother interrupts again, turning to Laura with an inquisitive expression. "Where's all this about wanting to be a model coming from? Where did you come up with such a ridiculous idea?"

Laura swallows hard. "I was just . . . asking. But it doesn't seem like a ridiculous idea to me."

"What you need to do is finish high school and go on to college. Once you've finished that, you can do whatever you feel like."

"But by then I'll be too old."

"Don't be silly," her mother objects. "You'll barely be in your twenties when you graduate."

"Yeah. Old. At that age lots of models have already retired."

"But what's gotten into you, Laura? Do you not want to go to the university anymore?"

"Of course I do! It's just that . . . Well, you yourself told me it's a good idea to explore all my options, right?"

"All the options at the *university*," her mother clarifies, holding up an index finger. "Choose any major you want, but choose one. Do you want to end up as some trophy wife or a go-go dancer in some disco in Ibiza? Because that's how ninety-nine percent of the girls who think they want to be models end up."

"I don't want to stop studying, Mom. It's just that . . ." Her voice trails off.

"Just that what?"

Laura shakes her head and purses her lips. "Forget it." She waves a hand. "It was just a stupid question."

"Are you sure?" her dad asks in a cordial tone, daring to butt in again.

"Sure." Laura stands. Picking up her plate and cutlery, she says, "I'm going to my room. I've got homework." Her expression neutral, she walks away down the hall, followed by her mother's worried gaze.

When she closes her door behind her, though, she's come to a decision.

12

"I want that report *now*!" On the phone, Sánchez raises his voice. "I don't give a rat's ass about the DNA sequencing and the VNTR. What I want is the autopsy and the analysis of fibers and prints. Yes, all of them!" he shouts. "You can do the other thing later. Are we clear?" He slams the phone down before the other person has a chance to reply.

The rest of the CID officers bend over their work, hoping to escape the flying shrapnel from the inspector's rage. It's not even nine-thirty in the morning and Sánchez is already tenser than the plumber on the *Titanic.* The meeting he and Superintendent Moncada had had the night before at the Ministry of Home Affairs must not have gone very well.

"Any news from the interrogations?" he calls to Raúl and Carla from his desk.

Raúl doesn't need to take out his notebook to review. "Nothing from the cleaning lady or the custodian. There was nothing on that night and the victim went to rehearse on his own, which was usual for him. They generally left him on his own in the theater until he was ready to go home, even after the cleaning lady left."

"So he had a key to the theater?"

"He always left by the emergency door. The alarm's disabled."

"Cameras?" Sánchez asks now, directing the question to Marcos and Nuria.

"There's a city CCTV camera at the corner of the street, but the streetlight was out and at night you can't see a thing. We sent the tape to the IT guys anyway, to see if they can work some magic."

"No other cameras?"

"There are two dummy ones inside a dollar store," Nuria says, "and one over the ATM in a Pakistani store selling cell-phone cases, but we still haven't heard from the security company."

"Well, insist. What else?"

"We've asked for a list of the people who work at the theater," Carla says, "and we've asked Financial Crimes to check Arturo Galán's accounts against the first victim's investment bank. There might be something there."

"Did you search his dressing room?"

"From top to bottom. No trace of drugs or whiskey bottles hidden in the closet. We found a couple of complaints about him from years ago, but as of now he had to be the most boring actor in show business."

"I don't buy it," Sánchez says suspiciously. "There's always something weird about those people. Are you searching his computer?"

"The IT guys have it, but since it's a Mac it's going to take them longer."

"Go through his email and see if it's related to the first victim somehow or to the Sons of Lucifer or any other satanic sect. There has to be some sort of connection."

"Between a reformed banker with a wife and kids and a second-rate actor down on his luck?" Marcos asks. "Sounds dicey."

"Maybe that's the clue." Nuria jumps on it before Sánchez can. "What if both of them have reformed? What were the complaints about?" she asks Raúl.

Now he does have to consult his notebook. "Assault and sexual abuse, but neither case went to trial. Both women dropped the charges before the hearing."

"They were paid off," Nuria theorizes.

"No doubt."

"Could you find them?" she asks.

"You do it," Raúl says. "I'm not your fucking secretary."

Nuria knows this isn't the time or the place, but a memory of her dad telling her when she got out of school never to let bullies push her around flashes through her brain. "If I did have a secretary," she shoots back, "it wouldn't be a jerk like you."

"That's enough!" Sánchez cuts them off. "I'm the only one here that gets to insult people, and the next person to piss me off is going to find himself in Traffic. Got it?"

"But—"

"Got it?"

"Yes, sir," Raúl and Nuria say through clenched teeth.

The department clock shows 11:58 when Antonia casually appears in the doorway with a file under her arm like someone out for a walk. It's her less-than-subtle way of telling Sánchez to stick his pressure and his rush where the sun don't shine.

"Fuck! Finally!" the inspector exclaims, slapping the table.

Carla and Raúl are at the theater talking to the employees, so the only ones there besides Sánchez are Marcos and Nuria who are compiling the names and phone numbers of Arturo Galán's friends and family.

"We worked as fast as we possibly could," the forensic pathologist says, setting the report down on Sánchez's desk. "I've sent you all an email copy," she adds.

"Well, give," Sánchez urges her. "Conclusions from the autopsy?"

"Same MO." Antonia crosses her arms, attempting to make some black-humor joke only she understands. "They injected him with curare and adrenaline for the same purpose, so he would be paralyzed but conscious while he was being skinned from head to foot—or rather"—she corrects herself—"from foot to head. From the angle of the cuts, we think he was already hung up when they flayed him. We believe he remained alive for more than two hours while the blood was draining out of him."

Nuria brings a hand to her mouth to stifle a cry of horror.

"What sons of bitches," Marcos murmurs.

"And the instrument that was used?" Sánchez asks.

"The same, apparently. A scalpel or something similar."

"Do you still think he doesn't need medical knowledge to do this?"

Antonia shakes her head as she takes out a Marlboro menthol and sticks it between her lips with no intention of lighting it. "Both murders could just as easily have been the work of a butcher or some kid who watched a few tutorials on YouTube. You don't need a degree in medicine to give someone a couple of injections and then strip off his skin."

"Any difference with respect to the first killing apart from the obvious?" Nuria puts in.

"Nothing important."

"And unimportant?" she persists.

"Nope, except for the proof that it's the same killer or killers. Given that the details about the curare and the adrenaline weren't leaked to the press, we can rule out a copy-cat."

"What about the fibers and the prints?" Sánchez intervenes. "Any concurrence there?"

Antonia smiles, reminding Nuria of the expression on Melón's face the day he'd wolfed down a sea bass she'd left thawing on the counter in the kitchen.

The pathologist takes a deep drag on her unlit cigarette. "That's where it gets interesting," she affirms. "We haven't found any similarity in the fibers or the prints . . . with one exception."

"What exception?" Marcos asks.

"It's a print with a sixty-eight percent probability of a match with the partial print we found in the bathroom off the bedroom of the first victim. Under other circumstances, sixty-eight percent wouldn't be enough to prove a reasonable correlation, nor would it be admissible in court. That's why the system didn't compare it to the National Police database. But now, nonetheless, we may just have the entire print."

"Good enough," the inspector says. "You two"—directing himself to Marcos and Nuria—"get onto the National Police database. Maybe we'll get lucky this time."

"That won't be necessary," Antonia says, her voice almost casual. "We already know whose print it is . . . though that's the weirdest thing of all."

"Weird? Why? Whose print is it?"

"Arturo Galán's."

"What are you saying?"

Antonia takes another fake drag. "I'm saying that the partial print found in Julio Alberto Álvarez de Cortázar y Luengo's bathroom coincides by sixty-eight percent with the prints of Arturo Galán."

"Fuck me," Marcos says.

Antonia throws him an appreciative glance as if calculating the benefits of following up on his suggestion.

"How is that possible?" Sánchez is thinking aloud. "Are you suggesting that victim number two murdered victim number one by skinning him alive and then two days later someone murdered victim number two in the same way?"

"I'm not suggesting anything," Antonia emphasizes. "I just put the facts on the table. Drawing conclusions is your department. I'm just a humble forensic pathologist."

Sánchez's look says *humble, my ass* so eloquently he might just as well have given her a T-shirt with the words stenciled onto it.

"What if . . ." Nuria ponders, "Arturo Galán isn't the killer? What if he was at the banker's house in the days before the murder for some other reason and his print just happened to be the only one we found?"

"A print in the private bathroom off the bedroom upstairs suggests a high degree of familiarity," Marcos points out. "In those luxury homes, they send their company to the guest bathroom."

"Exactly," Nuria agrees. "Which would imply that perhaps there was a relationship between the two, maybe even an intimate relationship."

Sánchez tilts his head like a dog who's heard a far-off sound. "Are you suggesting Galán and Álvarez were lovers?"

"Based on the evidence, it could be, couldn't it?" Nuria shoots Antonia a sidelong glance, realizing the forensic scientist has already reached the same conclusion. "That could lead us to believe that this was a crime of passion committed by a third party. Maybe there was a third lover in a love triangle who felt left out, or maybe a man or a woman who'd been rejected. Someone whom the victims trusted enough to allow him or her to overcome them without any sign of a struggle."

"Someone with means and opportunity who's fucked-up enough in the head to kill them the way they did," adds Marcos.

"A love triangle where one of the angles is a psychopath," Sánchez deduces thoughtfully.

"Makes sense to me," Nuria affirms.

"All right, then," the inspector agrees, apparently convinced. "Drop everything and go question the banker's wife and kids again. Find out if the guy was gay or if he had some sort of relationship with Arturo Galán. Maybe all that recent religious devotion was just meant to throw everyone else off. He wouldn't be the first," he adds. "But first, go with Antonia and her team to the actor's house to look for fibers or prints from the banker, just in case the visits went both ways. In case there's any evidence there of some relationship that the wife will undoubtedly deny." Picking up the telephone, he finishes by saying, "I'm calling Superintendent Moncada to give him the good news. We've finally got a bone to throw to the higher-ups that they can gnaw on for a while." Punching in the extension of the superintendent's office, he says, "I think we're very close to being able to close the door on this whole business."

13

Arturo Galán's apartment is only a few blocks from the theater, a sixth-floor remodeled unit on Rambla del Raval with high ceilings and good views. The property is in the name of Agapito Peláez, which turns out to be Arturo Galán's real name.

"Agapito . . ." Marcos comments as he enters the flat with Nuria at his back. "Holy shit. No surprise that he adopted a stage name." The forensics team, meanwhile, is waiting for them in their van parked on the sidewalk.

The first thing they see when they enter the apartment is a giant framed photograph of Arturo/Agapito when he was still young and famous. Nuria silently thinks that if this is what they found in the entrance hall, she doesn't even want to think what the rest of the flat will be like. It turns out she's not wrong.

The whole apartment, which measures around a hundred square meters, is a decadent monument to the life and work of the actor. Every square centimeter of wall space in the hallways, the living room, and the bedrooms is papered with yellowed movie posters for films she's barely heard of, theater productions, photos in which Arturo is shaking hands with second and third-tier celebrities, and a few minor awards and certificates of achievement.

In some ways, the apartment reminds her of her mother's, crammed with memories to the point where there's no physical or mental space to create new ones. The flat is like a mausoleum, a stage set for a production that's old and forgotten, a play that had lost its one actor the night before.

"Looks like he didn't have a wife or kids," Nuria comments, perusing the notes on her phone. "Just an ex he separated from twenty years ago."

"It might be interesting to talk to her," Marcos says as he moves through the apartment looking closely at everything.

"It might, except that she died some time ago."

"Oh, that makes it a little more complicated."

"Just a little," Nuria confirms, running a finger over a bookshelf filled with awards. There's not a speck of dust. She pulls a wry face at the realization that a dead man's house is cleaner than hers.

They explore the dwelling as if they're in a strange place where whatever they touch seems impossible to put back in its original location.

"It's a fucking museum," Marcos says. "It'll take hours to search. There are a million things here."

"Your worst nightmare if you ever want to move," Nuria adds, remembering with a chill the last time she had to change apartments.

"You begin with the bedrooms and I'll take the living room," Marcos directs, pulling out his phone. "I'll tell Antonia to come up in fifteen minutes."

"You'd better make it thirty."

Marcos looks around and nods.

Two and a half hours later the house looks like a hurricane hit it but they haven't found anything to tie Arturo Galán to the banker. No photos, no notes, no Post-its in the wastebasket. Neither is there anything related to Jordi Monells or the Sons of Lucifer, nor anything that points to the actor possibly being gay or bisexual. Given the over-the-top proliferation of photos, posters and pictures featuring his face, a more likely conclusion would be that his sexual preferences tended more toward a love affair with himself.

Nuria figures that when IT has finished searching Galán's hard drive and Internet history, they'll be able to see what type of porn he watched and what his true sexual tastes were. For the moment they can only speculate, but so far everything points to the conclusion that there's nothing overly odd in the actor's life save for his exaggerated devotion to himself.

"We're not doing anything here," she reasons, waving her arms to indicate her surroundings. "We need to make tracks for the widow's house—we don't want to get there late."

The widow is Margarita Bonanova i Roura, the grieving heiress to Julio Alberto Álvarez de Blablabla's fortune, and she's agreed to "grant them an interview" today, as she phrased it, as if she were granting an audience to a reporter for some gossip rag instead of the police who are handling her husband's murder.

With a hyphenated last name that's also the name of the neighborhood in which she was born—like being named Castellana in Madrid or Porvenir in Sevilla—Nuria's already forming a mental image of the woman, and she doesn't think the widow's going to make things easy for them. In her limited experience, people like her almost never did, pulling out their their address books at the first sign of pressure on your part and beginning to recite the names of your superiors like a prayer to the Olympian gods for protection.

"You're right," Marcos agrees, glancing at his watch. "Let's get going." They take their leave of Antonia and her team, dressed in their white coveralls with their little sample bags as they busy themselves at what they do, and descend to the street where they've left the black Cactus illegally parked next to the forensics van. They've left it in the care of a local cop; in this neighborhood, you never know what might happen.

Losing no time, they head for the Bonanova neighborhood. Margarita *idem* is currently staying with her two children at the house of a friend who's supposedly spending the winter in Dubai. She's assured them that they will be alone and undisturbed.

Slightly before one, they pull up at a luxury apartment building where they're received by the doorman. He directs them to use the service elevator since the main one is for the exclusive use of the tenants.

The proletarian who lives inside Nuria bridles at the suggestion, and she's about to make a rude comment to the doorman, but Marcos takes her elbow before she can open her mouth and pulls her toward the elevator. "He's just an employee," he says as they wait for the elevator at the back of the building. "It's not worth it to say anything. He might be a key witness on a case some day and he'll remember you."

"I know, I know," Nuria admits. "It's just that this archaic classist attitude makes my blood boil. What does he think, we're going to piss in the elevator?"

By the time they reach their floor, the housekeeper is waiting for them in the entrance hall. The place is a flat—only one apartment per floor. She asks them to follow her.

Margarita Bonanova awaits them in the living room, standing with hands clasped in front of her. She's wearing heels and clad in mourning clothes by Chanel, Prada, or some other ostentatious designer that to Nuria's eyes make her look like Jacqueline Kennedy Onassis.

She's surprised by how young the widow looks. According to their records she's fifty-two but at first glance seems barely out of her thirties. She's as tall as Nuria and slender, with that elegant bearing composed of equal parts confidence and condescension that's either inherited or absorbed along with mother's milk.

"Bloody hell," Nuria thinks, hating the other woman while at the same time sending up a silent prayer to look like her when she reaches forty.

They greet her with a handshake. "Good morning, Mrs. Bonanova."

"Good afternoon," she corrects them, inviting them with a vague gesture to take a seat on the sofa. "How can I help you? I already answered all your colleagues' questions."

Her smile and tone of voice are meant to be nice, but Nuria can tell—or she imagines—that she's looking at them like some sort of oompa-loompas from the underworld who have come to bother her.

"We know," Marcos says—being the veteran, it's his job to do the heavy lifting in the interrogation—"but we have some new questions based on the evidence we've gathered since then. I hope this will be the last time we'll have to bother you."

"I hope so," she responds coldly, taking a Gauloises and lighting it without offering them a cigarette or asking if her smoking will bother them. Nothing even vaguely like *whatever it takes to catch my husband's murderer*, just *I hope so* while she takes a drag. Her response has confirmed Nuria's suspicions that she's not going to make it easy for them. *She looks pretty relaxed,* she thinks now, *considering she's been a widow for all of seventy-two hours.*

Marcos lowers his voice an octave. "I beg you to be absolutely honest and to answer all my questions, no matter how strange or inopportune they may seem to you. Remember that everything you say will be held in the strictest confidence. Our only goal is to catch your husband's murderer."

This is the tone of voice Marcos uses when he's trying to seduce a woman. Nuria can see right through him and wonders if he's using it as a subtle interrogation technique or if he's actually trying to seduce the widow. Her partner's warning, nonetheless, puts Margarita Bonanova on alert. She sits up straight in her seat and regards them both warily as if she thinks they're going to ask what her favorite brand of vibrator is.

"Do you recall anything out of place these last few days? Any detail, no matter how trivial it may seem to you, could be useful to us. Did your husband display any unusual behavior or send any message that was out of the ordinary?"

"I already told the other officers no."

"Threats? Messages that were noteworthy?"

"Alberto was a banker," she replies. "Naturally he received threats. If you're the owner of a bank and no one's sending you death threats, you must not be doing things right," she says easily. "Ever since the preferred stock thing—and some of the media getting pissed off at the bank for doing something that was allowed by law and the National Securities Market Commission, my husband received so many threats we had to hire a private security firm. You can't even imagine what my family went through with all that."

Nuria thinks of the hundreds of thousands of ordinary citizens who were ruined by the banks and the hundreds of suicides that had resulted, including the death of her own father, and has to exercise a high degree of self-control to keep from jumping on the woman and telling her some truths to her face.

"According to your statement," Marcos continues, "you said that ever since those things happened your husband had become more religious. Why?"

"Isn't it obvious?" the woman responds. "All the news, all the unfair singling-out of Alberto affected him tremendously. He felt guilty, so he sought refuge in Jesus Christ our Lord. What would you do"—she addresses this to Marcos—"if you received a hundred emails a day wanting you to burn in hell?"

"Do you still have some of those emails?" Nuria asks.

"No, none of them," Margarita says, taking a drag. "At first we saved them in case we needed them some day, but once we'd accumulated thousands of them and the police didn't give a shit"—Nuria senses the resentment in her answer—"we decided to delete them as soon as they arrived. I went through them myself and destroyed them so Alberto wouldn't have to read them."

"Do you remember any of those messages mentioning anything related to the . . . circumstances of your husband's death?" she asks.

"Don't you think I would have mentioned that if there had been?" she snaps, almost as if she's spitting in Nuria's face.

"Any mention of the devil or satanic themes?" Marcos continues.

"Are you saying that because of the *666*? Do you think some satanists might have killed my husband?"

The widow's attitude toward Marcos is less unfriendly than it is toward Nuria; maybe his seduction technique is working. She decides to leave the rest of the questioning to him.

"We have to rule out every possibility, Mrs. Bonanova."

"No." She shakes her head as she takes a deep drag on her cigarette. "I don't remember anything like that."

Marcos turns over a page in his notebook and asks, "Do you know if your husband knew someone named Jordi Monells?"

"I'm not sure, but you can check his address book that you've already taken," she responds, reproach in her tone.

"Any relationship with the group the Sons of Lucifer?"

Margarita Bonanova jerks her head back as if she's just smelled something disagreeable. "Are you serious?" Her jaw tenses. "My husband was a good Christian. Have you come here to ask me questions or to insult Alberto's memory?"

"Arturo Galán?" Nuria puts in quickly. "Did you know him?"

"The actor?" Margarita asks, disconcerted by the sudden change of topic.

"Yes, the actor."

"I believe we might have seen him at some awards ceremony or something like that, years ago. But we never spoke to him that I can recall."

"Are you sure?" Nuria persists.

"Why?" the woman asks, confused. "What does that actor have to do with Alberto's murder?"

"Possibly nothing," Marcos clarifies. Pausing to take a breath, he says, "We need to ask you one last question, Mrs. Bonanova."

"I hope it won't be as stupid as the previous ones," she returns brusquely, exhaling smoke through her nose. She reminds Nuria of a bull about to charge.

"We need to know if your husband . . ."—Marcos swallows—"if you've ever suspected him of . . . liking men."

"Excuse me?" Her face freezes and she blinks incredulously.

"We need to know if your husband was gay or bisexual," Nuria puts in, tired of all the beating around the bush.

"How dare you!" exclaims the widow, going red with rage. She stands up so suddenly it seems to Nuria that she's about to climb onto the coffee table. "Leave this house immediately!" She points a finger at the door. "Out!"

<h1 style="text-align:center">14</h1>

"All things considered,"—Nuria shrugs on her parka as they're leaving the building—"that could have gone better."

"Or worse. At least now we know that—" Marcos's phone buzzes in his pocket, interrupting him. "Inspector," he says as he answers. "Yes, we're just leaving . . . A video? Yes, right now . . . Yes, sir."

"What did he want?" Nuria asks.

"For us to watch a video and then get back to the office as quickly as possible." Marcos clicks on a link and turns the phone horizontally.

On the *Daily Extra* web page, under the heading *Exclusive video footage of mass murderer* is a picture of Arturo Galán hanging upside down over the stage of the theater, naked and gagged. It looks like a still photo, but then the blade of a scalpel is seen as the camera approaches. The eyes of the actor, bulging with terror, are clearly visible as he understands what's about to happen to him. After barely ten seconds, the video ends as abruptly as it began.

"Shit," Marcos says. "This is going to complicate things for us even more."

"Is there no judge that can keep the *Daily Extra* people from publishing that? Don't they realize how much harm they're doing to the victim's family?"

"They don't give a shit as long as they rack up a lot of hits," Marcos snorts. "By the time the judges do something it'll be too late anyway."

"Yeah, this is a shitshow," Nuria agrees. "Though, who knows, maybe it will be easier to nab him if we can trace the origin of the video."

"I would be extremely surprised. These days, with VPNs and throwaway email accounts, it's almost impossible to trace an email. Though maybe that won't be necessary."

Nuria regards her partner with a frown of incomprehension. "What do you mean?"

"They've got a suspect detained at Egara. They're about to interrogate him."

"Who is it?"

"Sánchez didn't tell me." Marcos takes the keys, the ring embellished with a small cactus charm, from his pocket. "Just that we need to get there right now."

On the way, while Marcos drives, Nuria goes through her messages. There's a WhatsApp one from her mother asking if it's true about the satanic sect and begging her to be careful and letting her know that the whole congregation of the Reborn in Christ is praying for her that the Lord may protect and guide her and that the Satan-worshippers will be defeated through the power of Jehovah.

Nuria's a bit surprised by how religious her mother's language is and by her exaggerated references to God and the devil. It's as though she herself is the archangel Gabriel confronting all the devils in hell. Nuria has a worse feeling about the fucking Reborn than she does about the Sons of Lucifer.

Suddenly remembering the DNA analysis she's been waiting on, she calls the lab only to find out it will take at the very least one more day, according to Antonia's assistant. Their workload has increased substantially since the murder in the theater. Before hanging up, Nuria asks him to please get it done as soon as possible, reminding him that it could be important.

Next, her curiosity aroused by her mother's apocalyptic message, she logs onto Twitter to take the pulse of the most impassioned segment of the country, finding that the three main topics of conversation on the Internet are: #666, #SatanicMurderer, and #UselessCops.

"Shit," she mutters.

"What's up?" Marcos asks, taking his eyes off the road to glance at her. Nuria flashes her phone screen at him, showing the interminable series of messages with those three hashtags.

"Shit," he agrees. "Moncada must be having a shit fit."

"It hasn't even been three days," Nuria protests. "I don't know what they expect us to do. Magic?"

"This suspect they've got at Egara better be our guy because if he isn't the press is going to crucify us."

"We can't do more than we're already doing."

Marcos shrugs. "You know that, I know that, everyone in the division knows that," he snorts. "But just try to explain on TV that while we're able to nab most criminals because they're dumber than a bag of hammers, every once in a while one with half a brain comes along and then we've really got a problem."

By the time they reach the interrogation room, the suspect is already cuffed and seated in an uncomfortable metal chair, his hands on the table in front of him. Carla and Raúl are with him. She's seated and he's standing, his attitude belligerent. It only takes one glimpse through the mirrored glass for Nuria to see that they're using the classic good cop-bad cop tactic.

Standing next to her and Marcos are Sánchez and Superintendent Moncada, who is also observing the questioning, his face more serious than she's ever seen it. Nuria wonders if that's because he's gotten a call from the minister of home affairs or maybe because he's logged on to Twitter.

The suspect is a big, burly man. Unusually large, actually, like a middle-aged bear dressed in coveralls for work. He's bearded, with studs in his ears and a ring through his nose. His hair is greasy and uncombed and he has thick black eyebrows beneath which two dark eyes are looking out at Raúl with a contempt so palpable it's almost solid. Nuria notices a tattoo of the Spanish Occupy symbol peeking out from the neck of his shirt. It wouldn't surprise her at all if, underneath his blue electrician coveralls, he's wearing an ACAB T-shirt. He hasn't said a word yet, but Nuria would bet a year's salary that he doesn't fit into the half-a-brain category Marcos was referring to on their way there.

Sánchez has just finished explaining to them that his name is Manolo Buendía. He's the electrician who does maintenance work for the theater and has several priors for assault on a peace officer, resisting arrest, and disorderly conduct.

"Like half the young people in Barcelona," comments Nuria.

"IT found an email of his on the hard drive we brought from his house threatening Julio Álvarez with death. That connects him to the first victim as well."

"That's not much," Marcos says, scowling. "Does he have any motive for the murder of Arturo Galán?"

"This morning he posted a message celebrating his death and calling him a fascist oppressor because he supported España Primero in the last electoral campaign."

"And that's why you detained him?" Nuria inquires.

Standing in front of the window into the interrogation room, Sánchez crosses his arms. "That's why we detained him," he confirms. "With any luck, if we give him enough rope he'll hang himself."

But, as everyone realizes before much time has elapsed, this isn't going to happen. Maybe because he's been arrested so many times, the guy knows that his best weapon is silence and though he's probably dying to curse out the cops in front of him, he's biting his tongue. For now.

"We know about the threats you made to Julio Álvarez," Raúl accuses him, pointing a finger at him, "and that you publicly celebrated the death of Arturo Galán. Just that by itself is enough for a hate crime charge. Besides, you've got free access to the theater, your own key, and the know-how to deactivate the alarm system at the banker's house." He pauses so the suspect can process all these factors against him, then adds, "Where were you yesterday between eight p.m. and three a.m.?"

"At home," Manolo responds laconically, "scratching my balls."

"Was there a witness?"

"Sure, I've got two," he says, cupping his hand around his testicles. "Hanging right here."

"You want me to kick the shit out of them?" Raúl shoots back.

"After you suck them."

Raúl takes a step toward him and grabs him by the lapel of his coverall, bringing his face inches from the other man's. "You think this is a game, dickwad?"

Far from backing down, Manolo flashes a defiant smile. "It's the suck-my-cock game, pig."

"Raúl!" Carla exclaims as Raúl pulls his fist back and threatens to punch the other man in the face. Raúl's fist stops in midair, but he shoves Manolo backwards as he releases his hold on the suspect's coverall. "We need you to collaborate," Carla intervenes in her role of good cop. "That way we can rule you out as a suspect and you can go home."

"You can suck it for me too whenever you want," the electrician responds lewdly.

Behind the glass, Nuria still thinks he's not their man, though with that attitude she wishes he were.

Carla is unruffled. "We want to help you," she insists. "But we need you to help yourself by answering our questions. Do you understand?"

"First you can suck me and if you do it good I'll fuck you in the ass," Manolo leers. "You look like you like getting it up the ass. Am I right?"

"Look, Mr. Buendía." Nuria admires her colleague's ability to remain serene. She wouldn't be able to stay so calm. "Manolo," Carla corrects herself, trying to establish a bond of trust in her good-cop role. "If you don't clear up some points for us, we'll have no choice but to put you in a holding cell until you're ready to cooperate. Is that what you want?"

"Your holding cell's a spa for sissies." He bares his teeth in a ferocious grin. "I'm comfier than I am in my own fucking house."

"I don't think you're understanding the situation, Manolo. We have enough evidence to accuse you of double homicide."

"You're the ones who don't understand," he says unexpectedly. "You don't have shit. You just arrested me to justify your incompetence, but you know as well as I do that no judge is going to swallow your bullshit and that in three days max, you're going to have to cut me loose. The longer you keep me here," he adds, "the more obvious it will become how useless you are and how you don't have a fucking clue what you're doing."

The electrician's astute assessment of the situation surprises Nuria. She has to admit he's right and that she's prejudged him because of his appearance. He's not as stupid as he looks.

Who knows? Maybe he'll even end up being a viable suspect.

15

By eight o'clock that evening it's become clear to everybody, right down to the cleaning lady, that they're not going to get anything out of Manolo Buendía aside from profanity and provocation. After exchanging a few words with his public defender, the attorney leaves the interrogation room, his face red with rage, looking as if he's being tortured by bleeding hemorrhoids. Meanwhile, his difficult client goes directly to the holding cell without passing go.

Unless new incriminating evidence is found, Nuria very much doubts that any judge is going to allow a definitive charge of homicide to be entered against Buendía. What's also clear, though, is that he's going to be kept locked up for the prescribed maximum time of seventy-two hours, and if there were a way to double that, it would be even better. Ignoring the questions that are put to you and grossly insulting the officers who are questioning you—and even your own attorney—doesn't tend to be the best defense strategy.

"Go home," Sánchez tells the whole team. "Nothing more to do here. I want you all rested and here tomorrow morning early. We've got our work cut out for us."

His desk phone rings, interrupting him. "Go on, get out of here," he says, picking up the receiver and putting his hand over it. "You're going to bankrupt the department with so much overtime."

"See you tomorrow," Nuria says to her colleagues, exhausted after her almost twelve-hour workday.

Instead of going to her locker with the others, though, she makes a detour to the lab. She could call, of course, but this will only take two minutes and has the added advantage of being able to avoid Marcos and a possible invitation to have a drink. She doesn't feel like it today either.

When she reaches the lab, there's only one tech remaining to supervise the work that's mainly being done by the computers. Naturally, the DNA analysis she asked for still isn't ready, so after going to her locker, she heads to the parking lot. There, under the light of a streetlamp, leaning against the hood of his car, is Marcos, waiting for her.

"Are you avoiding me?" he asks.

"I had to go by the lab."

"You want to get a drink? We've got more time tonight."

"I'm tired."

Marcos gives her a seductive smile. "I know, so am I. That's why it would be a good idea to relax. Blow off a little steam."

Nuria looks around the parking lot. No one is left. "I don't see you inviting Carla or Raúl. They need to blow off steam too."

Marcos takes a step toward her and stands very close, almost touching her. "I don't like them as much as I like you."

"You can't fuck them," Nuria retorts.

"That too."

Nuria hesitates.

"Come on, a couple of beers. See what happens," Marcos urges with a wink, seeing a gap in Nuria's defenses. "It'll do you good."

Nuria checks her watch, more to give herself a couple of seconds to think than to see what time it is, then gives in. "One beer," she says, lifting her index finger.

Marcos's lips curve into a lecherous smile.

Two hours later, Nuria lies naked and panting across her bed. She's sweating in spite of not having turned on the heat. Next to her, Marcos steadies his breathing as he gazes at the ceiling.

"Holy shit . . ." he murmurs, his words coming in gasps. "I guess there was a lot of steam to blow off, huh?"

Nuria's not in the mood for jokes. She can still feel the quivers of her orgasm running through her nerve endings. Turning her head, she sees the semen pooling around the base of Marcos's penis. They didn't use protection, a stupid act of faith on her part since, in spite of what he's said, she's pretty sure he's fucking someone else. She'd needed to feel him inside her, though, without a film of rubber between them. She just hopes she hasn't caught anything.

"Are you okay?" he asks, reacting to her silence. In reality it's his way of asking her *was I good*?

"What do you think?" Nuria says with a long exhalation.

"I told you it would do you good."

"Yeah," she snorts. "You're so smart."

Marcos props himself up on one elbow, a sarcastic grin tugging at the corner of his mouth. "Any complaints?"

She points to the semen sliding down his hips. "Just wipe yourself off and don't leave a stain on my sheets. I just changed them yesterday."

Marcos looks down at himself and gets up to go to the bathroom. Meanwhile, Nuria sits up and starts to dress. Marcos returns and stands in the doorway, naked, watching as she pulls on the sweatpants she wears around the house.

"Is that a hint for me to get going?"

"It's late. Aren't you satisfied yet?" Nuria points to his flaccid member.

As Marcos watches her smooth her hair, her firm breasts and rosy nipples staring him in the face, a new erection begins to assert itself. "It's hard not to want more," he says, shaking his head. "You're really hot."

Nuria shakes her head. Picking her T-shirt up off the floor, she pulls it over her head. "That's enough for today."

Marcos lifts an eyebrow. "Does that mean there will be more another day?"

"It means it's time for you to go," she snorts, pointing to the door.

Marcos shrugs. "Fine. Just so you know, there's still gas in the tank."

Nuria picks up his pants and throws them at him. "Go on, get out of here," she insists, her tone friendly but firm. "Oh, and not a word of this to anybody."

Marcos runs his fingers along his lips as if zipping them shut. "My lips are sealed."

"They better be," she warns him. "Because if any of this ever gets out—"

"Relax."

"Okay," Nuria grunts, picking up his sweater and tossing it at his head. "Will you fucking get dressed now?"

Once her partner's gone, Nuria tries to get him out of her head while she heats a can of cream of pumpkin soup in the microwave. It's been weeks since she's had sex, and there's no way she's going to admit to Marcos that right now he's her only source of sexual—or any other—pleasure, not counting white wine and dark chocolate. Everything else in her life fades into a gray blur of work, work, and more work.

Melón is curled up on the couch digesting the copious dinner he's just wolfed down, and it occurs to Nuria for a moment that he's been eating better than she has lately. Once the case is over, she decides she's going to take some days off and, weather permitting, maybe go out sailing on the *Fermina* with her grandpa Pepe. It's been almost six months since they've been out, and not a whole lot less time since she's gone to visit him.

It's strange, she thinks, how she feels so much closer and has so much more trust in her grandfather than she does with her mother. For a moment this revelation produces a touch of shame but it's the truth and she has to admit it. It's also been her mother that, ever since her father's death, has taken a path completely opposite to Nuria's, anchoring herself in a past that isn't coming back and throwing herself into the arms of whoever is willing to offer her easy answers to her complex questions about life and death.

Trying not to think about this either, Nuria decides to check her email before climbing into bed. In her work account there's a new message from a surveillance company. It takes her a few seconds to remember that it's the company that monitors the ATM machine close to the Raval Theater.

Impatient, Nuria opens the email and finds a video zip file. She clicks on it, then pauses it to compare what she's seeing with a Google Maps street view.

The recording begins at six p.m. and it's already dark. Other than the light filtering from the display window of the store where the ATM is installed, the only illumination comes from a streetlamp at the right edge of the screen. The theater's emergency exit is barely visible at the left edge of her screen.

"That's as good as it gets," Nuria remarks to Melón. From his place on the sofa at her side, the feline opens one disinterested eye. Holding her bowl, she presses *play* on her laptop and begins to eat her soup that she's scattered a few croutons over.

A couple of minutes later, her eyes fixed on the emergency exit, she puts the video on fast forward and slips down little by little on the couch. People pass by the camera infrequently. The time on the video shows 8:00 p.m. and the foot traffic is drastically reduced, consisting mainly of kids going out to party and the occasional tourist on his way to his Airbnb, dragging his roller bag behind him. The door to the theater remains closed.

Little by little Nuria snuggles down further into the couch. Pulling the throw over herself, she draws in her legs and curls up like Melón. The fatigue of the day topped off by her roll in the hay with Marcos begin to take their toll and her eyelids begin to descend.

Fearing that she'll fall asleep and miss something, Nuria decides to turn off the video and continue watching it the next day at work. But just as she's extending her hand to stop the video, the emergency exit door opens. She looks at the time on the video: 8:43.

Pausing the video, she rewinds and plays it in slow-motion, her finger poised over the pause button. Again she sees the door open and someone unidentifiable emerge. It could be Arturo Galán or anyone else; the poor light and low definition of the video only allow her to see that someone opens the door.

What does make her sit up straight, though, is that suddenly, a silhouette appears in front of the half-open door, remaining there a couple of seconds. It's someone with his back to the camera, wearing a voluminous black coat. The person is also wearing a black hood that makes it difficult to estimate his body type, but Nuria calculates that he must be about a meter eighty centimeters tall and weigh between seventy and eighty kilos.

The silhouette appears to block the way of the person who's trying to leave—or, Nuria reasons, the other person might have opened the door for him, because almost immediately the first person steps back, allowing the other to enter.

It's one or the other: either the man with the hood is threatening Arturo Galán with a weapon in order to gain entrance, a weapon that's unseen because he has his back to the camera, or two: the actor knows him and allows him to enter.

Nuria realizes that, even though she's only seen the back of the second man, this is the first image they have of the murderer, an image that obviously doesn't correspond to the corpulent Manolo Buendía, who has to weigh almost double what this man does.

Her fatigue has vanished with the excitement of what she's seen, so Nuria takes advantage of this moment of lucidity to write up a brief report about the video and her conclusions and send it to Sánchez, marked "Urgent" so he'll read it first thing.

When Nuria finally returns to her bed, this time to sleep, the last thing she imagines before falling into the arms of Morpheus is being received early the next morning by the inspector and Moncada and walking through a crowd of colleagues, all of them applauding her with hurrahs and pats on the back.

74

16

"Fucking shit." These are the first words Nuria hears from her boss's lips the next morning as he watches the video on his computer screen. "You can't see a goddamn thing."

So, no. No pats on the back. "The definition's pretty bad," Nuria admits.

"That's putting it mildly. Give it to the IT guys to see if they can improve it."

"But at least"—Marcos intervenes in her defense—"we now have a first image of the murderer. That's a lot."

"*Possible* murderer," Sánchez corrects him. "The fact that the person was entering the theater doesn't mean he's our guy, nor does it mean it was just him. Maybe there were others who went in through the main entrance or through a window or the roof. We can't take anything for granted."

"But with these images, we can rule out Manolo Buendía as a suspect," insists Nuria, irritated at the way the inspector has dumped cold water all over her initial enthusiasm. "The person in the video isn't as big as Buendía."

"That's more a problem than it is a help," Sánchez retorts. "The guy in the video isn't him, but that doesn't rule out the possibility that he might be an accomplice or that he might have entered the theater some other way. No matter what the real story is, he's going to be sitting in that cell until the very last second of the seventy-two hours. Even if his buddies cause more trouble tonight."

"His buddies?" Nuria asks.

Sánchez stares at her, then at Marcos, whose face shows the same degree of cluelessness. "Don't you two watch the news? Yesterday there was trouble with the antiestablishment people and the Occupy movement in Las Ramblas. They were demanding that we free their homeboy and accusing us of police brutality and illegal detention. There were even insinuations in the media that we're not getting anywhere with the investigation," he adds, "and that we've arrested Buendía because of his anarchist political beliefs."

"Was there much destruction?" Marcos asks.

"The usual: they burned trash bins and motorcycles, broke display windows in high-end stores, graffitied the stock exchange . . . The usual, you know. But tonight the España Primero people are going to gather in Plaza Catalunya to protest the death of Galán and accuse us of not doing enough because he belonged to their party."

"Antiestablishmentarians and neofascists both demonstrating against us at the same time," Nuria says, raising an eyebrow. "We must be doing something right."

"Yep," Sánchez says, exhaling audibly. "However you look at it it's going to be a shit show. Both of them would love to get into a pitched battle and blame the other side . . . and then everyone else will blame us for not maintaining order. You know how it goes."

He gives them a look that takes in the rest of the team as well. "We've got to catch the murderer"—he raises his voice—"before the entire city descends into fucking chaos."

She's on her way back to her desk when Carla motions her over. She hesitates; since Carla became Raúl's partner, Nuria's distrust extends to her as well. Then she tells herself this is unfair and that at the end of the day they're all in the same boat.

"Have you seen this?" Carla asks her, lowering her voice and pointing to her computer screen. Nuria stands next to her and looks, seeing an image from a YouTube video frozen on the screen. For a minute she thinks maybe it's another clip recorded by the murderer but then realizes that this video platform has a very strict sensitivity filter that he wouldn't be able to get through.

"You've been investigating sects and all that, right?" Carla asks her.

"Um . . . yes, why?"

"Take a look at this," Carla says, passing her the headphones and starting the video. A moment later a guy who looks like a preacher appears, dressed entirely in white with a Bible in his hand. There's a large *666* in the background. After crossing himself he opens the Bible and fixes his gaze on the camera.

"The devil is among us!" he exclaims without preamble. "Satan has arrived on earth as the Scriptures have foretold. Read it here if you don't believe me! In Revelations 13:18 it says: *Here is wisdom. Let him that hath understanding count the number of the beast: for it is the number of a man; and his number is six hundred and sixty-six.* The man returns his gaze to the camera. "Can the word of God be more obvious? It says it clearly here!" The preacher is speaking louder and louder and Nuria's already getting a headache from listening to him. "Satan walks among us today and is killing us one by one! Two devoted Christians have been murdered in three days by the hand of man and the inspiration of the devil! And his number is *666*! What further proof do you want? It's the devil himself we're facing and no one is doing anything to protect us!" Lifting his index finger, he exclaims, "We must unite and protect ourselves because no one else will do it! Because as the prophet Daniel says in verse 9:27: *And he shall make a strong covenant with many for one week, and for half of the week he shall put an end to sacrifice and offering. And on the wing of abominations shall come one who makes desolate, until the decreed end is poured out on the desolator.*" This said, the preacher closes the Bible with a resounding thump and proclaims, "He who has ears to hear, let him hear."

Carla stops the video, which apparently consists of ten more minutes of ranting. "Fucking nut job," she says, turning to Nuria. "Did you know there's actually a documented *666* phobia? I've seen it on Wikipedia. It's called . . ."—she types something into Google and a page appears—"Hexako . . . sioihexe . . . kontahe . . . xaphobia." She tries to read the word without stopping without much success.

But Nuria barely hears her wrestling with the word because all her attention is focused on the name of the YouTube channel. Her heart sinks as she reads that it belongs to "The Church of the Reborn in Christ."

"Fuck, Mom." She manages to control her impulse to call her mother and order her to get as far away from the fanatical sect as she can because she knows her warning might have the opposite effect. Even so, she can't simply return to her desk and go on as if nothing has happened, so she decides to go to the lab instead. Not because she thinks they'll have anything new to show her, just as a way of getting out of the office for a moment so she can clear her head.

On her way downstairs, Nuria thinks about how to suggest to her mother that she stop having anything to do with the Reborn and concludes that this is a conversation she can't have over the phone. When had she said she would go visit her? Next week? Had she made that promise this week or last week? Her workdays are becoming so long it seems as if a month has gone by since the first murder when it's barely been four days.

She needs a vacation, she concludes by the time she reaches the forensics department and finds the team, all dressed in white lab coats and staring into their giant triple screens like gamers intent on the most boring game in the world.

A familiar voice salutes her. "Look what the cat dragged in." Nuria turns and there's Antonia Grau, lifting her gaze from the microscope she's bent over. "To what do I owe the honor?" she asks, removing the permanent unlit cigarette from her lips.

"Good morning, Antonia," Nuria greets her. "Actually, I just wanted to stretch my legs and get out of the department for a while. How's everything going here?"

"As you can see," Antonia says, gesturing toward a mountain of printed reports on her desk, "the work's piling up. By the way . . ." she adds, getting up and riffling through the folders, "I think this one's for you." She holds out one of the top ones to Nuria.

"What is it?"

"The DNA report you asked for."

"It's ready?" Nuria is surprised. "I thought . . . Well, it doesn't matter." She takes the file folder and opens it. What she finds is a sheet of paper with a series of differently colored bars plotted against a 2D graph. Below is a summary including the blood group, number of red blood cells, and several other pieces of data that she doesn't understand.

"Is this what you asked for?"

"Uh . . . well, yes, I think so. But I don't actually know how to interpret it."

Antonia approaches her and gives the report a quick glance. "It's an analysis of the DNA markers," she explains. "But it's useless if you're not comparing it to another one. You could say it's like a fingerprint, but of the blood."

"And can you compare it to others?"

"Sure, whose?"

Nuria considers this for a moment. She's not prepared for the question. "Um . . . I don't know. Would it be possible to compare it to all the other ones you have in the database?" she proposes, thinking that Antonia's sure to tell her she's crazy. "Like you do with fingerprints."

"Sure, no problem," Antonia says instead with a wink. "Shall I send it to you when it's ready or do you prefer to wait?"

This possibility surprises Nuria. "Wait?" she asks. "How long does it take?"

Antonia takes a drag on her unlit Marlboro menthol. "A few minutes. The mainframe computer does everything in the blink of an eye."

"Wow!" Nuria crosses her arms and smiles, thrilled to have an excuse for not returning to her desk. "I'll wait then."

It hasn't even been ten minutes when the screen of the computer terminal doing the comparison begins to blink and the image on the screen is edged in red like a fire alarm. "It's ready," Antonia announces, turning around on the stool where she's sat down again to scrutinize what's under her microscope. "And the winner is . . ." she adds, typing in commands on the screen. "Fuck me!"

"What?" asks Nuria. "Who is it?"

Antonia turns to her, her eyes very wide. "Where did you say you collected this sample?"

"From the basement of the headquarters of the Sons of Lucifer. Why do you ask? Whose is the blood?"

"Before I say anything else, I need to warn you that the sample could be contaminated, and even if it's not, there's a ten percent margin of error."

"Whose is it?" Nuria insists, disconcerted by so many preambles on Antonia's part.

"It's Julio Álvarez's," she finally says. "The first victim."

17

A mere two days after receiving the email, Laura finds herself standing in front of a nineteenth-century building on Consejo de Ciento Avenue, reading a plaque that says 5º 3ª: PYGMALION PHOTOGRAPHIC AGENCY.

She stares for an appreciable length of time at the intercom button without making up her mind to press it. Her heart is beating like a trip-hammer at the thought that touching that button could possibly change her life forever.

Checking her watch, she sees she's five minutes early for the appointment she made. Too long to just stand there and too short to go get a coffee. At last she takes a deep breath and presses the worn button.

"Yes?" a woman's voice answers after a few seconds.

"Hello, I'm . . ." Laura realizes she's speaking too softly. Swallowing, she tries again. "I'm Laura Gómez. I have an appointment for a photo shoot at five."

"Oh, yes, of course," the woman answers offhandedly. "Come on in." The buzz of the door opening invites her to enter the building.

After pushing the heavy metal-and-glass door open, Laura steps into a dark space that looks more like a cave than a lobby. For a moment she looks around for a light switch but then instead heads for the ancient elevator that's dimly lit by one sad yellow bulb hanging from the ceiling.

As the door closes and she presses the button next to the number 5, she wonders how good a photo agency that welcomes its models in this way can be. She can't quite imagine Gisele Bündchen in this archaic elevator. Though, probably, the first time they did her portfolio it wasn't in some glamorous studio in Manhattan overlooking Central Park either.

She's greeted upon reaching the fifth floor by a small, dark-skinned woman wearing an elegant black business suit with a white blouse who gives her a warm, welcoming smile. "Hello!" she says, shaking Laura's hand. "Glad to meet you. I'm the agency's admin and I'm here to help you with everything you need for the shoot."

For the first time in her life, Laura feels as if she's being treated like someone special. Straightening up to her full meter seventy-five centimeter height, she returns the admin's smile and speaks in a tone she hopes will communicate self-confidence. "Hello." She tries to make her voice an octave deeper. "Thank you very much."

Entering the agency, they walk down a long hallway flanked by closed doors, reaching finally an ample room painted white with large windows. There's an impressive array of electrical wires, lights, diffusers, and photographic spotlights. At that moment all her doubts about the professionalism of the agency vanish, and when a handsome, fiftyish man with graying, shoulder-length hair and an enormous reflex camera slung around his neck makes his entrance, her heart does a somersault in her chest at the realization that this is really happening to her.

"Good afternoon. I'm the photographer," he introduces himself, shaking her hand. "I'm delighted to meet you in person, Laura."

"It's . . . my pleasure," she mumbles, intimidated.

"You're even more beautiful than I'd thought," he says with a smile and an appraising nod. "Those green eyes of yours are a marvel. Have you ever seen such incredible eyes?" he asks the dark-skinned woman.

"Never," she assures him. As much as she tries to avoid it, Laura can feel herself blushing.

"Is this your first time?" he asks her with a feline smile.

Laura nods so her voice won't betray her nervousness.

"Don't be nervous," says the photographer as if he's read her mind.

"I'm not—" she mumbles, admitting then with a shrug, "Well, maybe a little."

"Everything's going to be fine," the admin assures her, setting her small hand on Laura's shoulder. "Don't worry."

"Okay," Laura responds in a tiny voice.

"Come with me," she adds, pointing to a white door on one side of the studio. "While he prepares the equipment, we'll make you up and see what we can find for you in the wardrobe. Did you tell your parents you were coming, finally?"

Laura shakes her head. "My mom's not a big fan of the fashion world," she confesses. "Is there . . . a problem?"

"No, no problem," the woman says soothingly. "It's actually almost better this way. Many parents have the wrong idea of what this is. But the day they see you on the cover of a fashion magazine, you'll see how proud they are of you."

"I don't know, I—"

"You'll see I'm right, love," she assures Laura. "With those incredible eyes and amazing body, they're going to be fighting over you. You'll see," she affirms with a complicit wink. "This is going to be the first day of your new life."

18

"Are you sure?" Sánchez stands in front of the screen with Nuria and Antonia in the forensics department, where he's deigned to appear in person after receiving the news of the DNA match.

"As sure as we can be in these cases," explains the forensic pathologist. "More or less a ninety percent probability."

"Repeat the test," orders the inspector.

"We've already done that," Antonia retorts. "Twice, and the result's the same."

"What do we do, boss?" asks Marcos, who's followed Sánchez to the lab. "Do we go get him?"

Sánchez nods, convinced. "Go get him," he confirms. "Get some backup and bring him here," he says to Marcos and Nuria. "And you"—he turns toward Antonia—"take your team and go to that house and find every last print or drop of blood. If Arturo Galán's been there too, I want to know."

"Consider it done," Antonia replies.

"I'm going to call the duty magistrate right now," Sánchez adds, pulling his phone from his pocket. "I'm going to ask for an arrest warrant and a search warrant too." As he types, he smiles, adding in a satisfied tone, "I think we've got the third corner of our triangle."

By the time Nuria and Marcos park their vehicle on Calle de la Princesa forty minutes later, Montcada Street is crowded with Mossos d'Esquadra and Municipal Police vehicles blocking the entrance and more importantly the exit to any person who bears even the remotest resemblance to the suspect. The rain is coming down hard again after a few hours' break that morning and the cops guarding the palazzo huddle under the portico in their fluorescent blue and yellow slickers.

The officer in charge gives them a formal salute when they reach the door. "Anything new?" Marcos asks.

"No one's come out or gone in," he informs him.

"Great. Keep waiting, radios on silent. She and I will go in first," he says, gesturing at Nuria. "The suspect may be dangerous, so be on high alert in case we need you."

"Yes, sir."

"Ready?" He turns to Nuria while setting his right hand on the butt of his Heckler & Koch P30.

"Ready," she says, pulling out her Walther PPK and holding it in both hands.

There are better, more modern handguns, but ever since Nuria had attended the Mossos police academy, years before, she'd decided she wanted to carry the same gun as James Bond. Perhaps the fact that her father had been an ardent fan of Ian Fleming's novels had had something to do with her decision.

"Well, let's go," Marcos says, pounding on the door. "Open up!" he shouts. "Police!" Behind them waits the officer holding the battering ram, ready to ram the wooden door if the occupant takes too long to obey.

"Open the door!" Marcos calls, pounding again. "Open up or we'll break it down!" Nuria counts the seconds, imagining the butler descending the stairs with the same lack of urgency as if this were a pizza delivery.

More than ten seconds elapse with no response. Marcos stands aside and motions with his head to the officer with the battering ram to proceed. Behind him, a team of Special Forces officers with their black uniforms, UMP submachine guns, and ballistic shields await their turn to join the action.

With the second stroke of the battering ram, the bolt on the large door gives. Like an invading horde entering a medieval castle the officers swarm into the central patio of the palazzo shouting "Police!" Before them the butler, standing in the middle of the open space, seems to have lost the stick he'd previously had shoved up his ass and stares at them in surprise and terror.

"What's the meaning of all this?"

Marcos cuts him off as another officer places plastic handcuffs on him. "Where's your boss?"

"What?" he asks, disoriented.

"Where is Jordi Monells?" Nuria intervenes, less imperiously than her partner. "Is he at home?"

"The master is not at home."

"Where is he?"

"I . . . I don't know. He hasn't returned since yesterday morning."

"He hasn't been back for twenty-four hours?" Marcos asks skeptically.

"A little over that, I would say," says the butler.

"Is that normal?" Nuria persists. "Did he not tell you where he was going?"

"The master never informs me when he goes out unexpectedly. I am his assistant," he affirms, recovering part of his aplomb, "not his mother."

"Well, we'll see what you are," Marcos says. Directing himself to a couple of officers waiting at the door, he adds, "Take him to Egara for questioning. Turn him over to Inspector Sánchez."

"Yes, sir," they reply, taking the butler by the arm and guiding him out of the house.

"You," Marcos says now to the Special Ops team, "search this floor and the upper one. We'll go to the basement."

"Yes, sir," says the sergeant leading the team, gesturing to his men to divide up between the two floors.

"Shall we?" Marcos asks Nuria.

"Ladies first," she says, pointing to the door that leads to the basement.

If the stairs leading to the Sons of Lucifer meeting room seemed gloomy the last time they'd been there, the sensation that now creeps up Nuria's spine is one of menace. She can feel the hairs on the back of her neck standing up the further they go on the narrow stairway, sweeping the steps with the beams of their flashlights.

"Jordi Monells!" calls Marcos. His voice echoes off the stone walls as if returning to him from hell itself. "Come out with your hands up!"

"We just want to talk to you!" adds Nuria.

No response.

They haven't been able to find the switch at the top of the stairs so they're descending step by step into the absolute darkness of the cellar. Nuria imagines that at any moment Monells is going to appear before them like a maniac, brandishing a knife. The fact that Marcos went ahead of her is cold comfort since there's no one to cover her back. Every few steps she turns around and shines the beam of her flashlight up the stairs. She's seen too many horror films not to know that black people, fat ones, and blonds are cannon fodder in situations like this.

When they get to the bottom of the stairs, Marcos sweeps the cellar with his flashlight while Nuria searches for the light switch. Finally finding it, she flips it on and the basement is suddenly flooded with light.

There's no one there.

"Shit," she mutters, putting her 007 handgun back into its holster.

Not even two hours after the start of the operation, Marcos and Nuria are already back in Egara, seated across from Luis Ambrosio Fuentes Meira, which is the full name of Monells's butler. Half a dozen officers from forensics have remained at the palazzo, focusing primarily on the cellar, taking prints and spraying luminol around in search of bloodstains like there's no tomorrow.

"I've already told you three times that I don't know where he is."

"Well, let's not make it four," Marcos says. "Where is Monells?"

"I . . . don't . . . know," the butler repeats, exaggerating his articulation.

"He doesn't seem to have taken any luggage or clothes," Nuria comments. "Does he often disappear like this for several days with just the clothes on his back?"

Luis Ambrosio shrugs. "Mr. Monells is a very peculiar man, as you will have had occasion to observe. He also has peculiar habits and friends, naturally."

"Peculiar habits like satanic sacrifices?" Marcos puts in.

"I don't know anything about that."

"For someone who spends the whole day at his house and devotes himself exclusively to waiting on his boss, you don't seem to know much."

"I didn't participate in his rituals, if that's what you're insinuating. They're just for the members of the association."

"And you're not a member?"

"Me?" Ambrosio seems almost amused by the question. "The people who form part of the association are a select few, specially chosen by Mr. Monells once they've passed a rigorous test to determine if they're suitable. Do you see me opening a hospital or writing a philosophical essay?"

"Talk to us about those people," Nuria said. "Do you have their names?" Ambrosio shakes his head.

"And these people?" Marcos gives him the photos of the banker and the actor. "Do you recognize them?"

"They look familiar," Ambrosio says doubtfully, bringing the photos closer to his face. "But I might have seen them in the newspaper or on TV . . . I really can't say. Are these the two that were killed recently? Is that why you wanted to see Mr. Monells?"

"We'll ask the questions," Marcos snaps. "Do you have a list with the names of the members of the association?"

"There is a list, yes, but Mr. Monells has it and I have no idea where he keeps it."

"We'll have to tell the IT guys to look for it on the hard drive of his computer," Marcos says, turning to Nuria.

"And the rituals?" she asks. "Do you know what they include?"

"I've already told you I don't participate in them."

"Yes, but surely you've had to take bottles of wine down to the cellar sometime. Or change the candles or clean the place. Because I can't quite picture Jordi Monells mopping or dusting the shelves."

"Only before or after they leave. They like to be secretive."

"Did you ever see blood? Or have to clean up something unusual?"

"Blood? No, I don't remember ever cleaning up blood . . . or any other weird substance. These are highly educated people performing initiation rites. Their meetings aren't like frat parties."

"But Monells told us that from time to time they also organize parties," Marcos reminds him.

"Yes, but never at the house. They rent venues for their parties or have them at other houses. Mr. Monells closely guards his privacy."

"And I imagine they don't invite you to the parties either," says Marcos.

Ambrosio makes a wry face. "What do you think?"

"I think you're not telling us everything you know," Marcos raps out. "How long have you been working for him?"

"I started working for Mr. Monells right before the pandemic."

"And in all that time you've never seen anything suspicious? Nothing out of the ordinary that you'd like to share with us?"

"I've seen a lot of strange things," Ambrosio says. "People who are born into wealth are all a bunch of eccentrics whose friends are even more eccentric than they are. They're people who grew up with more money than God and their only goal in life is to avoid being bored. So of course I've seen things you wouldn't believe: people coming into the house on horseback dressed up like Napoleon, a symphony orchestra playing Vivaldi in their underwear, destroying a new Mercedes in the patio with a hammer as a theater presentation . . . Things like that. But nothing having to do with satanic rites or blood or anything like that; simply . . ."—he searches for the word—"bizarre."

Nuria changes the subject. "Has he tried to contact you, or have you tried to contact him recently? We've been calling and the phone always seems to be disconnected or out of range."

"When Mr. Monells disappears this way, it's because he doesn't want to be disturbed. It's normal for him to turn off his phone."

"And on the previous occasions did he never tell you where he was going?"

"At times he's gone to Paris or London to shop, like someone going to the corner store," he explains. "Other times he goes to friends' houses or to his house in the Empordá. Did you already check there?"

"He's not there," Nuria says. "A patrol car was sent out to check."

"Actually, I have no idea," he admits. "With so much money and no job to go to, he could be anywh—"

The phone in the room suddenly rings, interrupting the butler. "Yes?" Marcos asks, unhooking the device that's connected to the other side of the mirrored window. "Right. We're on our way." Hanging up, he says to Ambrosio, "We'll continue this conversation later."

"What's up?" Nuria asks.

Marcos pulls on her arm and together they leave the interrogation room. "We've got an address," he explains. "They've traced the taxi that picked him up two days ago. It dropped him off on the outskirts of Esplugues." Grabbing his coat from the coatrack, he pulls it on as fast as he can. "Patrol cars are en route. We can be there in under a half hour."

19

When they reach the address on Josep Echegaray in Esplugues, they find the framework of a two-story house under construction. It stands behind a chain link fence bearing the typical admonishment found at construction sites about using a hard hat next to a sign announcing that this is a project of the Castells construction company.

The rain is coming down in sheets. Nuria puts on her cap and pulls the hood of her slicker up over it before opening the door of the Cactus. There are four other Mossos patrol cars parked outside the construction site, including the tactical team. The forensics van, due in a few minutes, will be bringing the protective gear and the equipment necessary for collecting samples—though it remains to be seen if there will be anything to collect. Carla and Raúl have arrived in another vehicle and taken their positions next to the fence.

"Proceed with caution." Sánchez's voice comes through the radio. "We don't know if he's armed." Nuria hasn't seen her boss arrive but imagines he must be with the first response team. The rotating blue lights on the patrol cars flash intermittently through the curtain of rain, reflecting off the puddles, the vehicles, and every wet surface, conferring on the construction site an almost dreamlike quality, like some science fiction film from the eighties. If Rick Deckard had appeared around a corner chasing a Nexus-6, it wouldn't have surprised her in the least.

"Nuria and I will go in from the back," Marcos communicates over the radio.

Raúl's voice responds, "Over. We'll go in from the front."

"Let's go," Marcos says to Nuria, gesturing to the edge of the fence that continues uphill for another thirty meters. Following the outside of the fence means toiling up the steep construction site. To keep from slipping, Nuria has to hook her fingers through the chain link as she laboriously makes her way through the mud behind Marcos.

Thanks to the dense rain and the reflections of the lights, it's hard to distinguish anything between the concrete pillars and the rebar that protrudes like black spines from the skeleton of some strange dead monster. Nuria doesn't believe Monells is still there. Too much time has passed. It wouldn't make any sense for him to be there, and even less so with the torrents of rain that are falling.

Although what will be the ceiling of the first story and the floor of the second is already constructed, rivers of muddy water flow over the ground beneath, carrying the dirt from behind the house where the yard will be. It's there, after skirting the chain link fence, that Marcos and Nuria discover they have again arrived too late, though they still don't know for what.

"Holy shit," says Marcos.

In the middle of the yard in back of the house under construction, someone has erected a rudimentary cross made of two boards nailed together. In spite of the rain and the distance, Nuria can make out three sixes painted with something that could be red paint.

Sánchez stands in front of the yellow tape with which they've closed off a radius of three meters around the cross. This is protocol to avoid contamination of the crime scene, though on this occasion it doesn't make much sense due to the incessant rain.

"Antonia, are you finding anything?" Sánchez calls from under his umbrella like a child who's not allowed to step on a freshly mopped floor. "Any print?"

Beneath a white tent bordered with spotlights that illuminate the scene, six forensic techs are going over the area like bloodhounds in search of a trail. The forensic pathologist lowers her mask to answer. "Nothing. Zip. The rain's erased all the prints, both finger and foot."

"Nothing on the cross?" Antonia shakes her head. "Nothing on the cross or anywhere else," she confirms. "Nothing more to do here."

They haven't even been searching the scene for a half hour, but Nuria's sure Antonia's right. Any trace would already have been washed away by the water.

"What do you think happened here?" asks Sánchez, turning to his team. "Why did he come here after you two went to see him? And why the hell did he leave us this cross?"

"He wanted us to know it's him," Raúl affirms confidently. "The asshole is a bored narcissist. For him this is all just a game."

"Do you think he wants us to catch him so he can be famous?"

"I think he wants us to pursue him."

"Well, he won't get very far with an Interpol arrest warrant on his head," Clara adds.

"If he left two days ago," Marcos argues, "he could be in Brazil or Thailand by now."

"But if that's the case," Sánchez asks meditatively, "why come here and put up a cross? Why waste the time? If he wanted us to know it was him he could have sent us a postcard from the airport."

"Maybe he just likes all the fanfare," Carla offers.

"Or he's just a nutcase," says Raúl, "and it's impossible to know why he does what he does. Maybe even he doesn't know."

"What he's done up to now doesn't seem like the work of a lunatic," Marcos objects.

"No? What do you call ripping the skin off someone? Just normal, everyday behavior?"

"I don't know. But someone who's so careful when he's murdering people doesn't fit that profile."

"We'll give him a psychological evaluation when we catch him. But right now, for me, he's a fucking maniac."

"And you? What do you think?" Antonia asks. Nuria raises her eyes and realizes the pathologist's words are directed at her. She swallows, uncomfortable at being the center of attention.

"I was wondering . . . why write those numbers precisely here? And why the cross?"

"Didn't I already say it's a message?" Raúl insists, spreading his hands.

"What message? That he's the murderer? We already know that if he was expecting us to follow him here, no? But why do it here of all places and in such an odd way?" Nuria waves her arms, encompassing the construction site from which all the other police detachments have left except for one. "And who is the message for? For us? For the press? For the construction workers? It makes no sense."

"I agree," Marcos says. "There's something we're not getting."

"Yes, but what?" asks Sánchez, looking around. "We've searched everything twice."

"We're missing something," Marcos agrees, huddling into his soaked raincoat.

"We're missing the victim," Nuria points out, her eyes fixed on the cross. "Whenever he's left the numbers, there's always been a victim right underneath them."

"Yes," agrees Carla. "But it's clear he didn't do that this time."

"Are we sure?" Nuria asks.

"We've searched everything," Sánchez repeats.

Nuria's gaze is fixed on the base of the cross. Clearing her throat, she says, "Not everything."

Night has fallen by the time the excavator finishes making a crater several meters wide and two deep immediately under the spot where the cross was. The incessant rain and the mud have complicated the task tremendously since the hole continually fills with water. In the end they've had to install a pump and run it at full speed to avoid the muddy hole turning into a small swimming pool. It took them several hours to get the city council to send the operators and the machines, and the fact that they don't know what they might find has forced them to work with a high degree of caution. The excavation was directed by Antonia, who's wrapped herself in a yellow slicker on top of her protective suit, a suit so covered with mud there's barely a square centimeter of its original white showing. The chief forensic officer reminds Nuria of the head of an archaeological excavation she participated in when she was in middle school a million years ago.

"Careful!" shouts Antonia, gesturing frantically at the excavator operator. "You're not installing pipes! There might be someone down there!"

The operator shoots her a look that shows her plainly how fed up he is. Since three in the afternoon he's been reminding the whole team that his workday ends at two. His expression says clearly that he would prefer to be anywhere else rather than here, working under the police lights when the temperature is hovering at five degrees over zero and the rain continues to fall in torrents like some biblical punishment.

At least he's dry, Nuria thinks. Even underneath her rain slicker she's wet to the bone. She stopped feeling her feet a while ago, and her initial enthusiasm wanes with each new shovelful of dirt that yields nothing more than a deeper and deeper hole.

Nuria can feel Raúl's eyes on the back of her neck, relishing the moment of humiliation for her that's sure to come soon, once they give up and allow the poor excavator operator to finally go home. That moment isn't far off. Half of the forensic techs have already decamped for home, and even Marcos is beginning to flag and let the occasional yawn escape him. Only Antonia still seems convinced that Nuria could be right. From the corner of her eye, Nuria sees Sánchez checking his watch for the third time in five minutes. She knows there won't be a fourth.

But then, above the noise of the rain, the excavator, and the pump, they hear a clunk.

"What was that?" Marcos steps forward, shaking off his lethargy.

"Stop!" Antonia orders the operator.

Without a second thought, Nuria grabs a shovel and jumps into the hole, which is now almost two meters deep, barely noticing that the water at the bottom rises to her ankles. Lifting the shovel, she drives it into the hole beneath her feet.

Clunk.

"There's something here!" she calls up.

A second later, Marcos is in the hole with her, holding another shovel. "It's wood," he affirms after stamping on the object beneath them a couple of times.

Nuria traces the outlines of the hole with the point of her shovel, trying to calculate the form and dimensions of the object. "Fuck, it's a coffin," she mutters, lifting her gaze to Sánchez, who's watching them from the edge of the excavation. "It's a coffin!"

Antonia orders the two members of her team who are still there to replace the small tent over the hole. They jump down and help move the mud away. Very quickly, what looks like a wooden box, approximately two meters long by half a meter wide, appears.

A sudden flash of inspiration makes Nuria take out her phone and punch in a name. A second later, they hear a ring tone.

It comes from inside the casket.

"What the hell?" Sánchez grunts, his face a mask of perplexity. Nuria shows him the screen of her mobile where the name of the person she's calling appears.

"I called Monells's number," she explains. "That's why it was out of range when we called."

"Fuck me," murmurs Marcos. "So . . . ?"

Before anyone can tell her to wait, Nuria drives the shovel under the top edge of the box, breaking the wood just enough to be able to insert a hand into the hole she's created. "Move," she directs the colleagues who are in the hole with her. Then, pulling at the top of the box with all her strength, she manages to lift the boards, which creak in protest.

"We should be doing this in the lab!" Antonia yells at her. But neither Nuria nor Marcos pay her any heed as he helps her pull the boards back until they've removed the entire top of the casket. As curious as they are, Sánchez doesn't make a move to detain them either. After all, the person inside might still be alive.

There at their feet, inside the coffin, lies the body of a man. The skin has been flayed from his torso and a bottle of compressed air lies between his legs. His fingertips are bloody and his eyes bulge from a face entirely transfixed by terror.

A face, nonetheless, that Nuria had not expected to see.

At her back, standing above her, she hears Sánchez ask loudly, "Who the fuck is this?"

20

In the CID conference room, Sánchez reads the text appearing on his computer screen aloud. It consists of the information on the ID card they'd found the night before on the body of the third victim of the "Satanic Assassin," as the press has baptized Jordi Monells in an outpouring of creativity. Outside the rain has finally stopped, but it's cloudy and an icy wind was blowing when Nuria arrived at the Egara offices that morning.

"Eduardo Castells Palí," reads Sánchez. "Born December 3, 1962 in Mataró."

"Why does that name sound familiar?" Marcos says to her in a whisper loud enough to be heard above the wind hurling itself against the windows. Seated at his side, Nuria motions toward the report she has open on her laptop in front of her. "Castells Constructions," Marcos reads. "Holy shit . . . so he's the owner of the land where he was killed?"

"Our killer has a peculiar sense of humor."

"According to the forensic report," Sánchez continues meanwhile, "after drugging him and skinning him, he was buried alive with an air bottle that kept him alive another twenty-four hours." He pauses so the meaning of this can fully sink in. "He destroyed his fingers and fingernails trying to claw his way through the top of the casket when he woke up," he adds, "but the poor guy didn't know he was buried under two meters of dirt, with no possibility at all of getting out of there alive."

"Unless we'd found him," Raúl points out. "Or arrested Monells from the beginning." Nuria suspects that even though her colleague is using the first person plural, in some way he's trying to place the blame for what's happened on her.

Sánchez ignores the comment and continues with the report. "No evidence of a struggle or prints of any type have been found, not on the body or on the coffin. But the presence of Monells's mobile phone definitely points to him being the main suspect. Possibly he dropped the phone while he was placing the body in the casket and by the time he realized it it was too late to recover it."

Nuria tsks involuntarily and Sánchez's gaze swivels to her. "Do you have something to say, Officer Badal?" She's about to say no, but then decides to share what she's thinking.

"It just seems awfully odd to me," she says. "Our killer has been extremely careful up to now . . . It just doesn't make sense to me that he would drop his cell phone and not realize it."

"Do you have an alternative theory?"

"No. Well . . . yes. What if he left it there on purpose?"

"Why would Monells leave his mobile phone at the scene of the crime on purpose?"

"Okay, but what if Monells and the murderer aren't the same person?"

"Explain yourself," says Sánchez.

"I'm not sure, Inspector. But I think we're assuming something that perhaps didn't happen the way we're thinking it did."

"The evidence is what it is," Sánchez affirms. "And unless memory fails me, you're the one who identified him as a suspect initially, no?"

"Yes, but— I don't know. It seems too obvious to me."

"Too obvious?" Sánchez snorts. "There have been three murders in five days and finally the murderer has made a mistake that gives us someone to arrest."

"But up to now he hasn't made any mistakes."

"*Everyone makes mistakes* sooner or later, Officer Badal."

"Yes, but what reason would he have to—"

Sánchez cuts her off. "That's enough. We have a viable suspect and all the evidence points in the same direction. We can ask him for his reasons once we have him in a holding cell. What we have to do now is find him. Is that clear?"

Nuria nods. Confronting her superior in the CID conference room isn't something that will yield a positive outcome in any possible universe. "Perfectly," she says.

"Great," the inspector says, satisfied. "Find out what Castells's relationship was with the two previous victims and with Monells. We need to lay a firm foundation for this case, and I'm sure it has something to do with that satanic sect, the Sons of Lucifer. One way or another, the four of them are connected." He adds, "If we can find out what the common link is, maybe we'll find Monells as well. All right?"

"Yes, sir," they all chorus in unison.

"What do we do with the butler?" Marcos asks. "Keep on tightening the thumb screws?"

"Keep on tightening them," Sánchez confirms. "Even if he's not an accomplice, he has to know something, even if he doesn't know he knows it. You can't spend years working at a serial killer's house without some detail surfacing that makes you suspect he's not right in the head: animals being tortured, biographies of Jack the Ripper lying around, ordering pizza with pineapple . . ."

Clara raises her hand. "Have the IT guys found anything on Monells's computer?"

"Nothing at the moment," clarifies the inspector. "Nor on his phone, but they still haven't been able to access some files that are in the cloud. Maybe the list of members of the Sons of Lucifer is among those files," he speculates. "Anything else?" He pauses. No more hands go up, so he concludes, rapping his knuckles on the table. "Well, let's get going. We've got a murderer to catch."

Midmorning finds Nuria sitting in front of her computer rereading the email that was sent to her, accusing the Sons of Lucifer of being complicit in the murders. It's straining her credibility that an apparently random accusation would have hit the nail on the head so directly. Who could have sent it? Why? Most importantly, why was it sent to her specifically? She's the youngest officer in the CID and the one with the least experience—not to mention the lowest one on the totem pole. If Nuria had wanted to point out a potential murderer, she would have written to the head of the department or looked for the personal email of some colleague. *But why her?* she asks herself again.

The crazy possibility occurs to her that Monells himself somehow knew of her existence and wrote to her as part of the macabre cat-and-mouse game he seems to be playing. If that's the case, she reflects, maybe he wrote her because he thinks she's the least competent officer in the CID—or the only one who would take seriously the idea of going to his palazzo in Borne. Nuria has to admit that if it hadn't been for that anonymous email, they'd be just as much in the dark as they'd been when the case began.

If her reasoning is correct and Monells is behind the murders and he's the one who's giving them clues that will lead them to him, Nuria can only think of two possibilities: that somehow, all at the same time, he's the most twisted, meticulous, and clumsy mass murderer in history . . . or that he's actually having fun leaving his little trail of breadcrumbs to make them think they have a chance of catching him.

If that's the case, Nuria reasons, it would make no sense for him to have gone to the other side of the world. If he really is leaving them clues so they'll keep following him, the logical conclusion is that he's somewhere nearby. When Nuria was a child playing hide and go seek, she'd learned that the way to win wasn't to hide in the farthest, most hidden place she could find, but rather, in a place from where she could keep an eye on her pursuer so she could adapt to his moves and change her position when necessary. The hunter never thinks he's being stalked.

She feels a sudden chill go up her spine when she considers the possibility that that's exactly what's happening to her. What if she's actually not the hunter . . . but the prey?

Carla and Raúl arrive back from their interrogation of Monells's butler. It's not hard to tell from their faces that it hadn't gone too well.

Marcos still asks, though. "How did it go?"

Carla bangs a file folder down on her desk. "I can't tell if he really doesn't know anything or if he's just leading us down the garden path. According to what he says, Monells was extremely discreet about all the activities related to the Sons of Lucifer. He made sure Ambrosio was never present, so he insists he has no idea who they were or what they did in that basement."

"So what are you going to do? Keep leaning on him until the regulation seventy-two hours are up?"

Carla shakes her head and lets out a tired sigh. "Sánchez has ordered us to let him go."

"Let him go?" Nuria repeats. "Why?"

"He's convinced he's not going to say anything, so he wants us to keep an eye on him twenty-four hours a day in case he's in contact with Monells and tries to contact him. He's asked for a warrant to bug his phone. If Ambrosio sees, speaks to, or dreams about Monells, Sánchez wants to know about it. You two?" she asks. "Any progress?"

Marcos leans back in his chair. "We're stuck again," he confesses. "That asshole seems to have vanished into thin air."

Just then Sánchez comes into the room, his expression mirroring the other officers'.

"Any news?" he asks, looking at Marcos and Nuria.

"We were just telling Carla right now that no, nothing," Marcos responds.

"Have you gotten any video images from around the construction site?"

"I've searched far and wide," Nuria speaks up, "but in that area there are no commercial establishments or traffic cameras, just single-family homes, and none within a hundred meters of the next."

"Don't they have cameras in the other houses?" asks Sánchez with a frown. "It's an upscale neighborhood."

"They have cameras, but all of them are focused on the interior of the properties. As you know, legally they're not allowed to take pictures of the exterior or the street."

"Well then, we'll have to do it the old-fashioned way. Go to the area and ask the neighbors if they saw any suspicious characters hanging around. The advantage of those neighborhoods is that anyone who's walking around there and isn't a resident sticks out like a sore thumb. Maybe someone saw him."

"Actually," Marcos says, throwing a sidelong glance at Nuria, "we're thinking he must have left there in another taxi. There's no public transportation in the area, and the car belonging to the construction company owner was parked nearby, so we know he got there on his own. Monells didn't take him there."

"Are you looking for that second taxi?" Sánchez asks.

"We're looking into it, but there are more than ten thousand licensed taxis in Barcelona, and half of them are shared by drivers who barely speak Spanish."

"Well, find someone from Traffic or some other department who can help you. If you need to, take someone with you who can speak Pakistani or whatever language it is. We have to find the person who picked Monells up and find out where he took him. It's the only clue we've got right now."

"It doesn't make sense to me," Nuria intervenes. "Why would Castells get together with Monells? By that time, the news was out about the deaths of the actor and the banker, and if they were all members of the Sons of Lucifer, they must have known each other. Wouldn't that have made him suspect something? We're missing something here."

"Your concerns are duly noted, Officer Badal." Sánchez leans toward her and speaks. "But what I want right now is for you to find that fucking taxi."

21

Laura stares fixedly at her own eyes in the mirror as the woman makes her up with the deftness of someone who's done the same thing many times before. After washing her face and smoothing on a super-expensive hydrating cream, she applies foundation with a brush, followed by a face powder that lightly bronzes her skin. Next she applies eye makeup and curls her lashes, which makes her green eyes stand out. Lastly, she applies pink lipstick that makes Laura look even more feminine.

After a half hour of work, the eyes that look back at Laura from the mirror are no longer those of an adolescent, but rather those of a sensual, devastatingly attractive woman wrapped in the white satin robe they've provided her with. On the one hand, it terrifies her not to recognize the person in the mirror, but on the other, she feels as if she's traveled into the future and seen herself as the breathtaking woman she'll be in a few years.

"What do you think?" the woman asks her with a satisfied smile.

Laura struggles to find the words. "It's . . . incredible."

"You're gorgeous, my dear," the woman says, giving her shoulder a squeeze. "All I did was bring it out."

"I . . . Thank you . . ."

The woman walks around her and sits on the edge of the dressing table. "Are you nervous?"

"Um . . . no. Well . . . a little," she admits. "It's my first time."

"Nothing to be worried about," the woman says soothingly, taking her hand. "But this photo shoot is a wonderful opportunity for you, and you need to be very relaxed for it to turn out well."

"I don't know if I can."

"Do you want me to help you relax?"

"Yes, please," Laura says.

The woman reaches into her pants pocket and pulls out a small plastic bag containing a few white tablets the size of aspirin. "Take one of these and you won't feel nervous anymore," she says with a wink.

"Is it drugs?" Laura asks, alarmed, recalling her mother's words. "I don't take drugs."

The woman gives a bark of laughter. "No, Laura. It's not drugs. It's just a tranquilizer for your nerves."

"It's just that I don't know if I should . . ."

"Of course, no problem. It's your decision." The woman puts the little bag back into her pocket.

Laura takes a deep breath. Her heart is pounding in her chest and she's feeling anything but calm. "It's okay," she says, giving in and holding out her hand. "Give me one."

"Are you sure?"

"Not really. But I don't want to cause problems for you."

"Well said," the woman says in a congratulatory tone, placing a pill in her hand. Laura pops it into her mouth without a second thought. "Okay then, now that we've solved the problem of nerves," she goes on, "what do you think about choosing what you're going to wear?"

"Sure," Laura says, running her eyes over the many outfits, each more attractive than the last. Suddenly she can't avoid smiling from ear to ear.

When she finally steps out of the dressing room, she's encased in a close-fitting black Versace dress that hugs her figure and emphasizes her curves. On her feet are black stilettos. Laura feels tall and powerful as she taps her way across the studio.

"Perfect," the photographer remarks as he lifts his gaze from the light meter to take her in. "Simply perfect."

A lazy smile curves Laura's lips. As the lights illuminate her she twirls, letting herself be carried away. Being there at that moment is like living a dream and though she doesn't know if it's her own emotion or the pill, she feels like she's floating a few centimeters above the wood floor.

"Go to the window and lean against the sill," the photographer indicates, raising the reflex camera that hangs around his neck. Laura obeys, placing herself next to the huge, modern, floor-to-ceiling window.

"Give me a sexy smile," he commands, and she purses her lips coquettishly, her green-glass eyes fixed on the camera. "Delicious," the man congratulates her as the shutter clicks away. "Move back and forth as if you're dancing," he directs. "Let yourself go."

Laura closes her eyes for an instant and seems to hear music. She doesn't know if it's real or in her head, but it doesn't matter. Letting herself be carried away by the tempo, she begins to sway her arms and then her hips in a sensual rhythm as if she's alone in the world and all that matters is right here, right now.

"That's it, very good. Very sexy." She hears the voice but it's strangely far away. "Keep dancing, lovely."

Laura does what he asks. She's experiencing a strange sensation; it's as if her body no longer belongs to her and she's just a spectator as her hands play with her hair and she bites her lower lip seductively.

"Wonderful," comments the man without taking his eye from the camera as he photographs her from different angles. But Laura is barely conscious of what he's saying or she's doing. All she hears is the voice of the man telling her what to do. She obeys blindly. Like when he asks her to slide one strap of her dress off her shoulder . . . and then the other.

Laura's not there anymore, she's just a foreign body that continues to move to the rhythm of music only she can hear as the silky black dress slides slowly down her skin.

97

22

Nuria's eyes are burning from staring at the screen and her throat is raw from talking so much on the phone. She's lost count of the hours she's been sitting next to Marcos trying to trace the taxi that supposedly picked up Monells at the construction site after he'd killed his third victim.

In spite of her exhaustion, they haven't finished checking on even ten percent of the taxi companies. On several of the calls, they needed the help of an Urdu interpreter and there have been no results yet.

"We're wasting our time with this," she says to Marcos, stretching her arms over her head. Her back and neck are aching as well; she's not used to spending so much time hunched over her computer.

"Stop saying that," Marcos orders. "You heard Sánchez."

"The fact that Sánchez said it doesn't make it true."

"No, but it does as far as we're concerned. If the boss says we have to look for the taxi, we have to look for the taxi, period. It's that simple."

"That makes no sense."

"It doesn't matter whether it makes sense or not, it's an order from a superior and we have to comply with it. If we find the taxi it might lead us to Monells and if we find Monells we've solved the case."

"That's precisely what doesn't make sense," Nuria argues, ignoring Marcos's argument. "Why, after we went to see him, does he decide to murder Arturo Galán and then Castells? Why risk it when he knows we're on his trail? And the tip that put us on his trail," she adds, "who sent it? And why? There are too many loose ends."

"Look, Nuria," Marcos responds, his tone revealing growing impatience. "I hate to say it, but in this case I have to admit Raúl's right. What we have to do is catch that son of a bitch before he kills anyone else. All the rest is secondary. Once we have him in a holding cell we can find out why he did what he did, how he did it, and just how crazy he is."

"But doesn't it worry you that everything we've achieved so far is thanks to an anonymous email?"

"These things happen, Nuria. A gossipy neighbor, a call to the local police complaining about a TV with the volume turned up too high . . . and by sheer luck we've snared an international drug trafficker."

"Yes, but still, it just seems like too great a coincidence that the only personal email account they wrote to happened to be mine."

Marcos closes his eyes and exhales lengthily through his nose. It's clear his patience has run out. "Just where are you trying to get with this?" he asks, obviously wanting to close the subject once and for all.

"I don't know, really. To the truth? It's just . . . I'm wondering if Monells is playing with us, or if someone could be manipulating us to get us to go after the wrong person."

"Monells is guilty," Marcos says conclusively. "If he weren't, he wouldn't have fled. Thanks to you discovering the blood in the basement, we have proof of his relationship with one of the victims—and that's not even counting the fact that the very day we went to see him a taxi brought him to the exact place where we found Castells buried two meters underground. This tells me there's no doubt at all that he's implicated. Whether he did it together with other people or with their help?" he asks himself. "Could be. It could even be that his accomplice, God only knows for what reason, sent you that email to your personal account. Maybe it's someone in his satanic club or his macramé circle that wants to get even because he stole the scissors from him. Who knows? But you know what the only sure thing is? That Jordi Monells is in on it. And the sooner we catch him the sooner we can resolve the case, win ourselves a little medal, and sleep eight hours in a row again. So just stop wasting time asking yourself useless questions," he concludes, returning his gaze to his computer screen, "and help me find this goddamn fucking taxi."

Evening is coming on, the sun has already sunk below the large windows of the department, and Nuria is still sitting in front of her computer screen, talking on the phone. "Yes, that same afternoon," she says into the receiver. "From Josep Echegaray Street or a street close to it . . . in Ciudad Diagonal, yes." There's a pause. "No, I already told you I don't know the destination, that's what I'm trying to find out." A longer pause. "You can't be sure . . ." she repeats, crossing a new name off her interminable list. "Right. Thank you. Good evening." She hangs up with a frustrated sigh and drops her head onto the desk. "This is useless," she groans, her forehead pressed against her notebook.

"Lower your voice, Sánchez is going to hear you," Marcos warns.

"Let him hear me, then," she retorts, turning to look at him. "I'm sick of making calls. I'm a cop, not some switchboard operator."

"That's what the job entails sometimes."

"Well, I'm fed up," she replies. "We've been making calls all fucking day instead of being out there pounding the beat."

"And you think we would have had better results pounding the beat?" Marcos fires back. "Monells is on Interpol and besides, we've blocked his bank accounts and credit cards. He can't get far."

"I don't think he's gone anywhere," Nuria insists. "If all this is a game for him, he's got to be close, keeping a watch on us, and I'll bet you he's got a good hiding place and a mountain of cash to keep him going. He's out there,"—she turns toward the window and the dark night outside—"hunkered down."

"Okay, fine. Maybe you're right, but we have no other clues and we have to take advantage of the fact that Castells's death hasn't gone public yet. As soon as that happens people are going to completely lose it and our bosses are going to have our backs to the wall before a firing squad."

Nuria already knows this. She lifts her head and looks at the wall clock. Still an hour to go before she can go home and time seems to have stopped. She stares at the minute hand until she sees it move imperceptibly from one little mark to the next. One minute, fifty-nine to go.

"I'm going to stretch my legs," she says, standing up.

"I'll come with you," Marcos offers, raising his head.

"I prefer to go alone. I need to think things through."

"Okay." Marcos shrugs. "Whatever you want."

Nuria takes her small purse and her coat and leaves CID, passing in front of Sánchez's desk and leaving a "be right back" floating in the air. The inspector, immersed in reading a report, seems not even to have seen her.

She goes out into the corridor and, just when she's about to take the fork that will lead her to the mezzanine balcony or the cafeteria, changes her mind at the last minute and goes in the opposite direction, toward the elevators that will take her to the parking lot.

Sánchez isn't going to like it, but Nuria's owed a ton of overtime, and today she feels like she needs to get out of there before her head explodes. On her way to her car she makes a call. "Hi Mom," she says. "Yes, fine. Thanks. Um . . . would you like me to come over for dinner? . . . Yes, I left early today . . . Okay, then, I'll go home and drop off the car. I'll be there in about an hour . . . Okay, great, see you then."

Her father had always told her that it was better to get things you didn't really want to do out of the way as quickly as possible. Thinking this, Nuria feels bad for putting a dinner with her mother into the category of things she doesn't really want to do, but then she reasons that it would be hypocritical not to, so one thing balances out the other. When she slides into the driver's seat and turns on the ignition she feels almost happy—for being an obedient daughter as much as for managing to escape the department before her last neuron dissolves.

"Hi." She greets her mother with a kiss on both cheeks when she opens the door to her apartment.

"Hi, Nurieta. So good to see you." Very few people use her pet name, Nurieta, any more: Grandpa Pepe, her friend Susana when she wants to tease her, and of course, her mom. Though she's pushing thirty, stands up to criminals on a daily basis, and has permission to use a firearm, for Estela Jiménez she will always be a little girl who needs help tying her shoes—which Nuria of course knows applies to pretty much all the mothers in the world.

"I snuck out of work early so I could see you," Nuria says, only half lying, as she enters the apartment. "It's been truly crazy the last few days."

"I can imagine," agrees her mother.

Nuria studies her mother's wrinkled face and tired features for a moment. Save for the color of her eyes, it's like looking into a mirror of her own future. She thinks briefly of how the passing of the years has affected her mother, but immediately turns her thoughts elsewhere when she realizes those same years will pass for her as well. If she's lucky.

"How are you?" her mother asks. "Are you hungry?"

"Very."

"Oh, that's great. I've made your favorite dinner."

"You made sushi?" asks Nuria.

"Sushi? No." Her mother makes a face. "I don't make that garbage. I've made you peas with ham and eggs. The way you like it."

This meal actually stopped being Nuria's favorite when she was twelve, but she puts on a game smile and nods. "Nice!" she says, hoping her mom won't notice she's lying. "Thank you."

"Well, then." She points at the sofa. "Get comfortable, rest. It will only take me a minute to heat up the food."

"Thanks, Mom," Nuria answers, taking her advice and relaxing into the couch cushions. When her mother leaves the room for the kitchen, Nuria lets her gaze wander over the furnishings and decor of the apartment. Everything is exactly the same as she remembers it from her childhood. The same wedding photos of her parents, the same photo of herself wearing a white dress at her first communion, the same small porcelain dogs, the same pots with the same plants in them, the same curtains, the same sofa where she's now seated, and the same carpet under her feet. Going to visit her mother is like traveling fifteen years back in time, one of the reasons she tries to avoid it as much as she can. She can't really say that that was the happiest time in her life.

True to her word, after one minute her mother appears again, holding two steaming plates that she sets on the dining-room table, which is already set. Mechanically, her mother reaches for the TV and turns it on. Nuria resists the temptation to ask her not to, understanding that the newscaster with his tie on the other side of the screen who is currently talking about the rise in the price of fuel is someone who keeps her mother company during the long winter nights. She doubtless sees him more than her daughter, so in spite of the annoyingly high volume, Nuria keeps her mouth shut and eats her peas.

"Is it good?" her mother asks. "Not too salty?"

"It's perfect."

Estela Jiménez smiles with satisfaction. "How's your work going?" she asks.

"Good, super busy."

"With all this about the Satanic Assassin?"

"He's not a satanic assassin," Nuria says. "He's just a murderer."

"With those numbers? I've seen them in both murders. It's the number of the beast," she adds, crossing herself.

Nuria stares at her, a little surprised. "What's that about?"

"I'm praying to the Lord to protect me from the beast and the satanic communist hordes."

Nuria has to force herself not to burst out laughing. "Satanic communist hordes? Where did you get that?"

"Haven't you been watching the news?" Estela motions toward the TV. "Murders with the number of the beast and the reds destroying the streets at the same time. Don't tell me that's just a coincidence."

Nuria blinks, disconcerted, as she tries to put the pieces of what her mother is saying together in her mind. "Are you referring to the demonstrations of the antiestablishment groups?" she asks, understanding what her mother is talking about. "We've always had those in Barcelona, Mom. They're happening now because we've detained one of their members in Egara. That's all."

"Oh! So the murderer is one of them?"

"No, don't be ridiculous." Nuria shakes her head emphatically. "But he's still being held and his friends aren't happy about it. How's it going for you with the Redeemers?" she asks, mainly to change the subject.

"The Reborn," her mother corrects her. "Very well. We get together to pray and they have talks once in a while. The other day a really nice man from España Primero came to explain to us why the country's going under because of the reds and the feminists."

"Fuck, Mom," Nuria says in exasperation. "The people in España Primero are a gang of—" She stops herself just in time. "I really don't think it's a good idea for you to fraternize with those people."

"You don't know them. They're good, decent people."

"I'm not saying they aren't," Nuria objects. "But the world is not the way they paint it, and the country's problems are not the fault of the people they blame."

"Well, maybe we'd better change the subject," her mother says huffily. "It's clear we'll never see eye to eye on that subject. How's dinner?"

It takes Nuria a moment to adapt to the abrupt change of topic. "Delicious, thanks. I haven't had anything this good in a long time," she says, exaggerating just a tad.

"That's good, I'm happy to hear that." Her mother nods in satisfaction. "By the way, my friends from the congregation got all excited when I told them you worked for the police and that you were in the CID. They asked me if you have any clues yet."

Nuria drops her fork onto the white porcelain plate with a clatter. "Goddamnit, Mom, I've told you not to tell anyone I'm a cop, and much less to say I'm in the—" She stops, thinking for a few seconds, then asks, "Hold on. When did you tell them I was in the Criminal Investigations Division?"

"Um, I don't know. A couple of weeks ago, maybe? Why?"

"Because a few days ago I received an anonymous email in my personal account from someone who knew I work there. Very few people know that."

"An anonymous email?" asks her mother, suddenly worried. "Were you threatened?"

"No, no . . . nothing like that. But, Mom, it's dangerous for strangers to know that I'm a police officer. Can you understand that?"

"They're not strangers," her mother argues, frowning. "They're members of my Reborn congregation and I've already told you they're good peo—"

"I don't care," Nuria says, interrupting her mother more brusquely than she'd intended to. "Even if they're angels with wings, I don't want you telling anyone what I do or don't do. Agreed?"

"All right," her mother says. Shaking her head incredulously she adds, "What a dour character you have. I don't know who you got that from. I guess I can't even tell people I have a daughter."

Nuria briefly closes her eyes to calm herself before answering. "It's not that, Mom. "The problem is . . ."

"Oh my God." This time her mother is the one to interrupt, bringing her hand to her mouth in shock. Nuria follows her eyes to the television screen.

On it is a video of Eduardo Castells in what will be his coffin, the air bottle between his legs, moments before being buried alive.

Only one word comes to Nuria's lips. "Shit."

23

In spite of the cold, Nuria decides to walk home instead of taking the metro. After her eternal day at Egara and then spending two hours with her mother, she needs some fresh air.

At this hour there are few people in the streets; the businesses and a good number of restaurants as well are closed and maybe because of that, when she crosses the Diagonal toward Gracia, at first she doesn't notice the absence of traffic. It's not until she's crossed the wide avenue that, at the intersection of San Juan, she sees dozens of blue police lights flashing in the night, competing with the Christmas lights. A little further on, the golden twinkle of several fires rises above the silhouettes of the vehicles.

Civic disturbances in Barcelona have become almost synonymous with the idiosyncratic nature of the city, and Nuria's always thought that in spite of the recurring vandalism, they're an expression of a restless society that feels the need to fight back. Once she read that the societies you really need to fear are the ones where nothing ever happens and all the citizens seem to be in agreement. Even as a cop, she fully agrees with this assessment. Surely, she thinks, her feelings in this regard must have a lot to do with the influence of her father and even more so, her Grandpa Pepe, who's always boasted about his youth that was filled with protests and running from the police. That his very own granddaughter ended up as a member of the Catalonian police force was a bitter pill that had taken him several years to digest.

Some pedestrians, like herself, have stopped in the middle of the crosswalk to contemplate the spectacle of lights, though most of them barely glance at it from the corner of their eye as they walk along, as though scenes like this one have become routine.

While she's still standing in the street, Nuria's phone beeps, letting her know she has a new WhatsApp message. It's from Marcos, who has sent her a link to a video that she hesitates to open, thinking it's probably the same one she just saw on the TV news at her mother's. She doesn't want to look at Castells's horrified face a minute before he's buried alive.

Even so, she clicks on the video. To her surprise, she sees the same Reborn preacher, dressed in white, staring fixedly at the camera with savage intensity. Nuria hastily turns up the volume when she realizes he's talking to the camera.

" . . . *the devil*," he's proclaiming at the top of his voice, "*and your will is to do your father's desires! He was a murderer from the beginning, and has nothing to do with the truth, because there is no truth in him!*" says John 8:44. "The word of God warns us, but . . ."—he wags his finger—"we pay no attention, sinners that we are. We turn our backs on the word of the Lord. More than anyone, the police and the corrupt politicians who have pacts with Satan and do nothing to keep the murderer from continuing to kill God-fearing believers. Because they are also servants of the devil! The serpent, who with his despicable hissing is coiled up in our society, turning to his will all those men and women who do not fear God! Let us go to the streets and show those corrupt Satan-worshipers that pure and decent people will not kneel before them and their machinations! Brothers Reborn in Christ, the hour to fight and defend ourselves from the evil that stalks us has arrived, with the help of our Lord! Because as Peter says in 5:8, *Your enemy the devil prowls around like a roaring lion looking for someone to devour."*

Nuria's seen enough. She clicks the video off, noting that it was uploaded just today and already has around five thousand views. It's not Ibai, the Spanish Internet celebrity, but five thousand views is still a lot for only having been up a few hours. Even if only one or two percent of the people who've seen it take it seriously, that's fifty or a hundred fanatics that could stir up trouble at any moment. Then the television coverage, anxious for any sort of spectacle, will make it look like it's ten thousand instead of a hundred.

Inevitably, whenever there's an accident, a pandemic, or a tragedy, there are vultures who are drawn to the carrion for their own benefit; it's a law of nature. But it's just as natural that when the time is right, those responsible, usually politicians, will seek to jettison the ballast by looking for scapegoats among their subordinates in order to save their own skins and their privileged positions.

Realizing that at moments like this, her head and the heads of the rest of the CID team will be the first to roll if push comes to shove, Nuria resists the temptation to touch her own throat. And the fact that her mother told the Reborn in her congregation that she's a cop who's participating in the murder investigation doesn't make her feel any better. No, it doesn't help at all.

In this mood, her mind preoccupied with the possible implications all this might have for her professional future, Nuria enters the Gracia neighborhood, crosses the Plaza de la Revolución, and turns her steps toward 77 Verdi Street.

The narrow walking streets of Gracia, always thronged, seem as deserted as the rest of the city and, perhaps because of this, despite being distracted, Nuria's able to make out, thanks to a flash emitted by a Christmas light, the silhouette of someone hidden in a doorway. The light has only illuminated him for a tenth of a second, but she could swear that it's someone with a hoodie on under a black coat.

Someone, in other words, dressed in exactly the same way as the figure in the video they'd gotten from the ATM. The figure that was shown entering the Raval Theatre through the emergency door on the night Arturo Galán was murdered.

For an instant, Nuria slows her steps, alarmed by the situation. It may be just coincidence, just someone waiting in a doorway for his girlfriend . . . but again, it may not. In the same way someone found out what her email is, she thinks, the murderer may have found out where she lives.

She has to act fast. The door of her building is less than twenty steps away. *Think, Nuria, think,* she tells herself.

Without altering her rhythm so as not to alert him, she keeps walking as if nothing's wrong, without looking in his direction. Now, from the corner of her eye, it's more difficult to make him out in the darkness, but she's sure there's someone there.

She opens her purse, looking for her house keys. Nothing happens. If he's thinking of attacking her, he'll do it when she turns around to open the door. She doesn't have her gun with her. Like every other night, it's locked away in her locker in Egara. But, as she searches in her bag, her fingers touch the handle of the extendible night stick she always carries with her. A cop's a cop twenty-four hours a day, she was reminded in the academy years ago, and right now she's regretting the fact that she doesn't have her gun with her.

Turning her back on the stranger, her ears on high alert, she jingles the keys while getting a firm grip on the night stick, expecting to hear the sound of footfalls any moment. And she does hear them, but not the way she's expected to. These are receding.

Nuria turns around and sees the hooded figure walking away up the street. She hesitates a moment, indecisive. What to do? Has he realized she saw him?

Is she just being paranoid?

"Hey!" she shouts. The stranger makes no sign of having heard her. "Hey, you! You in the hoodie!"

He's about twenty meters away now, but unless he's deaf he has to have heard her. Nuria decides to use the magic words. "Stop! Police!"

Saying this aloud usually yields one of two results: a) the one the words are directed to stops, or b) the one the words are directed to takes off running as if the devil's hot on his tail. Unfortunately for Nuria, this one is the second type.

"Goddamn it to hell," she swears and begins to run after him. He's got quite an advantage on her and even though she's in good shape and rested, she quickly loses ground.

The suspicious type turns the corner at Providencia. When Nuria gets there, a few seconds later, he's turning onto Verntallat and she's lost sight of him again.

Nuria accelerates her pace and feels how the unexpected effort of sprinting those hundred meters is beginning to affect her respiration. But she can't let him get away, so she clenches her teeth and runs even faster.

When she turns the next corner she sees him drawing away from her. She's not going to make it. Though she still feels the impulse to continue the chase, her steps shorten and she has to stop for a moment to catch her breath.

That's when he turns around and, lowering his hood, allows her to see the head of a young man wearing a watch cap. As she watches, he lifts the sweatshirt, revealing the acronym ACAB: *All Cops Are Bastards*. He flips her off and shouts, "Go fuck yourself! Fucking shithole pig!"

Nuria, her hands resting on her knees and her breath coming fast, feels surprisingly relieved, to the point of almost smiling at the young man's insult. No doubt he's one of the many antiestablishmentarians that live in occupied houses in the neighborhood. When she shouted at him to stop, he naturally fled. It's not something she can really hold against him, given the long history of skirmishes between antiestablishment people and the police.

Was it just chance that he'd been waiting almost right in front of her doorway? Who or what had he been waiting for? Had he known she was a cop?

"Well," she pants, "he certainly knows now."

The young man turns around and takes his leave by giving her the finger again. Nuria returns the favor and turns to walk back home. All she can think about now is taking a long hot shower and climbing into bed to make up all the hours of sleep she's lost recently.

That's when she thinks of Melón and the fact that she forgot to buy his canned food. She'll have to defrost a chicken breast and give it to him to keep him happy. He's become such a gourmet lately that if she dares give him dry food he'll probably throw it in her face.

24

Nuria opens her eyes to total darkness. It might be midnight or six in the morning. She's had a nightmare that she can't remember now, but her heart rate is still accelerated and she can feel the adrenaline rushing through her bloodstream.

Unwillingly, she looks at the clock. It's 4:12. Shit. Too late to take a sleeping pill and too early to get up. Nuria picks up her Kindle from her bedside table and begins to read, but realizes after three minutes that she's still too upset to focus, so she gets up, turns on the TV in the living room, wraps herself in a blanket, and lies down on the couch. Melón looks at her suspiciously from his favorite chair. It's one of those looks that says *don't even think about bothering me.*

Nuria pointedly avoids putting on the news and begins to navigate through her streaming channels in search of some series that's boring enough to put her back to sleep. She finds a thriller on Netflix that looks as if it will do the job, but a few minutes in it starts to get too interesting to turn off and by the time she realizes it, it's five a.m. and she's just watched an entire episode.

She turns off the TV, realizing she won't be getting any more sleep that night. Glancing at the clock again, she dithers for a while and finally decides to take a shower and go to work.

It's not even six a.m. when she parks in front of the Egara complex and walks by the Christmas tree that's been set up in front of the main door. At this hour only the night shift is working, and though this isn't the first time she's been at the office this early, the few people she runs across greet her with curiosity.

Of course there's no one in the division offices when she arrives, so she goes to the espresso machine and makes herself a strong coffee before sitting down in front of her computer screen.

An idea had occurred to her earlier while she was watching the thriller, but she's not sure it will yield any results. She logs into the Mossos databank and looks up crimes in the last few years that include the words *skin, flay, buried alive,* and *satanic ritual.*

She gets no matches from the Catalonian police archives, so she widens the search to include the National Police archives, covering the entire country and removing any time limits.

Here she finds a match: the case of the Alexander family. In 1970 Harald Alexander and his son Frank, Germans who had fled to the island of Tenerife after being accused of incest in their native Hamburg, murdered the mother of the family and two of the daughters in a never-before-seen orgy of blood and mutilation. According to the police report, Frank, the son, bludgeoned his mother to death while his father played the accordion to cover the noise of her cries. Later, using a straightedge razor and a pair of pruning shears, they'd cut off her nipples and ripped her heart out, hanging it from the ceiling. Two of the daughters met with the same fate, but were also drawn and quartered and their intestines removed and nailed to the wall.

Nuria has to read the report twice to believe it. She searches further in Google and discovers that father and son were captured and put on trial. They were found to be mentally ill and confined to a psychiatric hospital from which they escaped in 1995.

The escape had taken place thirty years ago, and more than fifty years had passed since they'd committed their horrendous crimes. Though the similarities with the current case were unsettling, both criminals had to be between seventy and a hundred years old now. Even if they were still alive, Nuria couldn't imagine them murdering people all over the city at the rate their murderer had.

"Good morning," someone greets her.

Nuria lifts her eyes from the screen and sees Sánchez coming through the door with a file folder beneath his arm. "Good morning, Inspector." She throws a sidelong glance at the clock on the wall in front of her. It's eight a.m.

"Have you been here long?"

"A couple of hours," she answers.

"Good, good." Sánchez nods. "Looking for the taxi, I imagine."

Nuria needs a few seconds to remember what he's talking about. "Oh, yes . . . sure. Though, speaking of that, I wanted to tell you—"

"Have you found it yet?"

"Uh . . . no, not yet."

"Well, let's not waste any time then," he interrupts, taking the file folder from under his arm and smacking it down on the table. "Urgent meeting when the others arrive. There's news."

Nuria vacillates for a moment, wondering if she should insist, but realizes she doesn't really have anything solid to offer Sánchez, just speculations. And there have been too many speculations lately, so she just closes her mouth and nods, concluding that it's better to wait.

Little by little the rest of the team arrives, and when Marcos walks through the door, last of all, Sánchez props himself on the edge of his desk, file folder in hand. "Eduardo Castells Palí," he reads aloud. "Sixty-three years old, builder, divorced with two daughters. No priors. Two sanctions from the national tax office for fraudulent tax returns that ended up going to trial. He was fined almost five hundred thousand euros, but there were no criminal charges. No relationship that we can see to the other victims, not even circumstantial. He never worked with Álvarez de Cortázar's Nostrum Investment Bank or hung out with Monells's circle and, according to his ex-wife, he hated actors and the theater, calling them narcissistic and useless. In other words," he adds, lifting his gaze, "he didn't seem to have any relationship at all with Monells or either of the other two victims."

"Are the circumstances of his disappearance known?" Raúl asks.

Sánchez nods. "According to the doorman at his property," he explains after finding the appropriate page in the report, "he took a taxi in front of his building in Tres Torres around six p.m. the day before his death. There's no call recorded in the phone records, so he might have gone out on his own or maybe received an email or a WhatsApp message—but we haven't found his phone yet."

"All the victims were wealthy," Carla comments. "A banker, an actor, a builder . . ."

"Arturo Galán not so much," Marcos puts in. "From what I saw, he was an actor who'd had his day."

"Okay, but his income was still upper middle-class, wasn't it?"

"Yes, that's true," Marcos concedes, "though I wouldn't call him wealthy."

"Enough with the semantics," Sánchez interrupts. "The fact is that the only thing the victims had in common with Monells is that they all had money—and despite that, robbery wasn't the motive in any of the deaths."

"It has to be the sect," Marcos emphasizes. "Just like we found Álvarez's blood in Monells's basement—even though his wife wasn't sure he knew him or that he was a member of the satanic sect—the same could be true for Galán and Castells. The fact that we haven't yet found proof that all of them were there doesn't mean that—"

Sánchez's phone rings stridently. Motioning to Marcos to wait, he picks up the receiver. "Yes? Oh, good morning. We're all here." A pause. "What? That's impossible . . ." Silence. "Are you completely sure?" Another pause. "Agreed." Sánchez raises his gaze to the assembled team. "Thanks for the heads up, I'll keep an eye out for the detailed report. Yes, see you later."

The inspector hangs up and shakes his head. He looks bewildered. "That was the forensic department," he informs them after a moment. "They've identified one of the prints we found next to Arturo Galán's body. Apparently," he adds after a longer pause, during which he takes the picture from the report lying on the desk in front of him, "it's Eduardo Castells's."

The verdict of the forensic department has approximately the same effect on the members of the CID as a confession from the Pope that he's really an atheist. Nuria sees on the faces of her teammates expressions ranging from perplexity to absolute incredulity.

"It makes no sense," Carla repeats.

"The actor kills the banker," Raúl says, lifting a finger as he speaks, "the builder kills the actor, and Monells kills the builder. Am I leaving anything out?" he adds.

"It makes no sense," Carla insists for the third time.

"They've all been killing each other?" Marcos inquires, as confused as the rest. "But why?"

"It's absurd," Nuria murmurs, trying as hard as she can to fit the pieces together in her head.

Sánchez meanwhile has gone to the magnetic whiteboard where the photos of the victims and Monells are posted. With a red marker he draws an arrow that goes from Eduardo Castells to Arturo Galán. Now each victim has his own murder suspect, each of whom is the next victim.

"They've killed each other one at a time," Nuria reasons, contemplating the whiteboard. "It's crazy, but it can't be coincidence, can it?"

The question isn't directed to anyone in particular but Sánchez is the one who turns to her. "We've got three victims and four suspects," he resumes, crossing his arms, something he tends to do when he's trying to concentrate.

"Three of whom are now dead," Nuria points out.

"Unless . . ."—Sánchez begins to draw black lines from Monells to the three victims—"Monells is our killer and somehow he's arranged to leave the prints of the others at the scene of the crime to implicate them."

"And how exactly would he do that?" Nuria demands. "Besides, what's his phone doing next to Castells's body?"

"Obviously, he dropped it," says Raúl, who is standing behind her.

"Give me a break," Marcos snorts. "There's *nothing* obvious about this case."

"What if he left it there on purpose?" Nuria asks, looking at Marcos from the corner of her eye.

Sánchez turns toward her. "Why would he do that?"

"So we'll come after him," Nuria says, for some reason compelled to say what she's thinking. "I think he's playing a cat-and-mouse game with us."

"I'll ask you again, why would he do that?"

"I don't know. Maybe he's bored or maybe he's completely nuts. But I'm beginning to think he was the one who sent me the email suggesting we go see him, and also the one who left the blood sample in the basement, hoping we'd find it."

"That's pretty farfetched, don't you think? What if you hadn't seen it?"

"Well, maybe he would have thought something else up. Who knows?" Nuria shrugs. "The truth is, if we've only got one murderer"—she points to the whiteboard, to the black lines Sánchez has drawn—"then the case begins to make a certain kind of sense, don't you think? At least,"—she picks up the eraser and wipes out the red lines—"more sense than thinking that the victims all killed each other in turn, like some kind of conga line of death."

25

"Conga line of death, huh?" Marcos murmurs to her as they make their way back to their desks. "Where on earth did you pull that out of?"

"It's the first thing that occurred to me," Nuria confesses.

"So you're still stuck on your theory that Monells is some sort of criminal genius that enjoys being pursued."

Nuria senses a hint of reproach in Marcos's comment, but keeps this thought to herself. "It's what I think," she shoots back. "Besides, it's the only theory that makes sense of all this. If that isn't the case, what alternative explanation is there? That all the victims have taken turns to kill each other in alphabetical order? Now *that* sounds crazy to me."

Marcos shakes his head. "Nothing about this case makes any sense," he admits. "At the moment the only thing we can do is try to find Monells, but the bastard always seems to be two steps ahead of us."

"That's because he must have had it all thought out beforehand. No doubt he created the Sons of Lucifer as a way to attract his future victims. He might have been planning this for years. I mean, think about it."

"But except for the banker's blood in the basement, there's no evidence that Arturo Galán or Eduardo Castells were also members of the sect."

"Both of them lived alone, so there's no one who can tell us any different," Nuria reminds him. "Álvarez de Cortázar is the only one who had a wife and kids, and he's the one whose blood we found in the basement."

"Too big of a coincidence."

"Not a coincidence at all," Nuria insists. "It's what Monells wanted us to see. I'm more and more convinced that he put the blood there himself. He's the one who sent that email to my address and later made sure I was the one to find it. He's been manipulating us from the beginning, the son of a bitch."

Marcos leans back in his chair, studying her thoughtfully. "You seem very sure of your theory."

"Do we have a better one?"

He lets out a long exhale. "No, truthfully we don't. But in any case, everything still revolves around Monells. We have to find him and we don't have a fucking clue about where he could be."

"I'm sure he's very close. I have a feeling."

"Okay . . . Well, whether that's true or not, the only thing we do have to go on at the moment is finding the taxi he might have used to leave the Castells crime scene."

"I have another idea," Nuria says.

Marcos raises an eyebrow in interest. "What idea?"

"It's a shot in the dark," she admits, "but before the rest of you arrived I was researching crimes that have had something in common with ours, whether in the method used to commit them, the victims, or the circumstances."

"Did you find anything?"

"Not yet, but there are still a lot of possibilities to check out."

"And you want to keep on with that instead of continuing to look for taxis. Am I right?"

"Give me three or four hours more. That's all I need."

Marcos considers for a few seconds. "I'll give you two," he says, consulting his watch.

More than three hours later, Nuria brings her search to an end. The only thing she's found is a murder committed in 2010, a homicide in which apparently a derivate of scopolamine was used to reduce the victim's resistance.

That's where the similarities end, though, since the weapon was a knife, found next to the body, that had been used to cut through the jugular. A very bloody way to kill someone, for sure, but a far cry from the showiness of their murders—and of course, without the presence of any sort of satanic symbol at the crime scene.

Besides, on that occasion, the guilty party had been caught, and the towering mountain of evidence had resulted in a sentence of twenty-five years and a day for premeditated murder.

The killer had turned out to be a woman, the partner of the victim. She'd been surprised in a state of confusion next to the body, covered with blood from head to foot and with the knife in her hand. No other prints or evidence that a third person had been present at the crime scene had been found, so in spite of the fact that the accused claimed not to remember anything or to have any reason to have killed her husband, she was still condemned to a term in prison that, even with a reduced sentence, meant she still had sixteen years to go in the Wad-Ras women's prison.

Nuria jots down all the relevant data in a notebook even though she knows it's another blind alley. Even so, she feels that the morning has been fruitful. At least until Sánchez's phone ring. After answering, he springs to his feet.

"Very good," he says, making a few notes. "We'll be there in ten minutes. Cordon off the area and don't let anyone in, got it?" He slams down the phone and turns to the rest of the team, all of whom are watching him attentively.

"We've got another body," he says briefly, picking up his overcoat from his chair and shrugging it on. "A local cop found it in an abandoned warehouse on Sant Quirze del Vallés, less than two kilometers from here."

When they reach the address and climb out of the cars under a fine, cold rain, they're in front of an ordinary-looking warehouse in the middle of an industrial park. A faded *For Sale* sign hangs from its façade. A little further away, an ambulance waits next to three local patrol cars, their flashing blue lights reflected in the puddles on the asphalt.

"Inspector Sánchez of the CID," the boss introduces himself as soon as he steps from the car. "What do we have?"

The local cop, whose uniform boasts stripes indicating he's a sergeant, salutes and points to the open door of the warehouse. "A patrol discovered that the door had been forced and went in to investigate," he reports as the rain drips off the visor of his cap. "They found the body and called it in. That's all. No one else has gone in since they were told not to."

"Anything else?"

"The officer is in a state of shock and is being attended to in the ambulance," the sergeant adds. "He hasn't been able to tell us much."

"Good," Sánchez says with a sigh. "Wait here." Turning to his team, he adds, "Marcos and Nuria, come with me; Raúl and Carla, you go in through the rear door."

"Yes, sir," the four reply in unison.

Sánchez pulls his gun from its holster and makes his way cautiously toward the half-open door. Nuria does the same. She peers over his shoulder, but the inside of the warehouse is totally dark and she can't see further than a couple of meters from the door. All three take their flashlights from their pockets and sweep them across the interior of the building, but the beams start to fade out about a dozen meters ahead of them. They're just able to make out a figure lying in the center of the warehouse.

"There it is," Marcos says.

"Let's go," Sánchez orders. "You two, fan out to right and left."

With no need for further instructions, Nuria and Marcos separate, going in opposite directions, their flashlights supported atop the barrel of their guns, pointing at what soon reveals itself to be a naked body. The head is covered by a rag and the arms and legs are spread wide and tied to pegs anchored in the floor of the warehouse.

A body that Nuria looks at in puzzlement for a minute, feeling that something is missing. The terrible understanding arrives quickly as she realizes that this body is missing its hands and feet, hands and feet someone has cut off and then replaced in the wrong place: the hands at the ankles and the feet at the wrists.

Nuria bites her lip to keep from screaming. Taking a deep breath in an effort to calm herself, she takes a few cautious steps toward the body.

It's not until she's standing right over it that she discovers that the genitals of the victim are flayed. The skin has been removed from penis and testicles.

Nuria feels the sudden pressing need to get out of there, to turn around and run away rather than keep confronting such horrors, rather than continuing to feed the nightmares that will pursue her for the rest of her life. But she can feel Sánchez and Marcos's eyes on her, so she forces herself to remain controlled. She wants to show them she's just as tough as any of them are. "It's my fucking job," she murmurs inaudibly to herself.

She steps even nearer the body, crouches, and with the barrel of her gun slowly lifts the cloth covering the head. She holds her breath as she does this, expecting to find the victim's face frozen in a final instant of unutterable terror.

Lifting the cloth, however, what she feels is the shock of pure surprise. She knows this face.

"Fuck me!" Marcos exclaims behind her. "It's Jordi Monells!"

Nuria brings her incredulous eyes even closer. The aristocratic features are unmistakably those of the leader of the Sons of Lucifer. Across his forehead, the numbers 666 have been carved with a knife.

Instinctively, she touches the victim's cheek with her left hand, as if she can't believe her eyes aren't deceiving her. To her astonishment, the body isn't cold, as she'd expected.

"But what—" she manages to get out, but can't finish her sentence because all of a sudden the man's eyes open wide as if about to bulge completely out of their sockets. His mouth opens, releasing a harrowing cry of agony that pierces her eardrums.

Twenty minutes later, Nuria is still sitting in the front passenger seat of the Cactus, her eyes closed as she tries to calm her heart rate by summoning up images of placid lakes and flaming sunsets seen from the deck of her grandfather's sailboat.

All around her is frenetic activity. The emergency team has stabilized Monells *in situ* and are now carrying him on a stretcher toward Sabadell Hospital.

The white van from forensics pulled up ten minutes ago, and without even waiting for Monells to be removed, the forensic team has begun to take prints and collect evidence, searching every square centimeter of the warehouse.

Marcos approaches the Cactus, holding a steaming cardboard cup in his hand. Opening the door, he says, "Here, drink this."

"The last thing I need is coffee, Marcos."

"It's linden tea," he clarifies, offering her the cup. "It will do you good."

Nuria hesitates a second. She detests the taste of linden, but he's right, it will calm her nerves. At least it's something hot. Taking the cup between her hands, she nods. "Thank you."

"Holy shit, what a fright, no?" he says with a bitter grin.

Nuria takes a sip of the tea as she tries to erase the image of Monells's eyes flying open right in her face. "I can't believe he was still alive even after . . ." She shakes her head.

Marcos lowers his voice as if speaking in confidence. "Apparently they cauterized the cuts as they amputated his hands and feet so he wouldn't bleed out. From what I heard Antonia saying," he adds, "he could stay alive that way more than twenty-four hours."

"My God . . ."

"Yep." Marcos tsks. "If there is a merciful God, it's pretty plain he didn't like him."

"Poor man." Nuria tries not to imagine the terror of witnessing your own mutilation. "But at least," she adds, "if he manages to survive the hospital food he'll be able to tell us who did this to him."

Marcos makes a wry face. "Haven't they told you?" he asks.

"Told me what?"

"His hands and feet weren't the only thing they cut off the poor guy."

Nuria stares at her partner, trying to guess what he means. Marcos hesitates as if just talking about it causes him pain personally.

"Monells isn't going to be able to tell us anything," he says, swallowing. "They pulled his tongue out by the root."

26

It's pitch dark when Laura finds herself standing in front of the lobby door of her family's apartment building. She looks at her watch and discovers in amazement that it's almost ten p.m.

She remembers almost nothing about the last five hours or how she got here, save for a vague recollection of a gorgeous black dress and a lot of lights shining in her eyes while someone spoke to her. All the rest is like one of those dreams that slips through your memory's fingers when you try to grab onto it.

Taking a small mirror from her purse, she sees that she's no longer made up, though her pupils are abnormally dilated. God only knows what was in that white pill the woman gave her. It definitely hadn't been a simple tranquilizer.

She feels too fuzzy to think clearly. It's as if she's just coming off a real binge. The one thing she does know clearly is that she doesn't want her parents to see her in this state. She might be able to talk her dad down with some cock-and-bull story, but that won't fly with her mom, and if she suspects Laura's taken some kind of drug, she'll be on restriction until the end of time. Even if she begged her mother and told her it had been against her will, she wouldn't care.

But she has no other choice than to go up to her apartment. If she arrives later than ten, her excuse, that she'd gone to Paula's to study, will fall apart and everything will go to hell. So she opens the lobby door a bit clumsily and takes the elevator up to her floor, praying that her parents are immersed in some show on TV and won't notice her arriving.

She can barely believe her luck when she opens the door to find a note from her parents saying they've gone to the movies and that her dinner is in the microwave.

Since she's not hungry, Laura goes directly to her room. After a quick shower, she gets her backpack ready for school the next day and climbs into bed, hoping the fuzziness she feels will be gone after a few hours of sleep. She doesn't even feel up to calling Paula as she'd promised her she would, to tell her all about it. Actually, Laura realizes, she wouldn't even know what to say.

The next day crawls by between an interminable succession of tedious classes and the machine-gun rapidity of the questions fired at her by her friend, who is obviously much more excited about the whole thing than Laura herself.

"Tell, girl!!" Paula demands, grabbing her by the arm in the hallway. "How was it??!!"

"Fine," Laura says a bit flatly. "I think it went well."

"You *think*??" her friend exclaims. "Come on, Laura! What do you mean, you *think*??"

"Well, um . . . It was fine. It was weird."

"Well, shit, of course it must have been weird. It's the first time you've done it!"

"Not that kind of weird," Laura specifies. "The other kind of weird."

"What do you mean? Did something bad happen?" Paula presses.

Laura shrugs. "I don't know . . . I don't think so, but the truth is I can hardly remember anything."

"What do you mean, you can't remember?" Paula asks incredulously. "Did you suddenly come down with Alzheimer's or something?"

"No, it's not that . . . They gave me a pill to relax me and . . . I don't know. Everything after the photo shoot started is like fuzzy, cloudy. Maybe it was nerves or maybe whatever it was they gave me didn't sit well."

"They drugged you?"

"No . . . I don't know. I don't think so, actually. They seemed very professional."

"What about the pictures?" Paula asks, changing the subject to what she's really interested in. "Have you seen them?"

"No, not yet. They said something about how they had to process them in another format or something. They said they would be ready in a few days."

"Wow! I can't wait to see them!" Paula squeals, clapping her hands in excitement.

"I know!! Me too!!" Laura lets herself be carried away by her friend's enthusiasm, imagining herself on the cover of *Vogue,* wearing that amazing black dress she barely remembers.

27

It's past seven by the time the CID team, the forensic techs, and all the other departments involved in the investigation gather together in the same conference room in Egara where they'd met six days before after the first murder.

Six days, Nuria thinks, amazed. It feels like six months have passed since the morning they found the first body.

"Four murders in under a week," Moncada is saying. He's standing at the front of the room in front of all the assembled teams. The dark circles under his eyes reveal the fact that Nuria's not the only one who hasn't been sleeping well lately. "It's the first time something like this has happened that we know of. There have been serial killers all over the world who have killed dozens of people, some possibly even hundreds: Ed Kemper, Ted Bundy, Jeffrey Dahmer . . . but they always committed their crimes over a period of years, even decades. Never in a matter of days. Still and all, we still don't even know if we're confronting one or several murderers, what his or their reasons are, or how they manage to carry out their crimes. In reality we don't know anything." He turns to the whiteboard, where Monells's name has now been moved from the list of suspects to the list of victims. "We don't have a single clue or a single solid theory, much less a suspect. After a week of investigation, we have nothing, nada, zip," he concludes, directing his words to his entire audience and particularly the CID team, "and that is completely unacceptable."

A guilty silence spreads through the room and for a few seconds the only sound to be heard is the rain beating against the glass.

"Do whatever you have to do," he continues. "Explore every possibility and don't leave a single stone unturned. This case is the Mossos's top priority right now. Besides having a serial killer on the loose in the city, the anarchists keep burning up the streets night after night, encouraging the Satanic Assassin to keep killing the wealthy. The religious fanatics and the far right are gaining strength and every day more come out to pray and demonstrate against the government and the devil—as if they were the same thing—and to top it all off, the opposition is using all this as a spear to throw at the president who won't hesitate to use us as a whipping boy to save his own skin. That means that not only are we in danger of losing our prestige and authority as an organization, but our very jobs and even our continued survival as a corps." His face is tense. "Your professional future depends on our catching this murderer *immediately,* do you understand?" Moncada passes his gaze over the men and women in front of him who sit in uncomfortable silence. "I hope you will act accordingly." He motions to Antonia Grau, who gets to her feet to speak.

In the brief interval between Moncada taking his seat and Antonia taking the floor, Nuria hears a fly buzz several meters away.

"I suppose most of you have read the preliminary report," the forensic pathologist begins. "But for those who haven't, I'll just sum it up by saying that we found Jordi Monells alive in an abandoned warehouse in Sant Quirze del Vallés. His hands, feet, and tongue were mutilated with a saw that we still haven't found and his penis flayed." From the corner of her eye, Nuria sees a few of her male colleagues apprehensively covering their crotches with their hands. "Nonetheless," Antonia continues, "we did find some surgical tubing and a blowtorch that was used to cauterize. Also, traces of curare and adrenaline were found in his system, as in the other cases. Apparently," she adds clinically, like someone reading a grocery list, "after the skin was removed from the penis, the tongue was cut out, followed by the extremities, which were cut off one by one, making sure the subject remained alive and conscious during the whole process."

A murmur of consternation runs through the room. Even the most senior members of the police cringe at the brutality of the act.

"With regard to fingerprints," Antonia goes on, turning over a page of the report she's holding, "we've found three unknown fingerprints on the handle of the blowtorch and more than a hundred different ones all over the warehouse. We're checking all those against the database. There were also a multitude of prints from shoes and tires, but those will take longer to process." She lifts her eyes from her report and asks, "Any questions?"

"Will he recover?" asks Joana, a young officer from the financial crimes division with horn-rimmed glasses and a mousy expression.

"Well, I don't think his hands and feet will grow back," Antonia answers, making a wry face, "but apart from that, it looks like he will live—if you can call that living, of course."

Now Carla's the one to raise her hand. "Do you think he left Monells alive on purpose? Or were we just lucky enough to find him before he died?"

Antonia shakes her head. "It's difficult to say," she affirms, "but the way he performed the mutilations, cutting off the circulation in the limbs with tourniquets and later cauterizing the wounds would suggest that his intention was to leave him alive. To do it that way had to have taken him much more time than would have been required simply to mutilate him and leave him to bleed out." She pauses before adding, "So yes, I would say he did it on purpose."

"It's a punishment," Nuria murmurs.

"Sorry?" asks Antonia.

Nuria gives a start, unaware again of having spoken aloud. She's got to learn to control that. Clearing her throat, she offers, "I was saying that it's a punishment. Someone is punishing those men for something," she adds. "This isn't just some random maniac running around with a knife. I think the murderer knows them and is punishing them or exacting revenge on them for something."

"The same way you thought Monells was a criminal genius that was playing with us?" Nuria recognizes Raúl's voice behind her; she doesn't need to turn around to know where the comment comes from.

"We all thought Monells was the killer," Marcos puts in, coming to her defense. "All the evidence pointed to it."

"Evidence that she herself supposedly collected at Monells's house."

Now Nuria turns around to face Raúl. "What are you insinuating?"

"Enough!" Sánchez interrupts them. "We don't have time for this." He goes on. "There has to be a common link connecting all these deaths, and we have to find it. We're dealing with a murderer who plans everything meticulously and we're way behind." He points to the whiteboard holding the four photos. "We still don't know his motivation or how he chooses his victims. We have no motive, no clues, no suspects."

"And what about the fingerprints?" asks Aleix, an officer from Organized Crime with a ponytail and tattoos. "My understanding is that at each crime scene prints have been found belonging to the next victim. Couldn't it be as simple as that? What if they have all been killing each other?"

Marcos brings his lips close to Nuria's ear and whispers, "Look, your 'conga line of death' theory."

"Right now we still can't explain the presence of those prints at the crime scenes," Sánchez explains. "We still haven't found any explanation."

Nuria raises her hand. "What if it's all part of some satanic ritual where the Sons of Lucifer agreed to kill each other off one by one?" she asks. "I know it seems absurd, but it would explain the prints that have been found."

"A ritual in which the members of a sect kill each other one by one and the leader of the sect is horribly mutilated?" Sánchez asks. "It just doesn't make sense to me, no matter how satanic they are."

"Well, there has to be some relation between the crimes, Inspector," Nuria insists. "It can't be coincidence: the satanic sect, the number of the beast, the blood, the prints . . . We just have to figure out how the pieces fit together. I think we definitely need to consider this line of investigation."

Moncada gives Sánchez a sidelong glance and the inspector nods almost imperceptibly. "All right," he says with a sigh. "You and Marcos get onto that. Any other proposals?" he asks, running his gaze over the audience. No one makes a peep. "Well, in that case, you all know what you have to do," he states, rapping on the table with his knuckles. "We've still got one murderer or several running around the city. Find them."

Everyone stands as Moncada leaves the conference room. Nuria can hear her colleagues talking in low voices, and most of their comments express discouragement.

"So now what?" Marcos asks, coming up to her. "Your speech was very inspiring but actually we're no better off than we were at the beginning."

"I know," Nuria admits. "We'll have to go over the evidence again to see if we missed something."

"In other words, you don't have the slightest idea of what to do."

"Not a clue," she confesses.

"That's what I imagined," Marcos snorts. "Though you got one thing right, at least."

Nuria turns around, curious. "What are you referring to?"

"This morning you said 'Monells is close by, I can feel it.' And look where he was." He gives her a wry smile. "Only five minutes from here."

"Yeah." Nuria frowns as their colleagues leave the conference room, continuing to converse in low voices. "I'm a bargain basement Sherlock Holmes."

Marcos glances at his watch and looks at her. "If you let me invite you to dinner I can talk to you about my theories."

"You don't have any theories."

"Yes I do."

Nuria lifts an eyebrow and crosses her arms. "What you want is to drink beer and get laid."

Marcos gives her a guilty smile. "That's a good theory," he says, "that we could put into practice. What do you say?"

"I say that you have a one-track mind."

"Is that a yes?"

"It's a no."

He steps closer to her. "But the other day you really enjoyed it," he insists.

"That was the other day. I don't want to today," Nuria says firmly, taking a step back. "Do you have a problem with that?"

"Jesus, Nuria. You don't have to get nasty about it."

"Nasty? I've told you no and you keep on insisting."

"Okay, fine," her partner agrees, raising his hands. "We'll leave it for another day. But it would do you good."

"Sure. Thanks for your concern," she replies, the irony obvious in her voice. Turning away from him, she leaves the room.

The truth is that she *would* enjoy going out and having a little fun, but not with Marcos, with whom she will predictably end up talking about work, his divorce, and what a witch his ex-wife is. She has no patience for that today and doubts whether she ever will again.

But neither does she feel like going home to her solitary pajamas-dinner-TV-sofa routine. She decides the simplest thing will be to look for some stranger on Tinder. She can tell him everything in her life is wonderful and maybe somehow she'll manage to convince herself that it's true as well.

After all, everybody's as happy as they want to be.

Or as they can be.

28

By the time the alarm goes off the next morning at six-thirty her Tinder date has left: a Brazilian mulatto with honey-colored eyes and a six-pack, recently arrived in Spain and with limited conversational skills due to an imperfect knowledge of the language. This was delicious for Nuria. There's no better way to keep from thinking than to converse with someone you can barely understand. Your communication is limited to smiles, repeated nonsense words, and playing footsie under the table. All Nuria had gotten from the encounter was that his name was Joao, that he was from Salvador de Bahía, and that he hadn't imagined it would be so cold in Spain.

After a brief dinner at the Thai restaurant in the Plaza de la Revolución, they'd gone up to her apartment, barely containing their mutual desire to rip their clothes off as they went up the stairs. Soon thereafter, any attempt at conversation was abandoned, replaced by moans and whispers into each other's ears, until at some point after her second orgasm, Nuria had fallen asleep, exhausted, and slept deeply until her alarm clock had yanked her out of her trance with its impertinent jangling.

When she opens her eyes, a black-and-white cat is sitting on the bed staring fixedly at her. "Good morning," she mumbles, her mouth furry.

The cat meows in response.

"Yes, I know . . . I forgot to feed you last night."

Meeeooooowww!

"Okay, okay, I'm coming." Nuria pushes back the comforter and climbs out of bed. The room is cold and she shivers when the air touches her skin. It seems that not only did she forget to feed the cat, she also forgot to turn the heat on.

Looking around for her clothes, she realizes they're probably spread all over the living room, so she abandons the search, heading directly for the shower instead.

Turning on the hot water, she closes the bathroom door as she leaves so that the steam will fill the small room. Next, still naked, she directs her steps to the kitchen, but realizes when she looks for a can of cat food in the cupboard that she still hasn't gone to buy any.

"Fuck," she says when she sees the empty shelf. Opening the freezer, she sees a frozen pizza, some vanilla and chocolate ice cream, ice cubes, and by sheer luck, one last chicken breast covered in ice crystals. "I don't know how long this has been in here, but it's what there is, my friend," she says to Melón who is observing her from the doorway of the kitchen with skepticism. He meows even louder.

"I give you my word that today I'll buy you lots of cans of the good stuff," she promises him while she shoves the breast into the microwave to defrost.

Melón continues to meow demandingly at her. Nuria puts her hands on her hips and regards him. "Excuse me, but some of us have a life. The fact that you don't have your balls anymore doesn't mean I can't have some fun."

Meoooooow!

"Yes, yes, I know . . ." she says as she walks by him on her way to the bathroom. "Just let me take a shower while it's defrosting and I'll grill it for your breakfast. You see, you're going to come out winning in the end."

The hot shower feels heavenly. Nuria doesn't know whether it's because of the sex, the cold air inside the apartment, or who knows what else, but she feels reinvigorated. Her mind is clearer than it has been for days.

After breakfasting on cereal with almost-expired milk poured over it, she cooks and serves the chicken to Melón, closes the door behind her with just enough time to make it to Egara, and goes out whistling despite the cold, gray day that greets her.

The traffic on the C-58 is surprisingly light, and it's not until Nuria turns on the radio that she discovers it's Sunday. Counting up in her head, she realizes she's been working almost two weeks straight without a day off.

Given the circumstances, no one on the team has dared to bring this to the notice of the boss. She hasn't even missed her days off, in fact. The thought that she prefers working to partying makes her feel melancholy for a moment, though the reality is that on a cold winter Sunday like this one, she would probably end up staying at home watching TV on the sofa with Melón on her lap. At most she might go out for a couple of beers in the neighborhood with Susana. That wouldn't be nearly as exciting, she concludes, as solving a series of mysterious murders that are turning the city upside down.

As she drives, the news alternates between the increasing civil disturbances plaguing the city, including the first skirmishes between the Occupy anarchists and the España Primero skinheads, and the macabre discovery of Jordi Monells in an abandoned warehouse, mutilated and barely alive.

As per usual in Barcelona every time there were antiestablishment protests by groups from the fringe left, half the anarchists in the rest of Europe took advantage of the disturbances to spend a few days in the city pouring as much fuel on the fire as they could. In consequence, small local protests grew into news-grabbing altercations that resulted in headlines all over the continent. What wasn't quite as usual was to see neo-Nazi groups and Franco supporters organizing their own demonstrations that "coincidentally" clashed with the anti-fascists in what ended up as pitched battles. This time it had happened on San Juan Paseo where, after a long night of rabble-rousing, not a single shop window had survived and a dozen cars had been burned out in the middle of the avenue.

Nuria feels a twinge of sympathy for her colleagues in the riot squad, but then she remembers the afternoon in May 2011 when she'd suffered the full force of a misguided blow at a peaceful anti-austerity rally in Plaza Catalunya and her sympathy fades. She has friends among the mobile brigade of the Mossos d'Esquadra and feels a certain solidarity with her comrades in arms—but she does recognize that in spite of being mostly good people just obeying orders and whose presence is necessary when things get out of hand, there are some who enjoy bashing citizens a little too much.

The newscaster is now saying that new contingents of both antiestablishment groups are planning to pick up the pitched battle tonight where it ended the night before. The Generalitat, on the other hand, is affirming that it's doing all it can with the resources it has, while the opposition is blaming the situation on the incompetence of the government and the Mossos. Finally, some extremists are calling for a nightly curfew, patrolled by military forces, until the situation is under control. Nothing new under the sun.

The good thing about all this, Nuria thinks, is that the murders are no longer front-page news, and that could give them a little more time to try to solve them. Though, judging by the progress they've made up to now, they're going to need more than a "little more time."

By the time she reaches the CID offices, she's ten minutes late. The entire team is already at their desks. Sánchez throws her a sidelong glance, then looks at the clock on the wall before burying his nose in the pile of reports on his desk again. Nuria doesn't need to be a mind reader to get the message.

"Good morning," she says to her colleagues at large as she approaches her desk. Marcos lifts his gaze from his computer screen and leans back in his chair. "You look like you didn't get much sleep," he says, crossing his arms over his chest.

"I went out for a few beers and didn't get to bed until late," she answers before realizing it would have been better to bite her tongue.

"Oh, so you were only too tired to go out with *me*, I guess. Who'd you go out with? One of your Tinder hookups?"

Nuria can feel a cutting retort on the tip of her tongue reminding him that it's none of his business but she counts to five instead, taking her seat behind her desk in silence. "How's everything going here?"

Marcos's eyes are fixed on her and he seems to be meditating whether to continue bugging her. Finally, in a theatrically reproachful tone, he says, "Working. I'm investigating the people around Castells," he adds after a few moments, "but he's a widow and his daughter lives in Berlin. He apparently has a woman, though, who goes to his house every morning to clean and cook for him. Find her so we can go question her," he orders Nuria brusquely. "The information is in the report."

"Right," she answers in the same tone. Privately, she considers it a waste of time to talk to the builder's housekeeper but she doesn't feel like arguing with Marcos. In fact, she doesn't even feel like seeing him.

Resigned to submerging herself in the tedious search, she turns on the computer. It takes her to the window she'd opened the day before while searching for past murders having something in common with the current ones.

Specifically, what appears before her eyes is the report on the murder of a man whose throat had been cut by his partner and in whose bloodstream traces of scopolamine had been found. The woman, Luisa Domínguez, has been in Wad Ras for ten years and is still claiming innocence. Even if she manages to get her sentence reduced, she'll still have a good number of years left to serve.

Glancing at her partner from the corner of her eye, Nuria makes a decision. Getting to her feet, she says, "I have to go out."

"What?" Marcos asks, disconcerted. "What are you talking about?"

"I have a clue that might be interesting. I need to go check it out."

"What clue?"

"A murder that was committed years ago. It's got some things in common with these. The perp is in prison and I want to go visit her."

Marcos hesitates a moment before answering. Pointing to Nuria's computer screen, he says, "Well, if she's locked up she's not going anywhere. So get with the program. I told you it's urgent."

"I'll do it when I get back," she says, taking her coat from the back of the chair and shrugging it on.

"Don't fuck with me, Nuria."

Marcos's language reveals a level of frayed nerves that Nuria decides to ignore. The more irritated he gets, the more she feels she's got to get out of there.

"I'll be back in a couple of hours," she argues, walking toward the exit. With her peripheral vision she can see Marcos shifting position in his chair, no doubt weighing whether he should shout after her or physically follow her out. In the end he does neither, just follows her with his gaze.

Nuria knows that one way or another, she'll pay a price for defying her partner this way, but she also knows that staying there just one more minute would have guaranteed consequences that would have been worse in the long run.

29

The Barcelona women's prison, the Centro Penitenciario de Mujeres, popularly known as Wad Ras, is one of those urban prisons belonging to the last century. Budgetary constraints have prohibited the move to a new facility on the outskirts of the city. The Moorish-influenced complex, constructed more than a century ago, is nothing more than a long building built inside Villa Olímpica that shares the block it's built on with some municipal athletic facilities. If not for the sentry posts, high walls, and bars on the windows, it could pass for an old library or a rather decrepit municipal office complex.

A little over eighty inmates in total are housed in the penitentiary, but Nuria's only interested in talking to the one who appears in the dossier she's printed out and that she now scans for the last time before getting out of the car. Once she's fairly sure she's memorized the most important information, she tucks the file folder under her arm and heads for the entrance to the jail.

Standing in front of the blue-painted iron door, Nuria presses the bell. The voice of an employee comes through the intercom. "How can I help you?"

"I'm Officer Nuria Badal from the Criminal Investigations Division," she says, holding her ID badge up to the camera. "I need to speak to an inmate."

"Do you have an appointment?"

"Do I need one? I need to ask her some questions related to an ongoing investigation."

"Everyone needs an appointment," the voice clarifies over the intercom. "Besides, today isn't a visiting day."

"It's not a visit," Nuria points out. "It's an interrogation."

"All the more reason you need to give advance notice," the person insists. "Is the prisoner informed about your visit? Is her attorney going to be present?"

Nuria swears under her breath. She definitely didn't prepare for this.

"No," she admits. "The prisoner isn't informed nor is her lawyer going to be present."

"In that case, with no appointment and no attorney present, you can't—"

"Listen," Nuria interrupts. "We're talking about a top-priority case. I urgently need to ask the inmate some questions. If it's really necessary, please let me speak to one of your superiors." She adds, "Unless you'd prefer to speak directly to Superintendent Moncada and personally explain to him why you haven't allowed me to do my job."

Nuria can hear the gears clicking in the employee's brain. After a few seconds of silence, she says, "Just a moment."

Two minutes later she's back. "Come in," the woman says gruffly. At the same time Nuria hears the buzz that opens the door. She steps through it to find herself in a small anteroom facing another, identical door. Lifting her head, she looks directly into the camera that's focused on her face and waits for the door to be opened.

After a new buzz granting her entry, she enters another small room where she's received by a penitentiary officer sitting behind bullet-proof glass. "You have to leave your weapon here," she says, pushing a metal tray toward her under the glass.

Opening her coat, Nuria takes her Walther PPK from its holster and places it in the tray.

The officer asks for her ID and fills out a card with a red V for visitor with Nuria's information. "First door on the right," she says laconically. "Up the stairs to the third floor. Director Carbó is waiting for you."

"Thanks," Nuria answers in the same tone. Following the employee's indications, she reaches a wooden door with a gold plate on it inscribed with the name *Dir. Eugenia Carbó.* She raps on the door a couple of times with her knuckles and a woman's voice invites her in.

Entering, Nuria finds herself standing in front of a woman with gray hair and a tired face sitting behind a chipped and peeling wooden desk. The office is small and, oddly, the window to the exterior is barred like the rest of them. For a second, Nuria wonders if this woman is also condemned to the position that's been assigned to her.

"Good morning, Director," Nuria greets her. "Thank you for seeing me."

"Good morning, Officer," the woman answers. Her voice sounds worn out, just like the furniture in her office. "Please take a seat. How can I help you?"

"I need to speak with one of your inmates." Nuria opens the file folder to consult it, though she knows the name by heart. "Luisa Domínguez."

"May I ask why?"

"I'm sorry, but all I can tell you is that it's related to a top-priority ongoing investigation."

"There are official channels you need to go through for this sort of procedure. Surely you must know that."

"Of course," she says. It's just a little white lie. "But we're dealing with an atypical situation here. If this weren't the case, I would have made my request through the official channels."

"Then you must realize your petition is highly irregular. Even more so when the inmate's attorney is not present."

"I understand," Nuria concedes. "But as I'm telling you, this is an unusual situation, and an urgent one. The lives of several people may be at risk."

Eugenia Carbó seems to turn this over in her mind for a moment, evaluating the pros and cons of the situation. "Regrettably, the current statutes prohibit me from authorizing an interrogation under these circumstances," she explains finally. "I could only allow it as an exception, a personal visit, and only if the inmate agrees."

"Fine," Nuria answers quickly.

"All right," agrees the director, standing up. "Wait here." She gets up and goes out of the office, leaving Nuria sitting with the file folder on her lap and a hive of doubts pricking at her confidence. When she'd made the decision to visit the prison while sitting in front of her computer in Egara, everything had seemed simpler. Actually, the main impulse for her visit had been her desire to get out of there.

As she waits for the director to return, she's acutely aware that she hasn't prepared any questions, nor does she have a clear idea of how to conduct the meeting. She arrived at Wad Ras with a general idea of what she wants to know, but without any idea of how to achieve her goal. In the police academy, they'd done practice interrogations of each other in order to learn different methods of questioning and their advantages and disadvantages, but here she's going to be sitting across from a condemned prisoner who, in addition to being unprepared, she can't pressure, since this isn't an official interrogation.

As the minutes pass, the house of cards that is her confidence collapses little by little and she feels more and more nervous. She even asks herself how she's going to explain this to Sánchez if he asks her where she's been when she gets back. She can't think of a single justification for her actions that's reasonable enough for her to avoid a severe dressing down.

Well, Nuria thinks, taking a deep breath, *there's no turning back now*. She'll do the best she can and accept the consequences of her mistakes. As her Grandpa Pepe always says, it's better to ask for forgiveness than beg for permission. Although that maxim might not fit an organization like the Mossos d'Esquadra too well.

After an eternal ten minutes more, the director finally returns and stands next to the door. "The prisoner has agreed to the visit."

Nuria's heart lurches in her chest. "Wonderful," she says, standing up. "Thank you."

The director nods and motions to follow her. "You have twenty minutes," she informs her as she leads Nuria down the stairs. "But the inmate has the right to cancel the visit at any time."

"Understood."

"The visit will be personal but there will be no contact," she goes on. "You will be in the same room but separated by bars. No physical contact is allowed."

"No contact," Nuria repeats. "I just need some answers."

Eugenia Carbó stops in the middle of the corridor and turns around to face her. "This is not an interrogation," she reminds her. "If you coerce or threaten the inmate in any way without the presence of her attorney, we'll both be in a world of trouble."

Nuria attempts to appear serene and sure of herself. "Don't be concerned, Director. I'll just ask her a few questions and then I'll be on my way. No threats or coercion."

The woman nods, though Nuria can still see a shadow of doubt in her gaze. Or maybe it's just the dark circles.

"Very well," she says, pointing to a metal door at the end of the corridor. "Wait in there and the inmate will be brought to you in a few minutes."

"Thank you, Director."

"Don't make me regret my decision," the other woman says. She turns around and walks away in the direction they came.

Nuria enters visiting room No. 2. It's a small space measuring approximately two by four meters, divided down the middle by a row of floor-to-ceiling iron bars. There's a chair on either side of the bar, fluorescent lighting, and four surveillance cameras, one in each corner of the room.

The walls are a faded green, marked with several sets of initials, dates, and a few hearts. A large window with a double row of bars looks out onto a gray sky and a few banana trees denuded of their leaves. The room itself is depressing, but the view of the outside isn't much better.

Uncomfortable, Nuria shifts her position in the plastic chair, trying to calm herself and think of a good strategy, but in spite of the chilliness of the room, she can feel herself starting to perspire under her sweater.

The wait finally ends when a steel door opens with a creak on the other side of the bars and a prison employee waves a small, dark-skinned woman into the room. She's wearing a loose fleece sweat suit in purple and yellow.

Nuria doesn't know if it's because of the eighties outfit, the emaciated look of the inmate, or both, but she immediately thinks the woman across from her is a junkie. "Good morning, Luisa," she greets her as soon as she takes her seat.

"Who are you?" the woman blurts. Her tone is aggressive, but the gravelly sound of her voice suggests a woman worn out by life.

"I'm Officer Nuria Badal, from the Mossos d'Esquadra," she introduces herself. "And I'd like to ask you a few questions."

"What questions? About what?"

Nuria hasn't planned on being the one answering the questions. "I'm working on an investigation and I would really appreciate your cooperation."

"My cooperation?" Luisa repeats, making a sour face.

"Yes, your cooperation. Would you be kind enough to answer my questions?"

"Fuck off," says the other woman. "What's in it for me?"

Something else Nuria hasn't contemplated. "I could," she falters, "bring you cigarettes, Tampax . . . anything you need."

"I don't smoke and I went through menopause years ago."

"What would you like, then?"

"To get out of here."

Nuria sighs. "I'm sorry, I can't do anything about that. I'm just an ordinary officer."

"So why the fuck would I help a damn cop?"

"You could help keep other people from suffering harm."

Luisa Domínguez twists her mouth in a cruel smile. "And why the fuck should I care about someone else suffering harm? Has anyone cared about what happens to me in the last fourteen years?"

"You could prevent a murder, Luisa."

This does get her attention and she sits up straighter in her chair. "A murder?"

Nuria senses her interest and turns the screw a little more. "What you tell me, Luisa, could save the life of an innocent citizen."

"I'm innocent," she shoots back, "and look where I am."

"That's exactly what I wanted to talk to you about."

"My case?"

"You claimed you'd been drugged and that someone else killed your partner. Is that right?"

"I got tired of telling the judge that," Luisa says, shaking her head. "I loved Felix. I would never have hurt him, much less killed him. Someone drugged me, killed him, and put the knife in my hand."

"In the physical exam they gave you," Nuria counters, opening the file folder, "there was no trace of drugs."

"Because they took so fucking long to examine me," she retorts. "What do I know? Maybe it was one of those drugs that disappears from your body in a few hours, like scopolamine. Why are you asking me this? Are they going to reopen my case?"

"I'm sorry, I can't give you any details about my investigation," Nuria says.

"Fuck that shit. You can't give me details, but you want me to help you in your shit investigation, did I get that right?"

Nuria turns over a page in the file folder and removes the photo of Jordi Monells. She hesitates for a moment but then shows it to Luisa. "Do you know this man?"

Instantly, Luisa's face transforms. Her dispirited expression turns to one of recognition, morphing next into something that looks like triumph.

"You're here because of the murders, right?"

"I already told you I can't give you details about my inves—"

"Cut the shit. I know why you're here."

Nuria leans back in her chair. "Oh yeah? Why?"

Luisa smiles, openly now, and Nuria notices that she's missing several teeth.

"You came because you want me to help you find that Satanic Assassin they talk about on TV."

Nuria tries to hide her anxiety and maintain her composure. "Do you know something having to do with the murders?"

Luisa crosses her arms. "Of course I know something about them."

Nuria waits a few seconds before realizing the other woman isn't going to say anything more. "Would you mind sharing what you know with me?"

"I'd be happy to share what I know with you," she says, mimicking Nuria's tone. "But I want something in return."

"What?"

"I already told you. I want to get out of here."

"I can't—"

Luisa stands abruptly, interrupting Nuria. "I don't give a shit what you can or can't do," she spits at her. "If you want to catch that murderer, you'll have to get me out of here."

She turns, walks to the steel door at her back, and raps on it with her knuckles. "Guard!" she calls. "We're done here!"

30

Sánchez is reading the brief report Nuria's just handed him while she stands in front of his desk waiting. From his own desk, Marcos observes her, awaiting the boss's verdict.

The inspector raises his eyes from the page a couple of times and studies Nuria over his reading glasses. His expression doesn't exactly convey satisfaction, she thinks.

When he's finished reading, he sets the paper aside, takes off his glasses, and stares at her fixedly. "What am I supposed to do with this?" he asks.

"That woman knows something."

"That inmate told you what you wanted to hear."

"You didn't see her. Her whole face changed when I showed her the photo of Monells."

"That picture's already been shown on the news," Sánchez points out. "She simply tied up the loose ends, figured out what you wanted, and tried to manipulate you."

"With all due respect, Inspector, you weren't there."

"Do you think I needed to be?" he shoots back. "Do you think this is the first time an inmate has tried to manipulate a cop to get something in return?"

"What if it's true? What if she really does have information pertaining to the case? Shouldn't we be taking that possibility into account?"

"Of course we can take it into account, Officer Badal. What we can't do is go to a judge and ask him to set a condemned murderer free just because she put on a little performance when you showed her a photo and then lied to you. No judge would even consider a request like that without solid evidence."

"But what if it *isn't* a lie?" Nuria insists. "What if I can unearth some proof that what she's saying is true? I'd like to thoroughly investigate her case and go back to see her again. Maybe I can get her to—"

Sánchez shakes his head. "I understand that you have doubts, Nuria," he interrupts. "An inmate who's been in prison for ten years and who has another who knows how many to go can be very convincing. Believe me, I had the same experience once and I was taken in too. But we can't afford the luxury of wasting time on this."

"But—"

He cuts her off again, this time more brusquely. "But nothing. We've got three and a half deaths on the table and one psychopathic asshole wandering around with a scalpel in his hand. We don't have the time or the resources to reopen a case from fourteen years ago. Have I made myself clear?"

"Um . . . Yes, but—"

"Is it clear?" Sánchez repeats, raising his voice.

This time Nuria nods obediently. "It's clear."

"Very well," he says, waving a hand toward her desk. "Then stop wasting time on this and get to work."

Nuria lowers her head, trying to contain her frustration. "Yes, sir," she says, gritting her teeth as she turns around and walks in the direction her boss has indicated with his index finger, back to her desk.

"How'd it go?" Marcos asks as she approaches, a little smile of satisfaction tugging at his lips.

Nuria knows he watched the whole scene, so she doesn't bother to answer.

"I warned you," her partner adds. "You can't just go up to Sánchez with something like that and expect him to listen to you. This is the real world," he states firmly, "not a detective series."

"I had to try," Nuria retorts as she sits down in front of her computer screen. "I'm sure Luisa Domínguez knows something."

Marcos shrugs. "Maybe yes, maybe no. But what's certain is that no judge is going to just let her walk scot-free."

Nuria's about to tell him she's sure she could get more information out of her if she could just talk to her again, but she understands it's useless to insist. Sánchez has the last word on the issue and he's made his stance on it abundantly clear.

Even so, in a last surge of pride, she murmurs, "We'll see."

The rest of the day is spent interviewing Castells's assistant. Marcos had found her hours ago, but apart from the revelations that he liked macadamia-nut ice cream and was obsessed with clean bathrooms, they learned little more about the third victim. No suspicious relationships, no weird habits and, of course, no satanic or even religious leanings. According to the woman, he was a divorced businessman who lived to work. About a significant other, male or female, she had no idea.

A search of the dead man's house also failed to yield anything meaningful. He'd lived in a luxury penthouse in the Tres Torres neighborhood with views of the small Sarriá cemetery. Though the apartment boasted all the indulgences someone in his sixties could buy, it gave Nuria the same feeling she'd had in Julio Álvarez's house: that this wasn't a home. If this is the culmination of a successful life, she thinks as she contemplates the showy but sterile surroundings, maybe it's not worth aspiring to.

On their way back to Egara, not one millimeter closer to solving the case, Sánchez calls to inform them that a new video has been uploaded showing the torture Monells was subjected to. Nuria clicks on the link and begins to watch it while Marcos drives, but in spite of the fact that the *Extra Diario* web page had the decency to pixelate the goriest parts, she can't watch more than a minute.

The camera seems to be mounted on a tripod and is focused on Monells's terrified face. When the murderer begins to cut off what appears to be one of his hands, the screams of the victim, even muffled as they are by the gag in his mouth, pierce Nuria's soul. It's the most gut-wrenching sound she's ever heard in her life.

The rest of the way back to headquarters is traversed in a heavy silence until Marcos, without taking his eyes from the road, asks, "Do you have plans for the afternoon?"

"I'm going to see my grandfather."

Marcos is silent for a few seconds as if expecting Nuria to say more. Finally he says, "And that's it?"

"That's it," Nuria confirms, suspecting which way the conversation is headed.

"No more hooking up with mulattos on Tinder?"

Nuria whirls around to face him. "Are you spying on me?" she says with a frown.

"Don't get too full of yourself, honey," he replies smugly. "A friend saw you having dinner with him, and since he knows you and I are partners . . ."

Nuria has to fight hard to control her irritation, taking three deep breaths before answering as calmly as she can, "It's none of your business who I go out with or don't go out with."

Now Marcos does turn to her for an instant. "I thought we were a team."

"At work," she reminds him. "What I do in my private life is strictly my own business."

Marcos puts on a plaintive tone. "What happened to us?" he asks. "Does that mean nothing to you?"

"*Us*?" Nuria shoots back, as if the word is incomprehensible. "There is no 'us,' Marcos. I thought I'd made that clear from the beginning. We hooked up a couple of times and that's it. Period. I'm not looking for a boyfriend, and even if I were, it would never be one of my colleagues from the Mossos."

"I see . . ." he murmurs dejectedly. "Evidently I was totally wrong about you. I thought you were different."

Nuria stares at him, incredulous at his words. When did all this happen without her noticing? She realizes that if she doesn't take a firm enough stand to stop this here and now, it might not be possible to stop it going forward. "Look, Marcos," she says, trying to soften her tone, "I don't know what kind of fantasies you've been spinning in your head, but I want to make this clear once and for all: there is nothing between you and me, there never has been, and I can tell you there never will be. So if you've got some romantic idea in your head, you can get rid of that right now because I assure you that's never going to happen."

Marcos continues to stare straight ahead in silence as if he hasn't heard her, but Nuria can see his tension in the rigid set of his jaw. She decides not to say anything further. She's said it all already. Emotionally exhausted, she props her elbow on the door and leans her head on her hand, turning her face toward the window and gazing out at the overcast sky hanging over the city of Sabadell.

That's when she hears Marcos mutter something barely audible under his breath: "You're all the same."

It takes Nuria the whole way home to calm down. As soon as they'd arrived at Egara she'd left without saying goodbye, risking a dressing down by Sánchez for not staying a minute longer than she absolutely had to—but once again, she needed to leave headquarters as quickly as possible, albeit for very different reasons than the ones she had the day before.

Once she's back in Barcelona again, she parks in the Barceloneta neighborhood. Her mood lightens and, bathed by the yellow glow of the streetlights that illuminate the narrow streets of the old fishermen's district, she allows herself to smile for the first time that day.

When she crosses Pepe Rubianes, her smile widens even more as she thinks of the unforgettable character her grandfather is with his wonderfully inappropriate comments. So by the time she's standing in front of the run-down four-story apartment building where he lives, with laundry hung out to dry between the balconies just like all the other buildings in the neighborhood, you could say she's almost in a good mood.

She pushes the bell and his voice comes through the intercom. "Yes?"

"Grandpa," she greets him. "It's me, Nuria."

"Nuria?" the voice asks after a few seconds. "I don't know any Nuria."

"Come on, open up. It's cold down here."

"Password?" he says.

"If you don't open up this door I'm going to give the bottle of wine I've got in my bag to the first person I see."

"Correct!" he answers with a laugh. A second later she hears the buzz through the intercom and pushes the door open.

31

Her visits to Grandpa Pepe are a hundred-eighty degrees different than the ones she pays her mother. The latter are an obligation Nuria always tries to avoid whenever she can, and which inevitably end up in an argument about how her life should be going and what she should be doing or not doing in regard to her work and personal relationships. In contrast, her visits to her father's father always involve plenty of bad jokes and good advice, with no biased judgments about her life or unsolicited opinions.

The door is opened to her by a white-haired man with penetrating blue eyes, attired in an elegant dressing gown and slippers to match. He's like a character out of a turn-of-the-century novel; if he's not wearing a suit and tie, it's because she's arrived without notice. Even wearing a robe, he looks more elegant than most people on their wedding day. The soft notes of a jazz trumpet issue from the old Phillips stereo in the dining room.

"Hi, Grandpa," she greets him again, kissing him on both cheeks.

"Hello, Princess. I'm so happy to see you."

"I managed to escape from work a little early today," she says, pulling out the bottle of wine.

José Badal smiles appreciatively and motions toward the interior of the apartment. "Make yourself comfortable. I'll go get a couple of glasses."

When he comes back, Nuria is seated at the coffee table in the living room under the Tiffany lamp that looks like a multi-colored glass puzzle. The soft light given off by the low-wattage bulb paints the ceiling with pastel tones, the same way Nuria remembers it when she would come as a child to this same apartment to drink hot chocolate. In those days she could barely hoist herself onto the chair.

"Everything good here?" she asks now, taking a sip of her wine.

"Everything is fine, thanks," her grandfather responds. "Did I tell you I've signed up for ballroom dancing on Tuesdays?" he asks her with a mischievous grin. The truth is that he had told her this the last time they saw each other, but Nuria says no anyway so he can explain again that he's learning to dance tango and that his partner is an enchanting woman ten years his junior who makes goo-goo eyes at him.

Nuria nods as enthusiastically as she did the first time and presses him for details about the classes and the marital status of his dance partner. "Have you introduced her to Fermina yet?"

"Uh, no," he says with a wave of his hand. "I haven't even asked her out for coffee yet."

"What are you waiting for?"

"Everything at its proper moment, Nurieta." He winks at her. "You've got to seduce women little by little so they think they're the ones taking the initiative. Let things mature until they finally fall like ripe fruit."

Nuria smiles wickedly. "Well, at your age, if you let things mature too much, she's likely to rot on the vine."

Grandpa Pepe lets out a guffaw that echoes off the walls of the small living room. "Very funny, Nurieta." He smiles and nods. "Better, tell me what's going on with you. How's work? Are you happy with the transfer?"

"I've already been at CID for several months, Grandpa."

"Is it going well?"

"Fantastic."

José Badal makes a wry face. He knows her too well. "What's happened?"

"Nothing, actually."

"Problems with your colleagues?" he guesses. "That's always the most difficult part."

"No, well . . ." she trails off. "It's just that . . ."

Her grandfather waits patiently for her to finish her sentence, only prodding her when it becomes clear she's not going to. "Personal problems or work-related?"

"Both."

"Hmm." He makes a sympathetic face. "Bad?"

"Maybe." Nuria sighs. "Just some bad decisions I made that I'm paying for now. Although what would really be weird would be for me *not* to make bad decisions, right?"

Her grandfather shakes his head. "Decisions aren't bad or good," he says. "They're just paths we decide to take based on the little we know. Later, the consequences may turn out to be good or bad, but many times that's not in our hands."

"Yeah, but when I take the wrong path so many times, maybe it's because my judgment isn't that great."

"Don't be misled, Nurieta." He shakes his head again. "We all make mistakes constantly. Everybody does it. The difference is that some people try to disguise their mistakes, others choose not to think about them, and still others simply blame them on everyone else. You, on the other hand," he adds, "blame yourself as if you'd known from the very beginning how it would all turn out. That's a mistake you've been making ever since I've known you."

"But in this case it's true," she insists. "I knew I was blowing it and I still kept on until I'd totally messed things up."

Don Pepe blinks thoughtfully a couple of times. "Is there something you can do to fix it?"

"I've done what I can, but I don't know if I've just made things worse."

"Well then, there you are." Her grandfather shrugs stoically. "If you've done everything you can to fix it, why worry? And if there's nothing else you can do . . ." he adds, lifting his glass, "why worry?"

Nuria finally smiles reluctantly and lifts her glass as well. "You're right," she admits, clinking it against her grandfather's and producing a delicate chime.

Actually, her worries haven't been assuaged at all, but she prefers to enjoy the moment and forget about the problems with Marcos and what her future in the department might be.

"Hey, now that I think of it," don Pepe says, setting his glass on the table, "What's happening with those murders? That's your department, isn't it?"

"It's the number-one priority for the CID right now."

"I can imagine." He nods. "I know I shouldn't ask you, but my curiosity's eating me up inside. Do you have a suspect? Is it true what they're saying, that the murders are satanic rituals?"

Nuria opens her mouth to give him the standard answer that she can't tell him anything but, perhaps because of the wine or maybe just because she has so much trust in her grandfather's discretion, takes a deep breath instead and answers. "We still know almost nothing," she confesses. "We don't know who's killing them, or how they're doing it, or why. This case is a nightmare, and all our superiors are doing is pressuring us."

"That doesn't surprise me. And to make matters worse, the whole city's going crazy, and each new death adds more fuel to the fire."

"I know. But I can assure you we're doing everything we can. Whoever is behind the murders is someone who's very smart and has been planning this for some time."

"In other words, he's not a satanic maniac the way he's painted by the media."

"Well, he can't be that mentally healthy if he's going around killing people," Nuria objects. "But if he is a maniac, he sure knows how to cover his tracks."

"And you still don't have any clues?"

"None."

Her grandfather fixes her with his gaze, scrutinizing her expression. "You don't seem very convinced."

"Well . . . There could be one, but Sánchez, my inspector, doesn't want me to investigate."

"Why?"

"Because he says it's a waste of time and no doubt he's right."

"But you don't think so," says don Pepe.

"I just think it would be worthwhile to make sure."

José Badal pauses pensively. "And what are you planning to do about it?"

"What do you mean?"

"You know what I mean." He looks at her astutely. "I know you well, Nurieta, and I'm sure it's eating you up inside. Am I wrong?"

"But what can I do?" Nuria spreads her hands. "I can't go against the orders of a superior officer, they'll open an internal investigation on me."

"That's never stopped you before."

"This time it's different."

"If you say so . . ." her grandfather counters.

Nuria crosses her arms and her smile widens. "You know you're a bad influence, right?"

"I'm just holding up a mirror to you, Nurieta."

"Yeah, sure," she answers, shaking her head while still smiling."

When she was small, her mother and her grandfather had been like the little angel and the little devil perched on each shoulder, whispering good and not-so-good ideas into her ears. Her mother always pulled her toward what was supposedly the politically correct thing to do, what other people would think, and societal norms, whereas her grandfather would pull her in the opposite direction, suggesting that she ignore the rules, take alternative paths, and trust in her own instinct.

Her poor father was the one who'd always had to mediate between his father and his wife, trying to show Nuria as he did so that the most reasonable thing to do was to take the middle road. But now that he was no longer there, and there was no one to show her the good and bad aspects of different ways of looking at the world, she had no frame of reference by which to judge when taking one path or another.

What she had now was her mother, her grandfather, and her own judgment, about which she had profound doubts. But it was all she had and, if she was going to blow it, she thinks now, it was better to do it following her own intuition rather than someone else's.

"How are you doing?" she finally asks in an attempt to change the subject. "Is your pension covering your expenses? You know that if you need it, I can pitch in."

"Bah, don't worry about it," says her grandfather, his indifference clear in his expression. "Fermina uses up most of it but then, I don't have many expenses apart from her."

"You haven't changed your mind about not selling her?"

"No, as long as I can keep paying the mooring fee," he says. "I have too many good memories on that boat and still owning her gives me hope about creating new ones in the future. If I sold her," he adds, "it would be like saying my life is over and that everything's going to go downhill from here until the day I die."

"Jesus, Grandpa, don't be so melodramatic. I'm also fond of Fermina, but your happiness doesn't depend on having a sailboat tied up at Puerto Olímpico."

José Badal lifts an eyebrow, amused. "Wow, look at that, you giving *me* advice now."

"It's not advice, it's just—" She finishes her sentence with a vague wave. "Do you want to go down there one of these days to swab her down and have a few beers on deck?"

"Do you even have to ask?" He grins happily.

"Well, enough said, then," Nuria says, lifting her wineglass again. "The next day I have off, I'll come by to pick you up and you and I will go down to the dock to wash Fermina's face."

This small decision also makes her feel happy and for a moment, while she rolls the subtle flavors of the robust Empordá red around on her tongue, she forgets about the murderer who's wandering loose in the city, the idea of disobeying Sánchez, the incipient problem she has with Marcos . . . She even forgets that she's forgotten to buy food for Melón once again.

32

Two weeks later, the agency still hasn't sent the photos, nor have they called her about the portfolio. In fact, they haven't contacted her at all, and Laura, pacing in circles in her room, wonders if she should call them or send them an email.

She finally opts for an email to avoid seeming over-anxious, but really because she's afraid of being caught flat-footed. If she writes the message she can go over it as many times as she wants to before sending it.

Half an hour later, after she's finally hit *send,* Laura decides to take a shower to clear her mind and try to let go of the whole thing. Maybe she'll even call her girlfriends to see if they want to go shopping downtown, though that will mean having to withstand yet again the barrage of questions they've asked her ever since they found out about the photo session. That's still better, though, than staying at home with her thoughts running in crazed circles in her head like a caged tiger.

Nonetheless, shortly after getting out of the shower, she hears the phone ring. She rushes to answer. "Hello?"

"Laura?" It's the voice of the photographer from the Pygmalion Photo Agency.

"Yes, this is she."

"I have something for you," the photographer announces, sounding as excited as if she's just won the lottery.

"The pictures?"

"Better," he answers. "An unbeatable opportunity to make yourself known."

"I don't . . . I don't understand."

"A party," he clarifies. "Next week. There will be very important people there, people who can launch your career and make you a star."

"A party?" she repeats, disconcerted. "But . . . what about the photos?"

"Forget the photos. Any pretty girl can get herself a model's portfolio. What I'm offering you is the chance for these people to meet you in person."

"What . . . people?"

"People with money, Laura. Money and contacts," he answers her with a touch of impatience, as if what he's saying is obvious. "The type of people you would never get to meet otherwise."

"I don't know, actually. I—"

He cuts her off. "I'm offering you a once-in-a-lifetime opportunity to attend a very exclusive party. There will be other professional models there with their agents. But maybe I was wrong about you," he adds, exhaling in what sounds like disappointment. "Maybe you're not ready."

Laura's heart does a flip at these words and she realizes this is one of those moments that may be a turning point in her life. A train has just pulled to a halt in front of her and the doors are about to close in her face. If she doesn't jump aboard right now she'll lose the opportunity forever.

"It's fine," she answers firmly. "I'll go."

The following Saturday she's ready, dressed in her most elegant outfit, a figure-hugging burgundy dress with matching heels and lipstick. On paper, it's the dress she planned to wear for the first time at her graduation, but not even in some alternate universe does she have the money to buy another one and she certainly can't ask her parents. In fact, she's told them she's going to a pajama party at Paula's house and has the dress and shoes packed in her school backpack.

Slightly later than the time she was told, her taxi drops her off in front of an elegant mansion on Tibidabo Avenue in the upscale part of Barcelona. From where she's standing she can see the whole city laid out at her feet.

From the exterior of the mansion there's no sign at all that a party is going on. Only the profusion of luxury cars parked in the surrounding area indicates that something unusual might be happening there. After checking the address a couple of times to make sure it's the right one, Laura presses the bell. A few seconds later a butler, wearing a black mask as if he were Zorro or something, opens the door and asks for her name.

Laura, disconcerted, hesitates a moment before reacting. "Um . . . Laura Gómez," she says. The butler, after checking with a list he's holding in his hand, stands aside and invites her to enter. She steps inside but comes to a halt almost immediately, her eyes like saucers.

The interior of the mansion is doubtless the most lavish she's seen in her life. The walls are lined with velvet and hung with enormous, gold-framed paintings. Chandeliers hang from the ceiling, each one of their crystal prisms flashing with reflected light.

But what's made her stop dead in her tracks isn't the furnishings but the discovery that the several dozen guests milling around the living room spread out before her are all masked, either simply, like the butler or the waiters moving among the throng, or elegantly, their masks encrusted with precious gems, feathers, or glittering trim.

"Shit," she thinks aloud.

Just then, the photographer's assistant comes striding toward her. Naturally, she's wearing a mask too. "Laura!" she exclaims, embracing her as if they were old friends. "I'm so happy to see you! I thought you'd changed your mind."

"Is this a costume party?" Laura asks, motioning toward the guests. "No one told me I had to bring a mask!"

"You don't need one, princess," the woman clarifies with a smile.

"What do you mean I don't need one?" Laura protests. "Everyone has one on!"

"Precisely." Laura senses a complicit wink behind her mask. "How are they going to see how lovely you are if you have a mask on?"

"But . . ."

"Relax, Laura. Just mingle, have a drink, and enjoy the party."

"Enjoy the party? But what am I going to do?" she asks, more and more upset. "I've never been in a place like this and I don't know anyone either!"

"Don't worry about that," the woman soothes her. "What matters is that they get to meet you. Just follow my lead," she adds as she takes Laura's arm and leads her into the aristocratic living room where some faces have already turned in her direction with great interest.

33

When Nuria leaves her grandpa's house, it's almost eleven. She calculates that by the time she gets home, showers, and climbs into bed it will be after midnight, and grimaces when she realizes she's not going to get enough sleep tonight either. But it was worth it; the long chat she had with don Pepe has not only lifted her spirits, it's also filled her with a determination she'd been far from feeling that afternoon.

On her way to her parking spot she glances at her phone, finding several missed calls from Marcos, but she has no desire to talk to him. Just the sight of the red icon on her phone screen makes her good mood vanish.

Next to her on the sidewalk, a Pakistani with a belly so large it looks like he's carrying triplets slams down the security shutter on his small grocery store. Only then does she remember Melón.

"Fuck," she curses under her breath, hurrying up to the man. "Excuse me, I need to buy something. It will just take a minute."

"Closed, miss," the man says, pointing to the closed shutter.

"Truly, it will take less than a minute. Please?" she pleads with a wink.

"Very late now." He shows her his watch.

Nuria extracts a five-euro bill from her purse and presses it into his hand. "Please take this for your bother," she says, showing him her best apologetic face. "It will just be a minute, I promise you."

The Pakistani looks at her, then at the bill in his hand. Bending over with some difficulty, he shoves the metal shutter up again. "One minute!" he warns her, raising his index finger.

When Nuria exits the grocery store with a satisfied smile, only slightly over a minute has elapsed. In her hand she carries two plastic bags containing every can of cat food the store had to offer.

The next morning, Nuria arrives at headquarters just before the morning briefing begins and goes directly to the conference room. As she's hanging her down jacket on a peg, Marcos comes up behind her. "I called you several times last night," he says brusquely.

Nuria turns around, hands on her hips. "I was busy," she says crisply. "Was there some emergency?"

Before he can answer, Sánchez's voice is heard inviting them all to take their seats. Nuria turns her back on Marcos. She still has no idea how to handle what's happened with him, but instinct tells her to keep her distance as much as she possibly can.

"Good morning to you all," the inspector greets them once everyone's seated and quiet. "Today we have to—"

The door of the conference room flies open and an officer strides into the room and up to Sánchez. He whispers something in his ear and hands him a small note. Sánchez reads it, shakes his head, and raises his gaze.

"The meeting's canceled. We have another body," he informs them, his voice somber. "Everybody to work."

This time the crime scene is in Sarriá, in a mansion on Ballester Street. Marcos hasn't opened his mouth once during the drive, for which Nuria is grateful, since she has no desire to talk to him. She knows the moment when she'll have to is coming, but the longer she can put it off, the better.

Circulating through the narrow streets in silence under the fine rain, Nuria has time to think about the fact that in only eight days, there's been almost the same number of murders as would normally be committed in Barcelona in a year. It's not surprising that the gutter press is making a killing and that the top story on every single news broadcast as well as every special news presentation is laser-focused on this case.

To top it all off, she didn't sleep well last night either. The civic unrest has reached all the way to the streets of Gracia, her own neighborhood, and the shouts, fireworks, and police sirens robbed her of sleep until the early hours. Now, in full daylight, driving through the tranquil streets of Sarriá, it all seems like a nightmare, but even so she can't rid herself of the sensation that the city's turning into a pressure cooker that's getting ready to explode.

Marcos speaks unexpectedly. "Is this fucking rain *never* going to stop?" Nuria doesn't know if this is an attempt at conversation or if he's just venting his anger on the weather. In any case she decides silence is the best response and continues to sit mute, her gaze focused on the windshield. "It's been raining for a solid week and fucking freezing at the same time," Marcos adds. "Where's the goddamn global warming?"

"That's how climate change works," Nuria replies at last.

"What?" Marcos barks, turning to look at her.

"I'm telling you that climate change doesn't just mean more heat and drought, it can also bring colder weather and more rain once in a while. Extreme climatology."

Marcos snorts. "So what's this? Are you the fucking weather woman now?"

Nuria rolls her eyes and returns her gaze to the streets they're driving through. She should have kept her mouth shut.

When they finally pull up to the address they've been given, Nuria feels relieved to get out of the car. Several police vehicles are already parked next to the wall of the garden surrounding the nineteenth-century mansion. It's three stories high with enormous windows. The entrance gate is standing open, and a uniformed officer waves them through once they've flashed their CID badges. "They're all in the back," he says, jerking his thumb behind him. "In the greenhouse."

"Thanks," Nuria answers, pulling her cap and gloves from the pocket of her coat. The white van belonging to forensics hasn't arrived yet, but she doesn't doubt it will be there in a few minutes. Enough time to take a look before the place is crawling with forensic techs in their white jumpsuits.

"You wait here," Marcos says to her, pointing to the ground at her feet.

"What? Why?"

"Because I say so. I've had enough of you walking around crime scenes taking pictures with your phone like some tourist. From now on we're going to do things differently."

"What the fuck are you talking about? I do my job!"

Marcos plants himself in front of her with a scowl. "Your job is to do what I tell you, Officer Badal," he replies coldly. "And as your superior, I'm ordering you to wait here and not come any closer until further notice. If you disobey, I'll be forced to inform the inspector and request that a disciplinary file be opened on you for insubordination. Understood?"

"You're a bastard."

Marcos takes a step toward her, shoving his face close to hers with the clear intention of intimidating her. "Understood?"

"You can't do this."

"I can, and I will," he underlines. "And if you try to get cute with me, you're going to be in such deep shit you're going to wish you'd never joined the CID."

"Is that what you want? For me to leave the department?"

Marcos bares his teeth in a cruel smile. "I see you're beginning to understand." He turns and walks away toward the back of the house, leaving her standing there.

Nuria has never felt so humiliated in her life. Her blood is boiling in her veins as she balls her hands into fists, digging her nails into her palms. Though the rain falling on her shoulders has intensified, she doesn't even feel it. Barely managing to contain her rage and frustration, all she can think of are slow, painful ways to kill her partner. Soon enough, however, she begins to assume some responsibility for the situation. After all, she knew she was taking a stupid risk.

She'd known that the situation with Marcos was going to become a problem, but she hadn't imagined it would go this far. She'd wanted to think that it would resolve itself one way or another and that even if things between them got complicated for a while, with time things would settle down and they could return to having a reasonable work relationship.

But now, standing under the rain, she comes to the painful realization that that had been a fantasy that was never going to come true. Now it's all gone to hell and there's no turning back.

Nuria lowers her head and gazes at her gloved hands, at the drops of rain sliding over the white latex, slipping between her fingers. Just like her future at the CID.

Could this be the end of her police career? Could her dream of being an investigator really end thanks to the infantile revenge of an offended partner?

Nuria lifts her head and stares at the group of officers entering and leaving the large glass greenhouse. "Fuck that shit," she mutters to herself, clenching her fists tightly.

<h1 style="text-align:center">34</h1>

Goaded on by the determination not to let her partner ride roughshod over her, Nuria comes to a bold decision. She doesn't want to show up at the scene of the crime and risk being publicly humiliated by Marcos. Maybe that's exactly what he's expecting her to do.

Instead, she feels for the keys to the Cactus in the pocket of her jeans. Even before a fully-formed plan has taken shape in her head, she's on her way to the car, her steps firm.

Nuria knows that making her own decisions under these circumstances is a reckless move, and that if she fails to achieve any sort of solid result she's risking a disciplinary file or worse. Even if she does manage to make a significant advance in the investigation, they may still open a file on her. But if she's clear about anything, it's that doing nothing will only take her down a dead-end street she doesn't want to enter.

By the time she turns the key in the Cactus's ignition, Nuria's convinced herself that the only way out of this is to risk it all.

Her first stop is the Sabadell Hospital, where Monells had been admitted into intensive care. After introducing herself to the doctor on duty at the ICU, a dark-skinned woman who is younger than Nuria and wears tortoise-shell glasses and a tired expression, the response she receives to her request to see Monells is a resounding no.

"Absolutely not," says the doctor. "No way. Totally impossible."

"Dr. Díaz, please," Nuria insists, reading her name on her ID badge. "It's essential that I speak with him. He's the only witness that's still alive that could make a positive identification of the person who did this to him."

"That doesn't matter. The patient is in critical condition and any effort on his part could prove fatal, especially if it involves reliving such a traumatic moment."

"I could get a court order," Nuria hazards, "but that would only take up more precious time."

"No you can't," replies the doctor, calmly shaking her head. "The courts have no jurisdiction here. I am the only one with the power to make that decision, and the answer is no." Nuria realizes she's right. "Now, if there's nothing else I can help you with," adds the doctor, turning to walk away, "I have many other things to occupy—"

Nuria grabs her arm as she's leaving. "If I can't speak to him, more innocent people are going to die. Do you want that on your conscience?"

Dr. Díaz stares fixedly at Nuria's hand on her arm until Nuria removes it, fearing that the physical contact may not have helped her case. Instead, the doctor says, "Speak to him? Even if he were fully conscious, how do you think a man without a tongue or hands to write with is going to tell you something?"

"Please just let me try," Nuria insists. She's almost begging now. "It's a matter of life or death. There are serial killers loose in the city and Jordi Monells is the only person who can tell us who they are."

The doctor looks back at the ICU ward behind her. After considering for a few seconds she exhales in acquiescence. "Five minutes," she says finally. "But if his vitals begin to show signs of alteration, you'll have to stop immediately. Is that clear?"

Nuria nods, slightly surprised at having gotten her way. "Thank you, Doctor."

"Five minutes," she repeats, holding up her open hand. "Not one more."

Without wasting a second, Nuria turns and heads for the bed the doctor has pointed out to her at the far end of the room. Lined up on both sides of the corridor are beds occupied by patients who are barely visible among the snarl of electrical wiring, intravenous lines, and tubes to help with respiration and surrounded by monitors and sensors, all emitting a chorus of erratic beeps, the only thread that keeps the patients moored in the land of the living.

When Nuria reaches Jordi Monells's bed, he's only partly visible behind the crowd of machines connected to his body that are keeping him alive. Two screens display his vital signs and some other numbers Nuria can't figure out. The only one she recognizes is the heart rate monitor, which shows that his heart is beating at a relaxed fifty-two beats per minute.

She approaches the head of the bed. The sight of Monells's face takes her back to the scene she was present at fewer than forty-eight hours ago, when he'd suddenly let out that desperate cry only a few centimeters from her face. Nuria feels the impulse to take a step back, as if afraid that horror will repeat itself, but she summons her composure and remains where she is.

Laying a hand on his shoulder, she says, "Mr. Monells . . . Good morning. I'm Nuria Badal. Do you remember me? I need to ask you some questions."

Jordi Monells has no reaction at all, not a blink, not an involuntary movement, not a change in his vitals. Nuria suspects that he's sedated to his eyeballs. "Mr. Monells," she insists, lightly shaking his shoulder, one of the few places where he doesn't have a patch stuck onto his skin or a tube entering his body. "Wake up, please. I need to speak with you."

Nothing. It's like she's shaking a corpse. For a second she thinks of asking the doctor to inject a coffee with two shots into his veins or something else to wake him up, but obviously she knows that's not going to happen and it would just take up precious time.

Looking around as she wonders what to do, she sees a hypodermic needle lying on a nearby tray. First making sure no one is watching, she picks it up and furtively pokes Monells with it, first just barely grazing the skin and next, when she gets no reaction, more deeply, until a tiny stream of blood trickles from the incision she's made.

Nuria quickly pulls the needle out, picks up a square of gauze, and blots the blood from the tiny wound. When she raises her eyes to his face again, Jordi Monells has opened his eyes and is observing her, his gaze foggy.

"Mr. Monells," she says rapidly. "I need to speak with you. You need to tell me who attacked you so we can arrest him." The man stares at her over his oxygen mask but makes no other movement beyond a slight blink. Nuria doesn't know if this is a reflex act or a sign of agreement, but her time is running out fast and she has no choice but to keep insisting.

His pulse monitor emits a beep and she can see from the corner of her eye that his heart rate has risen to fifty-eight beats a minute.

On her way to the hospital, a possible method of communicating with someone who has no hands with which to write nor tongue with which to talk has occurred to her. In her small notebook, she's written YES on the first page and NO on the last, and a letter of the alphabet on each of the pages in between. It's a slow, difficult method, no doubt, but it's the best she could come up with.

"Mr. Monells," she continues, holding the notebook in front of his face. "I need you to concentrate. If the word I show you is correct, blink. All right? Now, do you know the person who did this to you?" She shows him the page that says YES. He blinks. She waits a couple of seconds, then shows him the last page where she's written NO. He blinks again.

"Okay, we're off to a good start," she murmurs. Though she's confused, she decides to forge ahead.

Beep. The monitor shows sixty-one now.

"Was it a single person or a group?" she asks, realizing tardily that she's phrased the question wrong. She tries again. "Was it a group of people who attacked you?" She shows him the YES and NO again.

He blinks at NO.

Beep. Sixty-five.

"Was it one single person?" she asks, just to make sure. Again, he blinks at NO.

"Shit," she swears under her breath. This isn't working, but there's no Plan B. "Was it a man?"

YES.

Beep. Sixty-eight.

"Was it . . . a woman?"

YES.

Beep. Seventy-two.

For an instant, it occurs to Nuria that the killer might be transsexual, but then another possibility presents itself. "Was it a man and a woman?"

YES.

Beep. Seventy-six. The line indicating his heart rate is becoming more irregular.

"Did they tell you why they . . . did this to you?"

YES.

Beep beep. Eighty. The number is now in yellow.

"Were they members of the Sons of Lucifer?"

NO.

Beep beep. Eighty-four.

"Was it part of some satanic ritual?"

NO.

Beep beep beep. Eighty-nine. Now the number is orange.

"Was it for some financial or professional reason?"

NO.

Beep beep beep. Ninety-three.

"Was it for some personal reason?"

YES.

Beep beep beep beep. Ninety-eight.

Nuria hears the doctor's footfalls approaching behind her. To reassure herself, she asks again, "Was it because of a personal issue?"

YES.

Beep beep beep beep. One hundred three.

"Officer!" the doctor says behind her. "That's enough!"

Nuria sees Monell's eyes going to Dr. Díaz. She grabs his chin and forces him to look at her. "Focus, Jordi," she orders him. "This is very important. Did these people say any names? Is there any clue at all you can give me to help me find them?" She flips from page to page in her notebook.

YES.

Beep beep beep beep. One hundred nine. The numbers on the monitor are now in red.

The doctor grabs her arm, but Nuria twists free. "I just need a minute more," she says.

"Not one second more!" replies the doctor. "Can't you see what you're doing? This man is in critical condition!"

Nuria ignores her and turns back to Monells. "Do you have a name to give me?"

Monells blinks furiously and Nuria understands, or wants to understand, that he has crucial information he wants to give her.

Beep beep beep beep. One hundred fourteen.

Dr. Díaz has left and Nuria takes advantage of this to skim through the pages of the notebook one by one, attentively watching for Monells's blinks. Finally he produces the letter *M.* Closing the notebook, she begins again from the letter *A.* Before she can turn the page, Monells blinks.

MA.

Beep beep beep beep beep. One hundred twenty-one.

"Very good. You're doing so well," she says, turning over the pages again.

That's when a pair of hands takes hold of her like pincers, making her drop the notebook on the coverlet. Monells blinks emphatically. From the corner of her eye, Nuria can see that the page that's open is *R.*

MAR.

"What are you doing? Let me go!" she protests, turning toward whoever has her in a viselike grip. She finds herself face to face with the scowling faces of two hospital security guards who tighten their hold on her as if she's a drunk who's being tossed out of a discotheque at three a.m.

"I'm a police officer!" she protests. "Are you aware that you're interrupting an official investigation?"

"I'm just doing my job, miss," alleges one of the guards. His head is shaved and his arms are like hams.

"I warned you," the doctor says, shaking her head as the security guards guide Nuria past.

"This is important!" insists Nuria. "He was about to give me a name!"

"What is it you don't understand? This man is sedated and in critical condition," the doctor repeats as the two guards almost drag her out. "Right now he doesn't even know his own name."

Nuria doesn't know what to say to this and as she's rushed out of the ICU, it occurs to her that maybe Dr. Díaz is right.

But once again, she has no choice but to keep going.

35

Nuria leaves the hospital with more questions than when she went in. Not only have Monells's answers opened new possibilities, she can't even be sure of the accuracy of his responses. Was the real Jordi Monells the one who had answered her, or was it the opiates coursing through his bloodstream? To what point can she really trust his answer that it was a man and a woman? He'd seemed quite sure that the perpetrators weren't members of the Sons of Lucifer but, given the fact that she doesn't have the list of members anyway, knowing that doesn't make much difference even if it is true.

And what about those three letters? Would they be the first three letters of the first name of one of the killers? Or his or her last name? Maybe their initials? *MAR* could be anything.

As she walks toward the parking lot, the terrible feeling grows in her that what she's just done hasn't been helpful at all. It's all been for nothing except to earn herself a stern reprimand from her superiors if this incident should reach their ears, something that, judging by how upset the doctor was, Nuria thinks is more likely than not.

Oh well, she thinks, she had to try. As the saying goes, you end up regretting the things you didn't do more than the things you did. Her only reservation is whether or not this saying applies also to a police officer whose job is teetering on a tightrope at the moment.

Nuria climbs into the driver's seat of the Cactus and sits for a few seconds with her unfocused gaze fixed on the stains on the windshield. *Now what?* she asks herself.

She could return to the scene of the latest crime where she might still find the rest of the team. But why? The situation will be the same as it was an hour ago, but even more tense now that she'd left without letting anyone know she was going or where. What she just found out isn't enough to offer Sánchez. It won't make up for having gone over his head and visited Monells.

Suddenly, a name pops into her mind: Wad Ras.

The women's prison.

Luisa Domínguez.

But it makes no sense to go back there without any sort of deal to offer her. And there's no deal she can offer.

Or is there?

She enters the department at the Egara complex like a thief, looking from side to side and doing everything she can to avoid someone seeing her and asking her awkward questions.

Once she's assured herself that no one from her team is there, she makes a beeline for her desk, where she turns on her computer and begins to write furiously, attempting to make the document she's composing sound believable and official. Legalese has never been her forte, though, so after giving it a brief review to assure herself that it's complicated-sounding enough to be barely comprehensible—like any official document worth its salt—she cuts and pastes the logo of the Ministry of Justice to the top of the page and presses the *print* button.

With the printed copy in her hand Nuria reads it over once more, trusting it will be as convincing as it is confusing, though she knows that a good part of how credible any document is depends on the desperation of whoever reads it. She slides it into a manila folder embossed with the seal of the Mossos and slips out of the department, almost on tiptoe.

In the car again, she's just about to start the engine when her phone rings stridently in the pocket of her coat. Glancing at the screen she sees Marcos's name. Without a moment's hesitation, she puts the phone on silent, ignoring the call, and slips it back into her pocket.

"Shove that up your ass," she murmurs, turning the key in the ignition. If Sánchez calls she won't be able to do the same thing, but for now she tells herself she'll cross that bridge when she comes to it.

Nuria crosses the city at top speed and in slightly over a half hour finds herself sitting again in the office of Eugenia Carbó, the director of Was Ras. With the file folder in her lap, she nervously awaits the arrival of the official who arrives only after ten minutes have elapsed, her heels clicking smartly on the tile floor. Nuria doesn't need to be a psychoanalyst to see in her face that the other woman isn't happy to see her again.

"This is highly irregular, Officer," she raps out as soon as she seats herself in her office chair. "You can't just keep showing up here whenever you feel like it, skipping all protocol, and think that I'll simply look the other way."

"I . . . I'm sorry," Nuria agrees, contrite. "You're absolutely right, Director."

"The official procedures are there for a reason, not just because I say so. Do you understand? The inmates have rights, and I have many legal obligations with which I have to comply. If one of the prisoners decided to report me, that wouldn't be your problem, it would be mine."

"I'm aware of that, Director." Nuria experiences a sudden *déjà vu* of when she was in middle school trying to convince the principal not to tell her parents that she'd skipped a whole week of classes to go to the beach.

"You're sorry, I'm right, and you're aware of it," Eugenia Carbó repeats, her voice tinged with sarcasm. "Nonetheless, here you are again, sitting in my office and asking my permission to see an inmate in a totally irregular way."

"It's an emergency, Director. A matter of life or death."

"That's what you said the last time."

"And it's still true. There's been yet another victim since then, and we don't know how many more there may be. Every minute is critical."

"So if that's the case, why am I not looking at a court order granting you the permission you need right this minute?"

Nuria has no answer for this. "I . . ." She swallows and decides to lay it all on the table. "Look, actually my boss doesn't know about this visit. He thinks that speaking to Luisa Domínguez is a useless line of investigation and he's refused to support me. He thinks nothing she can tell me will have any credibility whatsoever and will only lead me to a dead end."

Eugenia Carbó leans back in her chair, the leather creaking under her weight, and interlaces her fingers. "And in spite of that, here you are."

Nuria looks at her and nods. "And in spite of that, here I am."

"Do you think you're going to achieve anything more than you achieved last time?"

"I don't know," Nuria confesses. "But I have to try."

The director ruminates for almost a minute, staring fixedly at Nuria as if trying to see into her, see what kind of woman she has in front of her.

"I like you, Officer Badal," she says at last. "I like women who are brave and determined," she adds, "maybe because I was one of them years ago . . . until I ended up here." She waves her hand in a gesture that includes not just her office but the whole of the Wad Ras prison and perhaps even the city of Barcelona. "It happened that one time I put one of my superiors in an uncomfortable position through my attempts to change things, and all of a sudden I found myself here with my butt stuck to this seat. Being brave and determined has its risks, especially if you're a woman."

Nuria nods. "I know. I may be totally blowing it, but I have to do what I believe is right, no matter whose knickers I get in a twist. That's why I became a cop."

Eugenia Carbó's face breaks into a smile that looks like it rarely comes out of hiding and she nods as well, satisfied with Nuria's answer.

Less than ten minutes later, Nuria is again waiting nervously in the visiting room for Luisa Domínguez to appear. In her planning she hadn't even considered the possibility that the inmate might refuse to see her but now that she's here, waiting for the door on the other side of the bars to open, her doubts begin to mount. She's thrown herself into the swimming pool head first, without looking, from the high dive, and now she's beginning to ask herself whether there's actually any water in the pool. In spite of the cold her hands are sweating, and small finger-shaped marks of moisture have appeared on the rough surface of the file folder.

When the steel door finally opens with a groan and Luisa Domínguez appears, wearing the same sweatsuit and expression of suspicious exhaustion as she had the day before, Nuria exhales in relief.

"You again?" Luisa growls.

"Yep, me again," Nuria says.

"I already told you everything I had to say," the woman affirms. "I won't say another word until—"

Nuria lifts the file folder so Luisa can see it clearly. The inmate's eyes narrow as she moves her head nearer to see what Nuria's holding. "What do you have there?"

"What you asked for."

Luisa blinks incredulously. She stares at the file folder, then at Nuria, and then back at the folder. "No way," she says warily.

Nuria opens the folder and takes out the document she just printed in Egara. "Here you go," she says, coming close to the bars and offering it to her.

Luisa looks at the document Nuria's holding out to her with suspicion, like a bad student unwilling to look at his grades at the end of the semester. "You're kidding me."

"See for yourself."

Luisa sticks her hand through the bars and takes the folder, her hand trembling slightly. Nuria doesn't know whether the tremor is due to nerves or some sort of abstinence.

With the zeal of a rabbi opening the Torah, Luisa takes out the sheet of paper and begins to read it avidly. Her eyes move impatiently from left to right and top to bottom like someone who's looking for a word in a word search game. After a minute, she raises her gaze from the document and fixes it on Nuria, her forehead creased in a frown.

"I don't understand a fucking word," she says. "But I don't see anything about how they're going to let me out."

Nuria nods with pretended calm. "No, it's there. It's a legal resolution that makes the revision of the judgment contingent on your cooperation in resolving this case. Obviously," she adds smoothly, "if you try to lie to us, the deal's off, but if you can really help us you'll be released."

"But here it says," Luisa says, pointing at the document in her hand, "that 'they will review the case,' not that they'll let me out."

An hour ago, while Nuria had been composing the document—which was more mendacious than a campaign promise—she'd wondered if she should have the so-called resolution mention an immediate release from prison in gratitude for services rendered, blah-blah-blah. She'd concluded, however, that to promise something like that wouldn't be believable and that the more limited promise she'd eventually decided on would.

Now she's regretting her decision.

She suspects that if, in addition to setting Luisa free, the document had said the government would be giving her a beachfront apartment and a convertible, the inmate would have gone for it. "Luisa," she says now, assuming her best poker face, "I believe you're innocent, and after an emergency review of the facts of your case, the judge also believes you may be. But official pardons are in the hands of the government and can take years. What I'm offering you is a chance to present your case and be tried again, but this time in a just manner, taking into consideration all the circumstances of your case."

"That's not what I asked you for. I don't want another fucking trial, what I want is to get out of prison right now!"

"What I'm offering you, Luisa, is the opportunity to do just that. You have to be realistic, it's the best deal you're going to get." Like a gambler pushing all his chips to the center of the table she adds, "Take it or leave it."

"Well, I'm leaving it," Luisa retorts. "Either you get me out of here or I give you nothing."

Nuria sighs and shrugs her shoulders. "Okay . . . if that's your decision." She stands and holds out a hand toward the bars. "Give me back the document and we'll forget the whole thing. I'm truly sorry for you."

Instead of handing it to her, Luisa glances at the file folder again. "I . . . don't know," she vacillates. "I'd have to show it to my lawyer."

Nuria swallows. "Of course," she says with a tense smile.

"Before I could tell you anything."

Nuria shakes her head firmly. "There's no time for that," she says. "There was a new murder this very morning. We can't waste even a minute."

"I've wasted ten years here."

"I know, and I understand you. But you must understand that what I'm offering you is a highly unusual deal—and that's because of the circumstances. If more people die while you're thinking it over, I can assure you the judge isn't going to be quite so benevolent."

Luisa Domínguez fixes her sunken eyes on Nuria as if trying to scrutinize her soul. A soul Nuria knows is assuredly going to hell for having so heinously deceived this poor woman. Only the consolation that doing this may save lives allows her to maintain her calm and her composure.

Finally Luisa takes a step back and sits down in her chair again, clutching the brown file folder like a life preserver. She warns Nuria, "Nothing I say can be recorded or used against me in the future."

The condition surprises Nuria but even so, she accepts without hesitation. "You have my word."

Luisa seems to vacillate again but at last she lowers her gaze to a point on the floor between them, as if her memories were to be found in the stains covering it. "All right," she says. "Now listen to me carefully."

36

"Years ago," she begins, "Félix, my partner, looked for pretty young girls on the chats and social media sites of the time like MySpace. The kind that dance by themselves now on TikTok or Instagram hoping everyone will see their reels and they'll get famous.
The girls he thought had potential he offered a free photo shoot and a professional portfolio they could use to begin their career as models."

Nuria waits in expectant silence.

"It was just that . . ." Luisa goes on, lowering her eyes again, "he would also offer them the chance to make a little extra money if they did . . . well, extra jobs."

"What kind of jobs?"

"You know . . . dates, massages, parties . . ."

"Sex?"

"Sometimes."

"You're telling me he lured young girls so he could prostitute them?"

"I wouldn't call it that."

"Of course not. And these girls, were they minors?"

"Some of them."

"Some?"

"Well, most of them. But you know, there are girls of fifteen who look like they're in their twenties."

Nuria bites her lip to avoid telling Luisa what she thinks about that. Especially coming from another woman. "What else?" she asks instead.

"Since he was a photographer, Félix was one of the ones who would find the girls, and I helped him sometimes at the photo shoots to make the girls feel more comfortable. That was all we did. It was other people who took care of everything else."

"Who?"

"I don't know, I swear it. Félix was in charge of all that, but I don't think he knew who was really behind it all either. It was all like very mysterious. Even the clients, when there was a private party, would all wear masks, like in that movie with Tom Cruise and Nicole Kidman. I think they got their inspiration from that movie."

"Are you telling me they organized orgies with minors?"

Luisa shrugs as if to say *that's life.*

Nuria feels a knot in her stomach and takes a deep breath, trying to calm herself. Luisa sees her and points a finger at her. "You gave me your word that none of this can be used against me."

Nuria feels like telling her to go to hell, but then remembers that isn't the reason she's there. "My lips are sealed," she reassures Luisa. "But tell me what all this has to do with my case."

"One time I went to one of those parties," the woman admits. "I was helping in the coat-check and I recognized one of the clients, Arturo Galán, the actor. He had a mask on, like all of them, but I recognized his voice and his bearing. I was a big fan, you know?"

"Are you sure?"

"A hundred percent."

"And you believe that whoever killed your husband and pinned the blame on you is the same person who killed Arturo Galán."

"Exactly."

Nuria crosses her arms and leans back in her chair. "I don't see the connection," she says, shaking her head. "Besides, more than fifteen years have elapsed between one murder and the other."

"Wait," Luisa says, raising her index finger. "There may be important people in that network, because some of the parents tried to report them to the Mossos, but they just deep-sixed the case and nothing happened in the end."

"What do you mean, they deep-sixed the case?"

"Just what I said, for fuck's sake. No doubt someone made a call to the judge or whoever and that was the end of that."

"You can't get away with that," Nuria says.

"Come on, don't give me that shit," Luisa scoffs. "And you're a cop? What world are you living in?"

"Where are you going with this, Luisa?"

"Shit, isn't it obvious? Someone, when they saw the cops weren't doing anything, decided to take justice into their own hands."

"By killing your husband and Arturo Galán."

"And no doubt all the rest as well," she affirms. "I'll bet you anything all those rich people who've been offed were members of that network or clients of the girls."

"You're talking about some sort of avenging father who decided to take justice into his own hands?"

"Why not? He wouldn't be the first."

"And the prostitution ring . . . is that still going on?"

"How am I supposed to know stuck away in here?" She waved a hand. "Maybe yes, or maybe the report the parents filed scared them. How should I know?"

"Do you have contact information for them?"

Luisa shakes her head vigorously. "I told you Félix was the one who dealt with them. I just helped out once in a while. They paid really well," she adds.

"So you told all this to the cop or the judge when you were on trial for the murder of your husband?"

"And have them lock me up for that too? No fucking way. I've got enough with one sentence."

Nuria reflects for a moment. "So then . . . the only thing you have is that you believe you recognized Arturo Galán's voice in one of those parties."

"I'm totally sure."

Nuria shakes her head, unconvinced. "It doesn't add up," she points out. "Maybe some father wanted to take revenge on you for turning his daughter into a prostitute, I'll give you that. Even that he might have had something to do with your husband's death, if he was the one that lured the girls in. But . . . to begin killing people in that network so many years later? That doesn't make much sense."

"There are people out there who are really crazy."

"And there are also people who are really horrible," adds Nuria, her gaze drilling into Luisa's. "But these murders have been especially cruel, and whoever committed them made a special effort to cause his victims terrible agony. To commit crimes like these, more than a decade later, the pain the murderer's been carrying around has to be far greater than just revenge for someone having induced his daughter to charge money for sex."

"Well . . ."

"Well, what?"

"The girls didn't always go along with it at first."

"Meaning what?"

"Sometimes it was necessary to give them a little push . . . You know."

Nuria frowns and leans forward in her seat. "No. No, I don't know."

Luisa seems to be looking for the appropriate answer somewhere in the small window of the room. "Let's just say that sometimes . . . Félix was forced to pressure them a little bit."

"Explain yourself."

"During the photo shoots we would usually give them something to relax them and . . . well, so they would lose a little of their initial embarrassment. Lots of them would get overly shy once the lights were on them."

"So you drugged them?"

"Just a minimal dose of burundanga. Just enough so they would relax during the photo shoot and go with the flow."

"You drugged them with scopolamine," Nuria sums up, her jaw tight. "And then?"

"Then we took photos," Luisa says. "First the normal ones, dressed, and then, once they were nice and relaxed . . . the private ones. The ones we showed to the clients."

"Pornographic photos?"

"Erotic, I would say," Luisa corrects her. "But well, there were all kinds, sure."

"And you were there."

Luisa Domínguez gives a quick nod. "I helped the girls to change and relax. It helped calm them if there was another woman present in the studio."

"And then you drugged them," Nuria says, barely containing her rage as she imagines the scene.

"I told you, just enough to relax them. I'm sure they got more wasted at the parties they went to."

"But you took advantage of it to take nude pictures of them."

Luisa shrugs. "That was our job," she explains, as indifferently as if she'd been talking about being a grocery stocker. "The photos were only circulated among the clients . . . unless the girls gave us problems."

"You blackmailed them with the photos?" Nuria says, understanding.

"And sometimes with videos we would take at the parties. It was just to guarantee that they didn't start running their mouths off—or if they refused to collaborate."

"If they refused to be prostituted," Nuria clarifies, imagining the terrible dilemma faced by the girls.

"I'm not proud of what I did . . . of what we did," Luisa argues. "But in the end most of the girls accepted it and they made good money. Lots of them were able to pay for their college with the money they made, you know?"

"And the ones that didn't?" Nuria asks. "What happened to the ones that refused?"

"I don't know."

"How can you not know?"

"I've told you several times, it was Félix who was involved with that, and he hardly told me anything. He always said that the less I knew, the better."

"You were making good money too, weren't you?"

Luisa shrugs again.

Nuria's still thinking the connection between the two cases is pretty flimsy, propped up only by Luisa possibly having seen Arturo Galán. Though the fact that they'd used scopolamine to take advantage of the girls and the murderer had also used it to subdue his victims might not be a coincidence.

Even so, it's still pretty small potatoes as something she can present to Sánchez to justify what she's done, disobeying him and manufacturing a false document with which to deceive an inmate.

"What about the photos?" she asks.

"The ones of the girls? We destroyed them," says Luisa.

"I don't believe you," Nuria says.

"When the parents filed the report with the Mossos, Félix got scared and erased everything. It all came to nothing, but he dismantled the whole thing just in case."

"What about the girls' names?"

"The same," Luisa says. "We burned everything, even the negatives."

"That's really hard for me to believe," Nuria says. "If those photos were your way of making sure the girls wouldn't report you, how is it that one did?"

"It wasn't one of the girls, it was her parents, after . . ." Luisa looks down, leaving the sentence hanging.

"What happened?" asks Nuria.

"It seems that she committed suicide," Luisa explains, almost in a whisper, as if lowering her voice will mitigate her guilt.

"And it was your fault?"

"How do you expect me to know?" Luisa snaps, defending herself. "All I know is that she killed herself. Her parents found some pictures and messages and decided it was our fault."

"They're the ones who reported you."

Luisa nods in silence.

"But the report didn't go anywhere," Nuria adds.

"They didn't investigate anyone, as far as I know."

"What year was this?"

"I think 2006 or 2007, I don't remember exactly."

"And you think those parents, seeking to avenge their daughter's death, could be behind your husband's death and the recent murders."

"Aren't you looking for a good motive to kill?" Luisa replies. "Well, there you have it."

Nuria thinks about it for a moment. It's true that it is a motive, and even if the evidence continues to be circumstantial, at least she's got a lead to follow up.

"What was the name of the girl who committed suicide?" she asks.

"I don't know."

"*What?*" Nuria explodes. "A young girl kills herself because of what you did and you don't even take the trouble to learn her name??"

"I didn't want to know it," Luisa murmurs, hanging her head.

It's becoming harder by the minute for Nuria to control her anger. "What about her parents?" she asks. "Do you remember their names or surnames?"

"Gómez," she answers, lifting her head.

"Gómez and what else?"

"I don't know," she confesses, spreading her hands. "I remember Félix mentioning it once during a phone call, but I don't even know if it was her father's last name or her mother's."

"That's not much help, Luisa."

"It's all I've got." She sighs as if a weight has been lifted from her shoulders. "I swear."

Nuria stands up, clenching her fists tightly. "It's very little. Too little."

Luisa holds up the file folder. "But we have a deal."

"Yes, but the deal was in exchange for information that will help us stop the murderer." Pursing her lips, Nuria adds, "I don't know if what you've told me will be enough for the judge."

"But we have a deal!" She shakes the folder.

Nuria represses the desire to tell her it's all been a farce and limits herself to turning around and walking away. At the door, without looking back at Luisa, she says, "I'll see what I can do."

37

When Laura opens her eyes it's morning. She stares up at the ceiling, her unfocused gaze tracing the convoluted designs. Confused, she blinks several times, trying to find something familiar, but there's nothing; this isn't her house.

Where am I? she asks herself, turning her head from one side to the other, discovering with surprise that she's in a luxurious room, its walls hung with oil paintings. There are several pieces of antique furniture set around the room and an ostentatious Bohemian crystal chandelier hanging from the center of the ceiling.

The morning light filters through the thick drapes, bringing her vague memories of the night before. She'd arrived at a party where all the guests were masked, and after the first drink she'd been offered the rest had been a blur.

Laura finally looks down. Lifting the silk sheets, she sees that she's naked. Instinctively, she touches herself between her legs. When she pulls her hand away, it's stained with dried blood.

"No, no, no . . ." she mutters, unable to hold back the tears. "No, please . . ." She's alone in a strange house, naked, and she's just discovered that some stranger has taken her virginity during a night she can't remember.

Bringing her hands to her face, she weeps disconsolately. Suddenly, the door of the room opens, admitting a woman with a blue uniform on and a kerchief on her head who's pulling a vacuum cleaner.

"Oh, sorry," she apologizes, catching sight of Laura. "I didn't know there was anybody left in the house."

Laura sniffs and wipes away her tears with the back of her hand. "What . . . what happened?" she asks. "Where am I? Who are you?"

The woman leaves the vacuum cleaner propped against the wall and approaches Laura. "I'm just the cleaning woman," she says. "This is a house that's rented out for parties, and I would guess you were here for the party last night."

"I . . . I . . ." Laura murmurs, sitting up in bed and holding the sheet over her breasts. "I don't remember anything."

"You don't remember *anything*?" the woman asks in surprise. "But . . . you know your name and all that?"

"Yes, I remember that. Just nothing about the party. Only that I arrived here, they gave me something to drink, and then . . . I don't know what happened after that."

"But are you all right?" the woman asks her, a touch of maternal concern in her voice. "Did they do something to you?"

A dozen different answers run through Laura's head, all with differing degrees of complaint and consternation, but in the end she just nods. After all, maybe it's not such a good idea to share all that with a stranger. "I'm fine," she whispers, her voice barely audible. "I just want to go home."

The woman remains standing by the bed. Laura can read the doubt in her eyes about whether she should press further but finally she nods and accepts the obvious lie. "Okay. Do you want me to call you a cab?"

Laura's about to say no, but she realizes that all she wants is to get home as quickly as possible. "Yes, please. Thank you."

Laura follows the woman with her gaze as she leaves the room in search of a telephone. Once she's closed the door behind her, Laura gets up and goes to the adjoining bathroom to pee, but remains rooted to the spot when she sees herself in the mirror.

The makeup she applied the night before has run and looks grotesque. She can hardly recognize her own face, partially hidden by her tousled hair. But what leaves her wordless are the bloodstains on her thighs and the countless marks and bruises everywhere on her skin, especially her breasts and buttocks.

She feels a dull ache in her nipples as if someone has twisted and pulled at them without mercy. Her vagina feels painfully irritated, and there's a sharp pain in her anus. Very delicately, she wipes it with a tissue only to find the paper stained an intense red, almost scarlet.

"The taxi will be here in ten minutes!" she hears the cleaning woman call from the other side of the door.

"Thank you," Laura murmurs, holding back the tears with difficulty.

You didn't need to be a genius to figure out what had happened the night before, and Laura's first impulse is to go directly to the police and report what's happened. But as she continues to clean the blood from her skin with a damp towel, she begins to think about exactly what she'll say to the police when they ask her what she was doing at that party, who'd abused her, and why she can't remember. She imagines the cop on duty looking at her suspiciously, casting doubt on her account of what had happened, and explaining to her that if there's consent, it's not rape—and if she can't remember how, when, or with whom she had sex, how can she be sure that she didn't consent to it?

Laura imagines the police not believing her. She imagines her mother blaming her for what had happened, the profound disappointment on her father's face. She imagines reporting the crime, the lengthy trial if they do end up believing her. She imagines the stigma, the blame that will always fall on her from those who believe that if a girl goes to a party with a bunch of strangers, she knows the risks she's taking.

Laura imagines all of this and much more while she gathers her clothes from the floor where they've been scattered and puts them on. By the time the taxi honks outside the door, she's made up her mind that it's better to say nothing and swallow her tears of pain and shame.

38

During the drive back to Egara under an overcast sky, Nuria tries to organize the jumble of information in her head in such a way that she can present it to Sánchez in a logical and reasonable way that will justify deceiving Luisa with a false document as the only way to obtain a clue she could never have laid her hands on otherwise.

Finally something about all this makes sense. There's a motive and some possible suspects, which is more than they've had up to now. But, well aware of the distrust with which the inspector will consider the confession of an inmate, Nuria decides that before saying anything to him, she'll look for the girl who committed suicide and her parents. Also the report her parents filed that, as odd as it seems, didn't end up being investigated.

For a moment she sees Luisa in her mind's eye embracing the file folder like a life preserver and she feels a stab of guilt for having lied to her. But then she remembers how the inmate had drugged those girls at the photo shoots and how she'd cooperated in blackmailing them and forcing them into a life of prostitution and the moment passes.

All of this goes through Nuria's mind as she parks in the lot and takes the elevator up to the CID offices. To her surprise, Sánchez is back and sitting behind his desk in his office. "Where were you?" he spits at her without preamble.

"I . . ." Nuria swallows. "I had to go follow up on a clue."

"Your place was at the crime scene this morning."

"Marcos made me wait outside the house," she shoots back immediately. "I thought there were better ways to spend my time than keeping watch over the car."

Sánchez fixes her with a razor-sharp gaze. "Your first obligation is to obey the orders of your superiors, including Marcos. This is not some travel club, it's a hierarchically organized police department in which orders are obeyed even though you may not like them. Are we in agreement about that? If you're told to wait outside, you wait outside, period."

"But—"

"No buts, for Christ's sake!" Sánchez snaps, jumping to his feet. "Are we good?"

"Yes, Inspector."

"I'm warning you, Nuria," he adds, lowering his voice. "I like you and I think you're a valuable addition to the team, but I will not tolerate you doing whatever you happen to feel like, going home whenever you feel like it, or ignoring orders when you don't like them. It doesn't work that way. If you ignore a direct order again, you will leave me no choice but to open a disciplinary file on you. Is that clear?"

"Yes, Inspector."

Sánchez takes a deep breath and sits down again. "Very well," he says, looking up at her. "Now explain to me about the clue you had to follow up on while the rest of the CID was working."

Nuria vacillates. Her plan had been to get all the evidence and information possible together before presenting them to the inspector.

"Well?" Sánchez prods, crossing his arms.

"I . . . need a little more time to check some facts."

"No, give me what you have. Now." He shakes his head. "It must be important for you to have gone off that way."

"Okay, well . . . I believe it could be important. We might finally have a motive and some suspects."

Sánchez leans forward, propping his elbows on his desk and interlacing his fingers in a show of interest. "I'm all ears."

Nuria wonders if she should sit down in front of her boss but, considering that he hasn't invited her to and it might just make matters worse, she decides to remain standing.

"You see . . ." she begins to explain while trying to recall what she's rehearsed on the way back to headquarters, "this morning I went to see Monells and then to the Wad Ras prison."

Ten minutes later, Nuria finds herself back at her desk staring at the blank screen of her computer while Sánchez types out a disciplinary file on her, his fingers pounding the keys with barely contained fury.

The fact that she'd shown up in the hospital by herself, without consulting him first, had irritated him, but when Nuria had confessed that not only had she gone to see Luisa Domínguez again, but that to get her to talk she'd created a false legal document signed by a fictitious judge, his eyes had started almost out of his head.

"You'll be lucky if they don't kick you out of the department," Sánchez had prophesied, shaking his head from side to side in incredulity. "What in God's name were you thinking?"

"I wanted to resolve the case," she'd answered simply, shrugging her shoulders.

"Holy shit, Nuria. We have rules and regulations to follow. You know that perfectly well. We're not gangsters or private eyes, we're judicial officers. We have to stay rigorously within the law to do our job. We can't just disregard it and do whatever the fuck happens to cross our minds at the moment. Ever," he reaffirms, tapping his index finger on the desk, "under any circumstances."

Nuria agrees contritely, insisting nonetheless, "It was the only way to get her to tell me what she knew. I assumed catching a murderer was worth taking a risk."

"Well, now you see it wasn't."

"Inspector . . . We now have a name that possibly begins with *MAR*, a motive, and a group of suspects."

Sánchez snorts, fed up. "The fuck we do," he snaps. "What you have are the ravings of a dying man drugged to the eyebrows and an inmate who would sell her own mother to get out of the slammer. A network of wealthy people setting up orgies with minors? Police reports that don't get investigated? Avenging parents who decide to take revenge for the suicide of their daughter nearly twenty years later?" Sánchez shakes his head again, disillusioned and ashamed for her in equal parts. "Are you listening to yourself, Nuria? Do you not realize this is an insane notion that makes no sense outside of some Hollywood movie?"

Nuria remembers then Luisa Domínguez's allusion to the movie *Eyes Wide Shut* with Tom Cruise and Nicole Kidman and her conviction rolls a few steps further down the steep staircase of reality. "I . . ." she murmurs. "I don't think—"

"I told you to forget about this line of inquiry for a reason," Sánchez interrupts her, more ashamed than furious at her. "I understand your reasons, but you've forgotten that you're a police officer, and I can't simply ignore that, even if I wanted to, which I don't. Because now that inmate is going to talk to her lawyer, who in turn will talk to a real judge, and before we realize it the CID is going to be buried in shit up to its neck and we're all going to be fucked." Sánchez pulls open his desk drawer and takes out a document. "I'm going to have to open a file on you and suspend you without pay until further notice, Nuria. I have no choice, do you understand?"

Nuria's brain is caught in a whirlwind of confusion and sorrow and she suddenly feels like a total idiot. *How could you have thought what you did was a good idea?* she asks herself. After a few seconds of silence she says, "I understand. I . . . I'm really sorry, Inspector."

"I'm sorry too, Nuria," Sánchez says quietly. "Believe me, I'm sorry too."

After her run-in with Sánchez, Nuria sits at her desk without knowing what to do next. She hasn't even bothered to take off her coat. What for? She's no longer on the case and possibly no longer even part of the CID. Hers has to have been the shortest stint as an officer of the CID ever. It's only taken her a few months to fuck things up so royally that she might even end up being expelled from the entire police department.

She makes a face, thinking she's doubtless beaten the record for incompetence. She'll probably end up being used as an example at the academy of everything you shouldn't do as a cop: hook up with your partner, disobey your superiors, falsify official documents . . . Looking at it from this perspective, Nuria realizes there aren't many red lines she hasn't crossed.

Sitting there with her arms folded, she realizes that her colleagues will be returning to Egara sooner or later, and she doesn't want to be there when that happens. Having to bear the inevitable looks of triumph from Raúl and Marcos is more than she can bear right now. She stands up, grabs her small backpack, and heads for the door.

Nuria passes Sánchez's office, expecting him to ask where she's going or who's given her permission to leave but he says nothing and Nuria feels strangely disappointed. It's as if he no longer cares what she does or doesn't do.

With tears forming in the corners of her eyes, Nuria walks down the corridor leading to the elevators, avoiding the eyes of everyone whose path she crosses. She can barely hold back the tears as she descends to the ground floor and heads for the parking lot. It's not until she reaches her car and throws herself into the driver's seat that she can open the floodgates and let out all the misery and frustration she feels at that moment. Putting her head down on the steering wheel, she abandons herself to disconsolate weeping, sobbing as she hasn't done since her father's death, weeping for what she's lost and what could have been and now never will. She weeps from shame and for how stupid she's been, for her character that always leads her to do things her way and ignore the rules as if they don't apply to her.

All she had to do was behave herself in a responsible manner, comply with the orders she was given without objecting, and keep her legs closed with her partner. But naturally, as always, she'd done exactly the opposite. "What the fuck is wrong with me?" she asks herself. "Jesus Christ, Nuria," she snorts. "This time you've really fucked things up."

When her tears finally taper off what seems like a long time later, she sits up, takes a deep breath, blows her nose, checks her mascara in the mirror to make sure it hasn't run all over her face and, with a deep sigh, turns the key in the ignition.

As she drives out of the Egara complex, Nuria realizes she has no idea where to go. The only thing that's clear to her right now is that she doesn't feel like talking to anyone, not even Susana or her grandpa. So the idea of going home, closing the door behind her and turning the heat up, sitting down with Melón in her lap and devouring a tub of macadamia-nut ice cream sounds very seductive.

There will be plenty of time to worry about things and think about finding some way to get herself out of the mess she's gotten herself into. But at the moment, all she feels like doing is withdrawing from the world and feeling sorry for herself for the rest of the day.

"Yes, that's a good plan," she concludes, merging with the dense traffic on the C-58. "Undoubtedly, the best one I've had so far today."

39

On TV, just after the announcement that a new polar vortex is headed toward the south of Europe and that heavy snowfall is expected even along the Mediterranean coastline, images of the mansion Nuria had stood in front of that very morning flash across the screen and the name of the latest victim of the Satanic Assassin is announced: Duke Francisco Ludwig de Hohenmohen.

After a warning to viewers about the starkness of the images to come, the screen fills with a video filmed in first person in the same way as the other ones that have already been published on the *Extra Diario* web page. Apparently, thinks Nuria, the remote in her hand, the bar for responsible journalism has been lowered many notches, and adding fuel to a serial killer's fire is no longer the exclusive province of the gutter press.

Nauseated but unable to drag her eyes away from the screen, Nuria sees the camera approaching a naked man tied to the trunk of a small palm tree inside a greenhouse. The image of the man's genitals is pixelated. He looks to be around seventy, with gray hair and a prominent belly. His blue eyes are starting from his head in abject terror and Nuria can see his mouth working around the gag that's stuffed into it, trying to make a sound, but it's useless. The camera gradually nears the future victim, and when it's less than a meter away, a knife appears in the frame, slowly approaching the unhappy victim's left eye, until the sharp point is driven into it, after which the video cuts off abruptly.

"Holy fuck." Nuria exhales, realizing she's been holding her breath. Melón, curled up next to her, raises his head for a moment just in case Nuria's words signal that dinnertime has arrived. "Don't look at me like that," she responds with a frown. "I was only trying to do what I thought was best."

Melón blinks, attempting to decipher her message.

"I fucked it up royally, I know," his owner adds. "But I couldn't just sit back with my arms crossed." The enormous black-and-white cat opens his mouth in a huge yawn and stretches his front paws. "What's that? Am I boring you with my problems? It's easy for you, you little fucker," she reproaches him. "You get to spend all day at home eating, shitting, and sleeping. I'd like to know what you would have done in my place, eh? Let innocent people keep dying just to keep yourself safe?"

Melón begins to lick his right front paw as if it were an ice cream cone.

"Well . . ." Nuria says thoughtfully, "maybe they aren't all that innocent if what Luisa Domínguez told me is true. But even so, you can't go around skinning people for revenge. That's what the law is for and the cops—to catch the criminals and judge them."

Apparently satisfied with the results of his ministrations, Melón now proceeds to lick his left paw.

"I mean," Nuria says to him, nodding, "it's true that, according to Luisa, a report was filed, but the case didn't go anywhere. But surely there's a reason for that. There probably wasn't enough evidence to warrant a thorough investigation, or maybe it was all a fantasy cooked up by some desperate parents with overactive imaginations, or maybe, as Sánchez said, it was all just invented by an inmate who would sell her own mother if it meant getting out of prison."

While reporters on TV are interviewing someone who must be a neighbor of the latest victim—she's wearing a pearl necklace and matching earrings just to hang around the house—Nuria takes a large spoonful of ice cream and puts it into her mouth.

The idea is to spend the afternoon on the couch feeling sorry for herself, to forget about everything related to the case and her dismal future with the Mossos, all while finishing a tub of Häagen Dazs. But she can't.

Well, not the part about the ice cream. That she can. In fact, she's almost to the bottom of the tub already. What she can't do is stop thinking about the case and how, if she weren't suspended, she could still be helping to catch the murderer instead of just devouring calories in front of the boob tube.

Though . . . Actually . . .

Suddenly seized by curiosity, she pulls her laptop toward her, opens the Mossos d'Esquadra page and, feeling like she's sneaking in without permission, types in her password. She discovers, to her surprise, that her access hasn't been canceled.

Maybe they forgot, she speculates. Or maybe the suspension hasn't gone into effect yet . . . The important thing is that she's in. She's aware that her presence on the site will be registered by the system and she's only adding more wood to her own funeral pyre. But what's the worst they can do to her? she asks herself with a wry smile. Fire her twice?

Now that she's in, the problem is what exactly to look for. She has no dates or names, only the feeble reference to the suicide of a young girl whose last name was Gómez in 2006 or 2007. It's very little, but maybe it will be enough, she thinks, typing the data into the search engine.

No results appear on the screen. She expands the date range by several years in case Luisa Domínguez was wrong. Still no results.

Nuria decides to eliminate the variable of the surname. This produces a depressing list of suicides of minors between 2005 and 2008, but there are no young girls named Gómez among them.

Deciding to attack the problem from another angle, she looks for the report the parents of the girl supposedly made on the death of their daughter, but again there are no results. This is getting strange.

It's possible that Luisa invented the whole thing from beginning to end and lied to her about it, but the truth is it hadn't seemed like she was lying when she'd been sitting across from Nuria on the other side of the bars. If she *was* lying, Nuria thinks now, she should definitely consider professional acting as a career when she gets out of jail. Or politics.

The suggestion that the Mossos or the judge had deep-sixed the case still seems unacceptable to her so she tries to narrow the search for the supposed report even further. Resigned to taking as much time as necessary, Nuria begins to examine all the reports filed in Barcelona during that time period one by one.

After two hours of looking at case files, her eyes are so tired they're beginning to water and it doesn't seem like such a good idea any more. Glancing at her watch, she looks at Melón and says, "Five more minutes and I'm giving this up."

But not even two have passed when a file appears on the screen that catches her attention immediately. Not because of what it contains, but because of what it doesn't.

Underneath the report number, the entirety of the document is redacted, every line of text illegible under the thick black line that's been drawn through it.

Incredulous, Nuria checks the two pages of the document, arriving finally at the end where a simple note at the bottom of the page says *Erroneous procedure.*

"What?" she asks the screen, then turns to Melón and asks him, "Can you believe that? Erroneous procedure? What the fuck does that mean?"

Looking at her, Melón's expression seems to say "What are you asking me for? I'm only a cat." Nuria nods understandingly. Picking up a scrap of paper, she jots down the report number.

"*Zero . . . eight . . . six . . . three . . . nine . . . eight . . . seven . . . seven . . .*" Next she types the number into the search bar but instead of seeing the name of the officer who filed the report, the judge who processed it, or information about the person who had originally reported it, what she sees on the screen is an error message. She tries again, typing the numbers in more slowly to make sure they're correct, but gets the same result.

"Shit," she muses. Nuria stares at the screen, wondering how to find out what's hiding under that file number, but can't figure out how to get past the Mossos' internal web filter.

"Maybe going to headquarters in person and asking," she murmurs, turning to Melón again. This time he doesn't even look at her. "No, of course. That's not a good idea."

Then she has a flash of inspiration. Pulling out her phone, she clicks on Susana's name. Her best friend picks up on the second ring.

"Wow, miracles do happen! I thought you'd lost my number!"

"Hi Susi . . . Forgive me, the last week or so has been intense."

"I can only imagine," Susana says understandingly. "Have you guys caught the murderer yet?"

"Um . . . no. I don't think so."

"You don't *think* so?" her friend repeats. "Aren't you on the team that—"

"Not anymore," Nuria explains before Susana can finish the question.

"Shit, what happened?"

"It's a long story."

"Did you fuck up and they took you off the case?" Susana questions her.

Nuria takes a breath and exhales it in a long sigh. "Am I that predictable?"

"Holy shit, Nuria," Susana says regretfully. "What happened?"

"Um . . ."

"You know what?" her friend interrupts her. "Let's meet at the Puzzle and you can tell me all about it over a beer."

"I don't know if—"

Susana cuts her off again. "One hour." She hangs up before Nuria can protest.

Nuria is left staring at the phone. She heaves a sigh of resignation. Going out is about as attractive a proposition right now as a punch in the gut but, after vacillating a few seconds about whether she should send Susana a WhatsApp message telling her she's not in the mood, she realizes that maybe a couple of beers with her old friend will be just what the doctor ordered.

40

After Nuria's summed up as concisely as possible everything that's happened in the last few days, Susana is left with her mouth open, shaking her head in absolute incredulity.

Their friendship dates from their academy days, and without a doubt, Susana is her best and almost her only friend, but it wasn't until now, seeing her freckled face, her tousled hair, and her sarcastic expression across the table that Nuria realizes how much she's missed seeing her.

"Fuck me, Nuria," she repeats for the nth time. "What in the name of God were you thinking? We're P-O-L-I-C-E officers," she says, spelling out the word to Nuria as if she's a little girl. "We can't just do whatever happens to grab our fancy. There are rules and regulations . . . We're agents of the law, for fuck's sake, not private detectives on some TV series."

"I know, I know, Susi."

"Well, Jesus Christ, it doesn't seem that way. Hooking up with your partner?" she adds, rolling her eyes. "How many times have I told you that's a no-no?"

"Well, never, actually."

Susana frowns. "Well, all the same. You must have known that."

"Yes," Nuria admits.

"And even so, you fucked him."

"More than once," Nuria corrects her heavily.

"More than once?" Susana takes a sip of her second beer of the night and stares at the ceiling for a few moments. "I hope it was worth it, at least."

Nuria purses her lips and gives a slight shake of her head. "Not bad, but not a ten."

"Anyway," Susana says, taking another sip of her beer. "Don't worry about it. I'm sure it will all work out in the end."

"Do you really think so?" asks Nuria.

Susana blinks a couple of times before releasing a discouraged-sounding sigh. "No, actually I don't," she says finally. "It would be hard to fuck up more than you have, Nurieta."

Nuria just looks at her friend. "Well, that's what I did." Grabbing her beer bottle like a shipwreck victim grabs a life preserver, she finishes it in one long draft.

"What are you planning to do?" Susana asks her.

"I don't know yet," Nuria confesses, setting down the empty bottle. "For the moment, I'm still digging, trying to clarify a couple aspects of the case."

"Hmm . . ." Susana says, leaning back in her chair and folding her arms across her chest. "I guess I was wrong."

"Wrong? About what?"

"About how you couldn't fuck up any worse than you already have."

"I can't just leave things like this," Nuria protests. "There are clues that, if I don't follow them up, no one else is going to."

"Well, that's probably for a reason, don't you think?"

"Yeah, I know Sánchez may be right and all I'm doing is wasting time and complicating things unnecessarily . . . but I can't just let these things go."

"Of course you can, for fuck's sake. They've suspended you and it's very possible they may kick you off the force completely. It's not your job anymore. What you should be doing is getting on a plane for the Canary Islands and planting your ass on the beach until they call you to testify."

"Yeah, I guess."

Susana gazes at her friend, her mouth twisted in a wry grin. "But you're not going to."

"You already know I'm not."

"Christ, you're stubborn."

"Just part of my charm." Nuria gives her friend a humorless smile. "What I need to know is if you're going to help me."

"You're going to do it just the same whether I help you or not, aren't you?"

Nuria shrugs eloquently, saying without words, *What else can I do?*

Susana lifts her hands, surrendering and abdicating responsibility at the same time. "Well, it's your funeral," she says with a sigh. "What do you need?"

"I need access to the information in a redacted document," Nuria explains. "It's a report that was filed at the time the girl died. The document's been sealed and marked as *Erroneous procedure.* Who the hell knows what that means. I know it seems impossible, but someone from higher up tried to hide all the information in that report."

Nuria sees Susana looking at her pensively, as if she's just remembered something. "You don't seem surprised?" she asks her.

Glancing suspiciously to her left and then her right, as if someone might be listening, Susana leans across the table toward Nuria and speaks in a low voice. "A few years ago, a small anti-corruption group was created within the Mossos to investigate Catalonian politicians. But only a year later," she adds, "the group was disbanded and each member was sent to a far-flung part of the country. All the files they'd been working on were redacted completely."

"Fuck, I didn't know that."

"Well, it's not something you chat about at a business dinner. At least not if you want to hold on to your job."

"Do you think they could be related to this?"

"I can't imagine how," Susana says. "What year was the case you're interested in?"

"I think around 2006."

Susana shakes her head. "What I'm talking about happened in 2010 and 2011."

"Do you remember who the superintendent was during that time?"

Susana rubs her chin and thinks. "No idea. But you could try to find out which officers were assigned to the case."

"I thought of that, but the names of the officers are also redacted and the platform claims not to have that information. And obviously I can't exactly go to Egara and start asking around. Although . . . now that I think of it," Nuria adds, narrowing her eyes, "wasn't there a guy in the records department that was hitting on you a few months ago? You could ask him to look for the original file."

"For fuck's sake, Nuria," Susana replies with a grimace, "that guy's a complete nonentity, not to mention uglier than the back of a refrigerator. If I ask him a favor like that he's going to want to take it out in trade."

Nuria puts her hands together in prayer position. "Please, Susi, it's really important."

"What you should be doing is forgetting about the whole thing. All you're going to get for your trouble is more problems than you already have."

"I'll owe you one."

"You already owe me lots more than one."

"This is the only opportunity I have to fix this," Nuria insists. "I know I'm clutching at straws and most likely it's going to bite me in the ass, but I have to try."

Susana raises her gaze to the ceiling of the bar where a few scattered bulbs glow in their paper and wicker shades, bathing the small space in a warm, relaxing light. Heaving a long sigh, she lowers her eyes to meet Nuria's green ones. "You just don't give up, do you?" she says.

Nuria gives her a guilty smile. "Will you help me?"

"I'll try to talk to him this week. If I can get him to—"

"Couldn't you ask him right now?"

Susana lets out a guffaw that dies instantly in her throat when she realizes that Nuria isn't kidding. "It's after ten at night," she says, tapping the screen of her smartwatch.

"That way he could look for it tomorrow morning first thing," persists Nuria.

Susana sighs again and pulls her phone from her pocket. As she types a WhatsApp message she says, "You owe me *big* time."

"I'm inviting you right now to eat at La Vietnamita."

"That's not even going to begin to cover it. But whatever." Susana snorts. "The truth is I wouldn't mind a nice hot bowl of pho."

41

"Tell!! Tell!!" Paula's interrogating her on the phone. "How was the party?"

Laura swallows, thankful that her friend isn't there in person to see her face, because she would know instantly that she's lying.

"Fine," she says listlessly.

"What do you mean, 'fine'? Holy fuck, Laura, what's going on with you lately? I want details!"

"I don't know, I mean . . . it was a normal party, the usual, elegant, full of people I didn't know."

"And? Did they introduce you to anyone interesting?"

"I . . . I don't actually remember. You know how bad I am with names."

"Holy shit, Laura. You don't remember *anybody*? How is that even possible?"

"I don't know . . . Maybe I drank too much."

"You got drunk?" asks Paula, scandalized. "Seriously? You go to some high-class party so people can meet you and you get hammered?"

"I guess I was nervous," Laura hedges, wanting the conversation to be over as soon as possible. "Maybe that's just not my world."

"What do you mean?"

"That I just don't feel comfortable with all that high-fashion stuff . . . I just don't think it's for me."

"Oh come on!" her friend protests. "How can you say that so soon? You haven't even begun!"

"Yeah, well . . . I think I've had enough."

"You're kidding me," Paula says doubtfully.

"No, really." Laura gives a tired sigh. "My mom was right, that world's a shithole. I'd rather keep studying and go to college."

There is silence for the next few seconds until Paula asks, "Did something happen to you at that party?"

"No, no, nothing," Laura responds too quickly.

"Fuck, Laurita. You're lying to me."

"Huh? No, really. Everything's fine."

"Do you swear?"

"You know I'm an atheist," Laura says.

"Well, you give me your word then?"

"I give you my word that I'm fine," Laura insists, trying to convince herself that she's not lying.

Another long pause on the line. Finally Paula says, "Something weird's going on with you. I don't know what it is, but something's wrong. You were crazy to be a model only a few days ago and now you don't even want to talk about it."

"Must be the hangover."

"That's bullshit. There's something you're not telling me."

"I like to act mysterious," Laura says in an unsuccessful attempt at humor.

"You're really good at it too," Paula retorts. "Well, if you don't want to tell me," she adds, "I can't force you."

Laura's about to answer her friend that she's not hiding anything, but decides she's already lied enough to her; better just to ignore the accusation. "I'm fine," she repeats, sounding even less convinced than she had the first time.

"Well . . . okay, then. If you decide you want to talk about whatever the fuck's happening with you, you know where to find me."

"Yes, I know. Thanks, Paula." Saying goodbye, Laura hangs up the phone.

That afternoon, she summons up her courage and sits down in front of her computer to write to the Pygmalion Agency. Though she knows she's done nothing wrong, she has to work up her nerve to do it. Just writing them to ask for an explanation of what happened the night before makes her burn with shame. Without mentioning details about the state she'd found herself in when she'd awakened in the morning, she insists that she doesn't remember anything about what happened and asks for clarification in a tone she hopes won't come across as that of a frightened adolescent.

After rewriting the email a dozen times, she presses the send button and turns off her computer, at once wanting and fearing that the phone will ring any moment and someone will give her answers she doesn't want to hear. She needs to know the truth but at the same time it terrifies her.

Tomorrow she'll find a pharmacy far from her house where they don't know her and buy a morning-after pill. Just thinking about that possibility makes a chill run up her spine from her coccyx to the nape of her neck. Tamara, a girl from her class the year before, had gotten pregnant. They'd given her a pill to abort at the health center and her parents hadn't found out, but Laura would hate to have to go through that. Above all, knowing how awful Tamara had felt the next few days, with pains in her abdomen and vomiting. Of course, however bad she'd felt, though, it was preferable to the alternative.

Again she feels the urgent need to shower, even though she's already showered twice today. She can't seem to wash off the unbearable feeling of being dirty and that everyone else can see the marks all over her body as if she's been obscenely groped and pawed by dozens of filthy, greasy hands.

The sound of a message arriving on WhatsApp jolts Nuria out of her sleep. She tries to ignore it and keep sleeping, curled up under her thick down comforter, but the memory of the night before and the favor she asked Susana gradually worms itself into her brain.

With her face buried in the pillow, she tries to convince herself that the message will still be there even if she sleeps another half hour, but the persistent worm of curiosity won't leave her alone, and finally she gives in to the impulse to check the screen of her phone.

Nuria stretches out her arm and gropes around on her bedside table without opening her eyes. Her hand knocks something over that clinks when it hits the floor. Next she bumps into the lamp. Finally her fingers feel the familiar outline of her phone. With no small effort, she turns over in bed and, finally opening her eyes, touches the screen. The bright light momentarily blinds her like a pair of oncoming headlights and a sharp pain like a knife pierces her eyes and her brain all the way to the nape of her neck.

"Fuck me," she mutters, rubbing her eyes to mitigate the effects of her hangover, one of the usual consequences of going out for a drink with Susana.

When her headache has subsided to a mere annoyance, Nuria slowly opens her eyes again and touches the green WhatsApp icon on her screen.

Effectively, the message is from Susana.

Mission accomplished: the officer in charge of the case was Sergeant Ismael Flores González, retired in 2007. No address, but there is a phone number: 767346228. I have to have dinner on Thursday with the clod from the filing department. You owe me BIG TIME.

Nuria blinks sleepily and rereads her friend's message. It's a quicker response than she'd expected, and now an unexpected doubt assaults her: *is pursuing the case further really the most intelligent decision?* She's forced to admit it isn't. Not by a long shot. What she should do is take her friend's advice and go off to the Canary Islands to lie in the sun until such time as things come to a natural resolution, one way or another.

Though, if she looks at it from another angle, this may be her only chance to redeem herself and get her job back. If she can find the serial killer that's terrorizing the city, not only will they not be able to kick her out, she might even get a promotion. *Who knows?* she thinks, picturing herself receiving a medal in front of a multitude of photographers.

Taking a deep breath, she shoves the comforter off. A black-and-white blur leaps from the bed with a meow of protest. "Oops!" she says. "Sorry, Melón, I didn't see you."

Melón pauses in the doorway to throw her a look of reproach, then stalks out of the room with an injured air.

"What a grump," Nuria says, sitting up and swinging her legs over the side of the bed. A brief dizzy spell makes her pause for a moment before standing up. Her stomach churns queasily and her head feels as heavy as if she's wearing a lead hat.

"Shit," she mutters, putting her hands to her forehead. Every time she goes out with Susana she drinks too much, something she always ends up regretting the next morning. But as often as she promises herself this will be the last time, it always turns out to be the next-to-last.

Stumbling slightly, she gets to her feet and heads for the kitchen, thinking about strong coffee and Ibuprofen. Only after that will she attend to Melón's breakfast, her own, and a hot shower. Once she's in possession of her physical and mental faculties again, she'll this Sergeant Ismael to find out where the rabbit hole takes her next.

"Yes?" The gravelly voice of a man obviously afflicted with a cough answers on the third ring.

"Ismael Flores?" Nuria asks.

"Who is this?"

"Excuse me. My name is Nuria Badal, and I'm a CID officer in the Mossos d'Esquadra. Are you Sergeant Ismael Flores?"

"Retired sergeant," he corrects her pointedly.

"Yes, I know. It's nice to meet you. I'm calling because I need to ask you some questions about an old case that might be relevant to a current one."

"An old case?" the man asks curiously. "It must be really old. I retired more than fifteen years ago. What year are we talking about?"

"2006."

"Oof," Ismael grunts. "That's a long time ago and my memory's not what it used to be."

"It's about the suicide of a minor who was apparently blackmailed into becoming part of a prostitution network. After her death, her parents filed a report, but the investigation was closed and the filed documents have been redacted. I'm not sure, but the family name may have been Gómez." Nuria pauses to give him time to process this information, then asks, "I believe you were in charge of the case?"

Ismael Flores takes almost a minute to respond. Only his gravelly breathing tells Nuria the sergeant is still at the other end of the line. Finally he says, "Surely you can find the information you need in the archives at headquarters."

"That's the problem, Sergeant. As I said, the report is redacted and labeled as an 'erroneous procedure.' All I've been able to find out is that you were the one who handled the case. That's why I called you."

Ismael pauses again before murmuring thoughtfully, "I . . . I remember a bit about that case. The father was completely undone. It was the mother who wanted us to investigate, but almost all she could tell us were incoherent ramblings or mere suppositions. We were really busy at the time and the inspector decided to take over the case himself."

"The inspector took over your case?" Nuria asks in astonishment.

"It didn't seem like it was going anywhere—no clues, no solid basis for the report," he clarifies. "There really wasn't a case at all, in reality," he adds. "So a short time later, the inspector mothballed it."

"Didn't it seem odd to you that the inspector relieved you of the case? That's not usual."

After another pause, Ismael asks her, "How long have you been in the CID, Officer Badal?"

"Not very long," she admits. "But what does that have to do with anything?"

"That's what I imagined. Your voice sounds pretty young."

"Not that young, I fear."

"See . . ." he says. "With time you learn that it's better to keep your mouth shut and do as you're told if you don't want your career with the department to go to hell. Do you understand what I'm saying?"

"I have a good idea."

"If you value your job at all, I recommend you stop nosing around in the past and forget all about this case, or you're going to be stepping on someone's toes, someone who has the power to fuck your life over."

"Is that what happened to you?" Nuria asks. "Is that why you retired less than a year after this case came along?"

Ismael takes a deep breath and exhales tiredly. "I'm sorry, I'm going to be late for an appointment, Officer."

"But—"

"I'm sorry, I can't help you."

Nuria fears he'll hang up any second. "Wait!" she says hastily. "Do you remember the name of the girl or the parents?"

"No, I already told you it was a long time ago."

"And the name of the inspector that took over the case? You do remember his name, don't you?"

The sergeant wavers, but ends up giving her a name. "Inspector Samuel Coixet. But I don't think he'll be able to help you much."

"Why?"

"Because he died six years ago."

Nuria can't avoid a grunt of frustration. "How about the judge who heard the case? Do you recall his—"

He interrupts her. "I don't remember anything else. I'm sorry, Officer, but there's nothing more I can do for you."

"I understand . . . Thank you for your time, Sergeant. If by any chance you do remember something, please call me at this number?"

Instead of agreeing, Ismael says, "One more thing, Officer. You told me you're investigating a possible link to an ongoing case, right?"

"That's right."

"Could you . . . bring me up to date on the current case?" he asks. "Maybe that way I could be of some help."

Nuria hesitates a moment. Under any other circumstances, even with a retired officer, it would be highly irregular to discuss an open case. But then, everything she's done lately is highly irregular as well, to put it mildly. So . . . "I'm investigating the murders that have occurred over the last two weeks in Barcelona," she explains.

"The Satanic Assassin ones?"

"I don't believe there's anything satanic about them," Nuria corrects him. "But yes, those are the ones."

"And why do you think these murders may be related to a case of suicide that happened more than fifteen years ago?"

"I don't know. It's actually . . . just a hunch I had," she confesses. "Shortly after the suicide happened, the photographer who had been filming her for the web was murdered and his wife was found guilty. But there are certain things that don't add up and make me suspect that the murder of that photographer and the present-day murders might be related."

"You don't seem all that convinced."

"Yes . . . Well, no. I don't know. Like you, I don't have any evidence or anything solid to hold onto, but I still want to follow up that lead as far as I can and see where it takes me."

"Your boss at the CID is Inspector Sánchez, right?"

"Do you know him?"

"Well enough to be surprised that he would allow you to follow up a line of investigation based on a hunch."

Nuria swallows. Maybe it had been a mistake to call the sergeant, she reflects. But it's too late to turn back now. "Yes, well, actually it's sort of a parallel investigation that I'm doing on my own. My intention is to update him on my progress once I have some hard evidence."

Ismael is silent for a few seconds and Nuria sends up a fervent prayer that she hasn't just blown it again. Finally he says, "I understand." He sounds sincere. "I hope you find the evidence you need."

"Um . . . yes. Thanks. Me too."

"If I remember anything, I'll let you know, don't worry."

"That would be fabulous," Nuria says.

"Good day, Officer Badal," the ex-sergeant says a bit brusquely in farewell, ending the call.

Nuria's left staring at the screen of her phone incredulously. "What the hell just happened?" she asks out loud, turning toward Melón, who watches her from the couch with very little interest. "First he tells me to forget about the case and then suddenly he gets interested and tells me not to worry. Does any of that make sense to you?"

The cat says nothing, but Nuria can't shake the feeling that she's missing something, something she's not seeing even though it's right in front of her nose.

43

The call with ex-Sergeant Flores has left her with more questions than she'd had before, and she hasn't been able to get any important information out of him either. The only option she has left is to call the investigating judge but, as absurd as it might seem in a milieu as bureaucratic as the judicial one, it was impossible to find out which judge it had been. It's as if someone has taken all the time and energy necessary to eliminate every trace of that report. The question is, who? And even more important, why?

For a moment Nuria considers calling Susana again and asking her to press her "friend" in the filing department to dig a bit deeper, but she understands that by doing so she would be taking unfair advantage of their friendship, not to mention implicating Susana even further in something that could eventually involve her as collateral damage.

Seated in front of her laptop, Nuria massages her temples as if doing so might stimulate the neurons that have recovered from her hangover. "Think, Nuria . . . think," she mutters to herself, but the only thing that occurs to her is to Google news articles about the suicide of a young girl in Barcelona and its environs during 2006.

Nuria's aware that it will be like searching for a needle in a haystack but at the moment she's not really up to thinking of a better idea. With a noisy exhale, she gets up to prepare her second coffee of the morning. She has a sneaking suspicion it won't be the last.

Several hours later, her cup sitting on the table, emptied of its third *espresso intenso*, Nuria finally finds something. The June 7 issue of a local paper called *Vilaweb* contains a piece on the suicide of a young woman with the initials L.G.M. in the Sagrada Familia neighborhood, a short distance away from the unfinished cathedral. The article, barely two paragraphs long, doesn't offer further details, but there is a byline for someone named Mar Alonso.

Without a second's hesitation, the caffeine still coursing through her veins, Nuria calls the newspaper only to be informed that that particular reporter had left her job at the paper years before.

"Could you help me to localize her?" Nuria asks. "It's important."

The suspicious voice at the other end of the line says, "Who did you say you were?"

"Nuria Badal, officer with the Mossos d'Esquadra. I'm investigating a case in which Miss Alonso could be of assistance to us."

"Okay . . . Don't take this the wrong way, but how do I know you're who you say you are? You would need to submit an official petition for me to be able to provide you with personal details for an ex-employee. I hope you understand."

Nuria takes a deep breath and suppresses a snort of impatience. "I understand," she replies. "But time is of the essence in this case, and I would very much appreciate your collaboration. If you could just give me her phone number that would be enough. I just need to ask her a question about an article she wrote in 2006."

The young woman on the other end of the line seems to be reflecting on this for a few seconds. Finally she says, "If what you need is information about an article, they're all archived in our database. I could give you information on that if there's nothing confidential. What article are you referring to?"

"It was published on June 7, 2006, on the suicide of a girl named L.G.M."

"Just a moment," murmurs the young woman. Nuria can hear her fingers flying over the keyboard. "Yes, here it is," she says after a moment. "What is it you need to know?"

"Everything," Nuria says immediately. "Any information you could have might turn out to be relevant."

"What I can give you," says the young woman, "is the name of the parents and their address. Would that be all right?"

"That's exactly what I need," Nuria says.

When Nuria arrives at the address she's been given, she finds herself in front of a seven-story building on Lepanto Street, barely two blocks from the Sagrada Familia cathedral and a twenty-five minute walk from her own home.

One of the things Nuria likes most about Barcelona is that you can walk anywhere. A pleasant two-hour stroll will take you from one end of the city to the other. So, in spite of the cold and the threatening black clouds churning in the sky above the rooftops, she'd decided to walk to her destination rather than taking the metro or calling a taxi.

Pressing the button on the intercom that corresponds to the sixth floor, apartment two, she waits. Only a couple of seconds later, the voice of a woman is heard through the loudspeaker. "Yes?"

"Good morning. I'm Officer Badal from the Mossos d'Esquadra, and I'm looking for María Martínez and Alfonso Gómez."

"The police?" the voice asks in surprise.

"Yes, the police," Nuria confirms. "Are you María Martínez?"

"No, no. You've got the wrong floor. There's no one living here with that name."

"Could you please open the door for me?"

The woman appears to vacillate for a moment, but in the end says reluctantly, "Yes, of course." A second later the buzzer sounds, indicating to Nuria that the door has been unlocked.

Once she's inside the lobby, she goes to the mailboxes and confirms that in fact, the names María Martínez and Alfonso Gómez don't appear on the box corresponding to 6º 2ª. Glancing rapidly at the other boxes, Nuria realizes there's no one by either of those names in the building.

When the elevator arrives, she goes up to the sixth floor and knocks on the door with a gold-colored *2* on it. A second later, the woman she spoke to at the entrance opens the door and stands there observing Nuria suspiciously. She's around forty, with straw-like hair, a green house dress, and a face that looks as if all she eats is Swiss chard.

"Are you a cop?" she asks her again, looking her up and down. Nuria's already well used to people doubting that she's a police officer when she's not in uniform, especially with her blonde hair, air of general dishevelment, and unusual height. So in a movement that's become almost automatic, she pulls her wallet from her pocket and shows the wary woman her ID card.

"Good morning, ma'am. I'm looking for the Gómez Martínez family. I was told they live at this address."

"Well, you're wrong. It's not here."

"Would you be so kind as to show me your official ID?"

"What for? Are you calling me a liar?"

"No, ma'am. But it's my duty to check it. Please forgive the inconvenience."

The woman continues to stand in the doorway as if wondering what to do. With some difficulty, Nuria maintains the friendly smile she's plastered on her face.

"Just a moment," the woman finally says and turns around, shutting the door in Nuria's face with a bang. A few seconds later she reappears and hands her national identity card to Nuria without a word.

"Mariana Lombau Becerra," Nuria reads. "Is this you?"

"Of course it's me, can't you see?"

"How long have you lived here?"

"I don't know, nine or ten years. Why?"

"Did you meet the Gómez Martínez family?"

"I don't know who they are. I've never heard of them."

"Apparently they were the people who rented this apartment before you."

Mariana crosses her arms impatiently. "Okay, great. What does that have to do with me?"

Nuria takes a deep breath, making a huge effort to keep smiling. "Do you know if there's some neighbor who's lived in the building for twenty years or more?"

"I have no idea. I'm not friends with the neighbors."

"That's odd, you seem so nice," Nuria says.

"Excuse me?" Mariana says.

"Thanks for your help," Nuria says, smiling even more broadly as she hands back the woman's ID. "Have a nice day."

The woman grabs the card out of Nuria's hand with a grunt and slams the door in her face.

Nuria rolls her eyes. Turning around, she presses the elevator button, pondering how to find out which neighbors had known the Gómez Martínez family.

That's when the door to apartment 6º 1ª opens with a slight creak of the hinges and the face of an elderly lady peers through the crack like a frightened mouse. "Are you looking for the family that lived across from me?" she asks Nuria in a quavering voice.

"Did you know them?"

"Of course. They were a nice family, not like . . ." She throws a quick glance at the closed door across the hall. "Such a terrible thing that happened to them."

"What do you know about what happened to them?"

"Know? Well, I know what everyone knows. That the poor girl killed herself and the parents were devastated. Every day I could hear María, the mother, sobbing inconsolably. It must be terrible to lose a daughter like that," she adds, crossing herself. "And then, what happened with the father . . . Terrible, just terrible," she repeats.

"The father?" asks Nuria.

The neighbor looks at Nuria questioningly, giving her an appraising glance. "Aren't you a police officer?"

"I'm an officer with the Mossos d'Esquadra," Nuria explains, showing her ID card. "What happened to the father?"

"I thought you knew," explains the old woman. "Less than a year after Laura's death, the father also committed suicide."

"Fuck me," Nuria mutters. "No, I didn't know."

"Well, yes, you see." The woman shakes her head in regret. "The poor thing couldn't stand the pain."

"And the mother? Do you know what became of her?" Nuria asks.

"María?" says the elderly woman, raising her eyebrows and nodding as if they were talking about one of the great mysteries of the universe. "A few days after her husband died, she packed her bags and left without saying anything to anyone."

"She didn't say where she was going?"

"She didn't even say goodbye," says the elderly lady with poorly concealed reproach. "It's not as if we were friends, but she could have at least said goodbye, don't you think?"

"Yes, of course . . . And you haven't heard anything about her since?"

"No, nothing."

"Do you know if she could still be in contact with some other neighbor? Someone she was . . . closer to?"

"I was the neighbor she was closest to, believe me. If she didn't say anything to me, she didn't say anything to anyone else."

"I see. What else can you tell me about María Martínez? Do you know what she did? Did she have other family?"

"Doctor," answers the elderly lady. "I think she was a gynecologist, if my memory serves me. And I don't think she had any other family. She told me once she was an only child, so . . ."

"Do you know where she practiced?" Nuria asks.

"What's that?"

"I'm asking if you know where she worked. In some hospital?"

"Oh, yes. She was in the private sector and I believe she worked at several places."

"Do you recall any of them?"

The elderly lady puts on an expression of concentration and rubs her chin. "Maybe in Teknon?" she says after a few moments. "A couple of times the mailman made a mistake and put some letters addressed to her in my mailbox. They had Teknon Clinic as their return address. Maybe they were paychecks or something?"

"Great." Nuria congratulates herself. At least she has a clue. "Do you recall anything else? Any detail could be of great importance."

"It was almost twenty years ago, dear," sighs the woman. "My memory isn't what it used to be."

"That's fine. Thank you so much," Nuria says, pulling a business card from her purse and handing it to the woman. "You've been a great help. If you happen to remember anything else, whatever it is, you have my number here. Don't hesitate to call me."

When Nuria steps out onto the street again, the rain has started once more. She carries a small pink umbrella in her bag, but the walk to the Teknon Clinic is long and uphill, so she lifts her hand and signals the first taxi she sees with its green light on.

44

The taxi winds its way through the Versailles-like gardens that surround the exclusive private clinic and stops in front of the salmon-pink neoclassical façade of the main building. Nuria gets out of the vehicle without bothering to open her umbrella. The glass doors open wide as she nears the entrance. Before her extends a lobby that has apparently conserved elements of the original Vilana palazzo.

Right inside the entrance doors, standing behind a glossy walnut counter, a young receptionist with a smile that reminds Nuria of a toothpaste ad greets her with a slight dip of her head. "Good morning. How can I help you?"

"Hello. I'm looking for the Human Resources department?"

"Are you here to turn in a résumé? You'll need to go to—"

Nuria interrupts. "No, no. I'm a police officer," she explains, showing her identification. "I need information about one of your employees."

"Oh, well, in that case, make your way to the adjoining building," says the young woman, pointing to her right, "and go down to the lower level. There you'll see signs for the Human Resources department."

"Thank you," Nuria says. Following the wide walkway in the indicated direction, she enters the next building and goes down a staircase of immaculate marble. As she walks through the west wing of the building, she's surprised at how few people she encounters. Her memory of public hospitals is of constant hustle and bustle, with doctors, patients, and visitors going every which way. This medical center, in contrast, seems like a luxury hotel during the low season.

When she reaches the door labeled *Human Resources*, she raps on it with her knuckles and then enters without waiting for an invitation. Half a dozen administrative workers are scattered around the spacious office, concentrated on their computers. Not one raises his head to see who's come in.

"Hello," Nuria says to no one in particular.

Only one of the employees, a heavyset woman with short hair and the sort of glasses secretaries used to wear in the seventies, lifts her eyes from her screen and asks, "Can I help you with something?"

"I hope so," Nuria says, walking in her direction. "I need information about a doctor who worked here." She flashes her ID card before the woman can object.

The admin holds Nuria's ID close to her face, narrowing her eyes to scrutinize the photo as she compares it to the blonde woman with a ponytail and a cap on standing before her. "Are you a police officer?" she asks, still sounding suspicious.

"Officer Badal from the Criminal Investigations Department," Nuria clarifies, adding immediately, "I need all the information you can give me on María Martínez, a gynecologist who worked here until 2006."

Reticent, the woman looks around as if searching for someone. "I . . . don't know," she murmurs. "You might need to present a written request to the head of the department and then he can—"

"It's a matter of life or death," Nuria cuts her off, leaning forward with her hands on the woman's desk. "There's no time for written requests. I need the information right now."

"But—"

"Life or death," Nuria repeats. "You decide."

The woman blinks a couple of times indecisively but in the end bends her head over her keyboard. "María Martínez Oller," she reads from her screen in a moment. "Born in Manresa on July 3, 1969. Studied gynecology and obstetrics at the University of Barcelona. Her college ID number was 32411. She worked here from July of 2001 to January 2007 as a gynecologist. Would you like her address and telephone number?"

"Phone number, please." The admin jots it down on a yellow Post-it note and hands it to her. "Anything else?" asks Nuria.

"That's all."

"Is there a photo?"

"No, none. The personnel files don't include photos."

"All right. Does it say there where she went after she left Teknon?"

The woman glances at the computer screen again and shakes her head. "No, that's all it says."

Nuria thinks for a moment, hoping that another question will occur to her, but again this seems to be just another dead-end street. "Okay, then," she says with a sigh, sticking her hand into her pocket. "Here's my card in case you remember anything more. Thanks for your help."

As soon as she's out the door, Nuria pulls out her phone and enters the number the woman gave her. An instant after she finishes typing it in, a recorded voice comes on and informs her that the number is no longer in service.

"Big surprise," Nuria mutters under her breath, ending the call and sticking the phone back in her pocket.

Once out on the street again, she decides to walk home. It's more than a half hour, and that's at a brisk pace, but it's downhill and will give her time to think about her next move . . . if there's even a next move possible, that is. Because every time it seems she's about to take a step forward she runs into a new wall that blocks her way.

The idea of throwing in the towel occurs to her as she unsuccessfully Googles María Martínez Oller. She then looks her up on social media, discovering to her surprise that there is no information whatsoever alluding to a gynecologist by that name. Not on Facebook, not on Instagram, not on Twitter or LinkedIn. There's no mention of her on any blog, medical search engine, or web page. Nothing. Zero. It's as if she never existed.

Nuria knows that in 2006 the social media networks weren't what they are now, and that search engines like Google weren't as voracious either, but even so, almost twenty years have passed since then and it's hard to believe there's not a single trace of María Martínez on the Internet. Even Nuria's own mother, opposed as she is to anything even faintly redolent of the twenty-first century, appears on the screen when she types in her name.

Only two possible reasons occur to her that might explain this strange vacuum: either she herself has erased any trace of her digital alter ego, or—what seems more likely to Nuria—after leaving her apartment and her job, she'd taken the same path her husband had, leaving no record of her death anywhere.

At any rate, the result is basically the same: María Martínez has disappeared for all practical purposes. Nuria suspects that no matter how long she's willing to continue the search, the results will be the same.

Walking home, Nuria stows her phone in her pocket and huddles down into her coat. The rain is taking a short break, but the cold hasn't released its grip on the streets of the city, like an invisible hand that freezes everything it touches. The condensed vapor released by the heaters of the businesses along the streets and the tailpipes of the passing cars brings a wry smile to her face as she wonders if there's some paranoid theory that attributes some sort of mind-control power to the vapor as well, like the power some people attribute to the supposed chemtrails left by aircraft. It would be amusing, she thinks, to watch some conspiracy theorist holding his breath to avoid becoming contaminated by the vapor of his own exhale.

Though it's fun to think about such things, Nuria pushes these thoughts from her mind in order to focus on what's actually worrying her right then. She continues to be trapped in a loop of suppositions, with no evidence or even a plausible theory to offer her superiors. No matter where she's gone, she's run into a wall or at best, a dead-end street.

There's nothing more she can get out of Monells or Luisa Domínguez, or the police database, or the Internet itself. The only loose end left to her was María Martínez and her possible motive, avenging the death of her daughter Laura, but with no one to question and no lead to follow up to find out whether she's even still alive, it's an enigma she has no chance whatsoever of solving.

On the other hand, there's Ismael Flores, but the ex-cop doesn't seem to have much more to tell her, nor would he want to even if he could. The officer who was his inspector at that time is now pushing up daisies, so he isn't going to be much help, so there's no one left she can ask.

Or is there?

What if to redact that report it had taken someone with even more restricted access than an inspector? Nuria asks herself. *Could it be that someone even higher up in the Mossos food chain had also known what was going on or had even been the one to make the decision?*

Immediately, she takes her phone from her pocket again and types into the Google search bar: *Superintendent Mossos d'Esquadra 2006.*

A photo appears of a fiftyish man with an authoritative bearing, abundant, graying hair under a superintendent's cap, and an inquisitive look that seems uncannily familiar to Nuria. She reads the name under the picture and her mouth drops open in amazement. "Fuck me . . ." She repeats the name aloud so she can hear it and be sure she's not imagining it. *Jordi Soler i Casas*, she reads incredulously. *Superintendent of the Mossos d'Esquadra from 2001 to 2008. Since 2022 he has held the post of Minister of Home Affairs of the Generalitat of Catalonia.*

As she's reading the Wikipedia text for the second time the phone suddenly rings and the name *Susana Román* appears on the screen. "Hi Susi," she answers promptly. "What's up?"

"I just heard it on the police radio," Susana says urgently. "They've found Judge Martina Mas Serret dead."

Nuria gives a start and her heart stops beating for a second. "Was she . . ."— she takes a breath before finishing her sentence—"murdered?"

"Her fucking head was skinned," Susana says. "So I'd say yes."

"Holy shit."

"No kidding."

"Do you know . . . anything else?" Nuria asks. "Did they paint a 666 in blood or anything like that?"

"I don't have any details yet, Nuria. I just found out by chance and the press doesn't know yet, but it seems that they butchered the woman. I'll bet you anything," she adds, her tone confidential, "that she was the judge on the case you're working on and that she was the one to dismiss the complaint."

"You said her name is Martina Mas Serret?"

"Was," Susana corrects her.

Nuria makes a mental note of the judge's name so she can investigate her as soon as she gets home. "Great. Thanks so much, Susi. If you find out anything more—"

"Yeah, yeah, I know," her friend answers. After a brief pause she adds, "But you be careful, you hear me? Whoever's behind this, he's a fucking psychopath."

"No worries, I'll be careful."

"Right. Who are you trying to kid, Nuria?" Susana fires back. "You're never careful."

<h1 style="text-align:center">45</h1>

That night Nuria has a hard time falling asleep. Well past two in the morning, her gaze is still fixed on the ceiling, her brain going round and round while Melón snores at her side.

The death of the judge, surprisingly, hasn't been leaked to the press yet, but it's only a matter of hours until it is. Something like that can't remain a secret, even if secrecy is beneficial to the investigation.

Susana, nonetheless, had called her at midnight to confirm that the usual aspects of the murder had indeed been present: the triple six, painted in blood, the torture that preceded the end, the paralyzing drugs, and the slow, terrifying death—in this case, flaying the skin from the head of the unfortunate woman with what was suspected to have been a not-particularly-sharp kitchen knife.

Apparently the CID was still in charge of the case, but the murder of the judge might just be the straw that broke the camel's back, showing up the Mossos and leading to the case being transferred to the National Police or the Civil Guard, which would put the very existence of the entire police force of Catalonia in jeopardy.

According to the grapevine, Susana has told her, the shitstorm that went down when the Minister of Home Affairs met with the higher-ups of Egara had been epic and had included an ultimatum: if the murderer wasn't caught in the next twenty-four hours, heads would roll in the CID.

For a moment, Nuria considers the possibility of contacting Sánchez and bringing him up to date on her inquiries, but the truth is she still doesn't have any solid evidence to show him. In fact, her theory that Laura's suicide might be the motive for the crimes is foundering without a police report and with the father dead and the mother vanished seventeen years ago. Nonetheless, the murder of Judge Martina Mas Serret points decidedly in that direction. Even though she hasn't been able to confirm that Mas Serret was the magistrate assigned to the case, Nuria's convinced that she's the one who shelved the investigation, a decision that in the end cost her her life.

If she follows the macabre logic of the killer, there are at least two names remaining on his blacklist, the two people who are still alive and who both bear a certain responsibility for not bringing those responsible for Laura's death to justice: the officer in charge of the case, Ismael Flores, and the current Minister of Home Affairs and former superintendent of the Mossos, Jordi Soler i Casas.

Nuria decides it's time to stop beating around the bush and talk to the person who can really give her answers to her questions. The small impediment to this is that the Minister of Home Affairs of the Generalitat of Catalonia is unlikely to grant an urgent appointment to a suspended police officer. Because it's one thing to "forget" to mention the detail of her suspension to a civilian, and quite another to try to weasel information out of someone who occupies a high-ranking government post, someone who also just happens to be her boss and can permanently destroy her career with a snap of his fingers.

The first idea that occurs to Nuria is to try to pass as someone else: a journalist, for example. That way, she thinks, she could possibly gain access to the former superintendent and be able to question him without raising suspicions.

Without giving it any further thought, Nuria Googles the phone number of the Press Operations Department of the Ministry of the Interior of the Generalitat, calls it, and asks for an appointment to interview Jordi Soler i Casas.

"What media?" asks the admin on the other end of the line.

Shit, I should have planned this better, she thinks, then says the first thing that pops into her mind. "Um . . . newspaper."

"What precisely would the interview be about?"

Fuck, I definitely didn't think this through. "Uh . . . About the general state of things at the moment. A little of everything. You know."

"No, I don't know."

"Well . . ." She swallows and decides to go for it. "I'm working on the Satanic Assassin case"—she almost chokes on the name—"and I'd like to ask the minister a few questions about it."

She's pretty sure she hears a snort at the other end of the line. "I'm afraid the minister's calendar is completely full," the voice says. "I'm sorry."

"But—"

"Thank you for your call. You can try again in February if you'd like. Perhaps he'll have some time available then."

"I can't wait that long."

"Well . . . You'll have to forgive me, I have another call," says the admin. "Have a nice day." She hangs up without another word.

Nuria is left staring at the phone incredulously. It definitely hadn't been a good idea to mention the case. She's played what was perhaps her best card, and now she doesn't have many more to play. In reality, she has only one left, she concludes after thinking about it for a moment.

"Okay, then," she mutters, shoving the comforter off her and setting her bare feet on the thick wool rug. "Might as well be hanged for a sheep as a lamb."

By midmorning, Nuria's standing in front of the main entrance to the Ministry of Home Affairs on Diputación Street, a few meters from Tetuán Plaza. It's a ten-story building of glass and steel, flanked by another that looks like a fin-de-siècle mansion with a certain Parisian air. One didn't have to be overly observant to deduce which of the two housed the offices of the low-to-middle-range government employees and in which the professional politicians with chauffeurs and expense accounts worked.

At the door, Nuria is admitted into the interior of the building without issue, thanks to her police credential. After speaking to the concierge, she directs her steps to the minister's office which, as she'd suspected, is located in the neoclassical building. She finds a hidden corner of the corridor from where she can keep an eye on the door to his office without drawing attention to herself.

After ten minutes, she's bored. Stakeouts have never been her thing, and standing in a hallway that's practically deserted, transited only rarely by some clerk or other who is completely engrossed in his paperwork, is especially tedious.

Keeping her peripheral vision trained on the door to the minister's office, Nuria pulls her cell phone from her pocket and begins to scroll through the social media sites, both to distract herself and to calm the nerves that have formed a knot in the pit of her stomach.

She's beginning to suspect that what she's doing is nothing more than a waste of time when, after more than an hour of waiting, the elevator door slides open and the minister strides out of it, his steps hurried and an expression of concern on his face. He's followed by a small entourage of bureaucratic employees who are trying to keep up with him.

"Minister?" Nuria says as he walks by her. He halts for a moment and throws her a quick glance.

"Yes?" he says impatiently. The ex-superintendent is a man in his late sixties with an exuberant mane of hair that hints at capillary transplants in Turkey. He's wearing a bespoke blue suit, a perfectly knotted silk tie, and a gold watch that no doubt cost more than Nuria's car. In person, he's much shorter than she'd expected, but his body language and sharp gaze make it clear that his size is not an impediment and that he's obviously been in charge for many years.

"Could I speak with you alone for a moment? It would only take a minute."

"I'm very busy. Make an appointment with my secretary," he says, pointing at someone behind him and beginning to walk again.

Nuria sees that in a matter of seconds the minister will disappear behind the door to his office. Without a second thought, she raises her voice and blurts out the first thing that comes into her mind to get his attention. "It's about a redacted file from when you were superintendent of the Mossos in 2006."

The minister stops again and turns toward her, his eyes narrowed behind his Armani glasses. "Who are you?" he asks warily.

"Officer Badal, from the CID," she says.

The minister frowns. "Well, in that case, *Officer,*" he replies, verbally underlining her rank in the police hierarchy so she can't help but be aware of the difference between them, "you should know that this is not the way to approach your superior. If you wish to speak to me, follow the established procedure."

"It's about something extremely urgent, Minister. I don't have time to go through administrative channels."

Jordi Soler i Casas taps the face of his watch with his index finger. "I'm the one with no time to lose," he retorts, turning around. "Ask my secretary for an appointment." Before Nuria can think of another objection, the minister opens the door to his office and disappears inside along with the three people following him. The door closes behind them.

"Well, that went well," Nuria murmurs aloud. For a moment she continues to stand there in the middle of the hallway feeling a bit foolish and with no idea of what to do next.

The minister had reacted when she'd mentioned the redacted file to him, but he hadn't given any sign of wanting to talk about the subject.

Nuria makes a wry face, realizing that at that very moment the minister may be looking her up. If that's the case, it won't take him long to find out that she's been suspended. At last she shrugs, coming to a decision. Now that she's come this far, there's no turning back.

A couple of hours later, Minister Jordi Soler i Casas exits his office and strides quickly toward the restrooms on the second floor. Congratulating himself that there's no one there he needs to greet, he enters the first cubicle. Lowering the zipper on his pants, he relieves himself after having sat through an interminable call with the president of the Generalitat. Finishing, he zips up with a sigh of pleasure and leaves the cubicle in order to wash his hands but stops dead in his tracks when he sees a tall blonde with green eyes leaning against the bathroom door, her arms crossed over her chest.

"What are you doing here?" he asks as soon as he's recovered his composure.

"Waiting for you," Nuria admits naturally.

"I believe I made myself quite clear. Ask my secretary for an appointment."

"And I've told you that it's urgent. I just need you to answer a couple of questions."

"Just who the hell do you think you are, interrogating me? Do you understand I can have you thrown out of the police department immediately?"

"Right this minute, my police career is the least of my worries," Nuria lies, hoping he won't realize it. "June of 2006," she begins. "A minor named Laura Gómez Martínez commits suicide after becoming involved with an organization that forces her into prostitution. Her parents file a complaint but no one moves a finger and the initial report ends up being suppressed."

"I don't know what you're talking about."

"You were superintendent at the time."

"And what does that have to do with it?"

"I need to know the details of that case and why it was hushed up. It could be the key to stopping the current wave of murders that's worrying you so much."

The minister shakes his head. "I don't see what the two cases have in common."

"Possibly nothing," Nuria admits. "Or possibly everything. That's why I need to gain access to that file and learn why the report was dismissed instead of being investigated."

"And how do you expect me to remember a case that was dismissed almost twenty years ago?"

"I'm sure you have access to the original report and can find out what really happened with the case."

"And why should I help an officer who's been suspended and had a disciplinary file opened on her?"

"I see you haven't wasted any time."

"And you are going to lose your job."

Nuria makes a wry face and snorts. "Maybe. But if I'm right, you could be next on the murderer's list."

The minister's eyes widen. "What are you saying?"

"I believe someone is avenging Laura's suicide. First he went for those who abused her and now, beginning with the murder of the judge, he's intending to kill everyone who did nothing to stop the guilty parties."

"What does that have to do with me?"

"You tell me," Nuria replies. "That's why I need the file that was redacted."

"I didn't authorize anyone to redact a file."

"Well, someone did."

The minister takes a few seconds to think it over while meticulously washing his hands. "Everything you're telling me . . . are your superiors aware of it? Why is this the first I've heard of this?"

"I'm suspended, remember?" Nuria says. "Precisely for this. For following this line of inquiry."

"They can't have suspended you just for that."

"Well, I might have overlooked a few rules and regulations in the process," Nuria confesses. "But in this case I believe the end justifies the means, don't you think?"

The minister fixes his gaze on her, assessing her and her words. "I'll speak with your inspector who's in charge of the case," he affirms after a few moments. "All of this is highly irregular."

"Could you get me the original file? The key to all of this may be in there."

"I'll see what I can do."

"Thank you," Nuria says.

Jordi Soler i Casas shakes his head. "Don't thank me too soon, Officer Badal. I still haven't decided what to do with you."

"Do what you have to do, Minister," Nuria answers, trying to sound off-hand. "I'll do the same." With a last look at her, he squeezes past and leaves the men's restroom without another word.

When the door has closed behind him, Nuria sticks her hand in the pocket of her coat and clicks the recorder off.

46

Several weeks have elapsed since that fateful night, and only a day less since Laura wrote the agency asking for an explanation. In fact, ever since that afternoon, she's written them at least ten times and called many more times than that, but it's as if the agency has been swallowed up by the earth. Not a single response, not a single message left. Nothing.

The tone of urgency in Laura's messages has grown as the days have gone by until she's finally accepted that they're ignoring her and that the best thing to do is simply turn the page and hide that horrendous experience away in the darkest corner of her memory. In fact, she finds that each day she thinks less about it until finally there are whole days during which she almost succeeds in avoiding the memory of that morning.

That is, until the day the phone rings again and when she answers, she hears the voice of the photographer greeting her breezily, as if nothing's wrong.

Laura freezes. Ever since it happened, she'd thought of a thousand things she wanted to reproach him for, demand from him, even threaten him with. But now that the moment has arrived, she finds that she's mute, with no idea what to say.

"How's everything going?" the photographer asks her as if he's an old friend she hasn't seen for a while. "There's another party this weekend," he adds casually, "and I need you to be there. There will be some really big names from the fashion world there and—"

"No!" Laura yells with her whole being. "No!" she repeats, emerging from her stupor at last. "They drugged me and raped me! Do you realize that? They abused me at that fucking party! I should have reported you! I should have reported all of you! You're all a bunch of fucking sons of bitches!" she explodes. "Fucking assholes!!"

"Calm down, Laura."

"*Calm down??!!*" she roars. "How am I supposed to calm down? They raped me! Did you not hear me??"

"These things happen," the photographer says calmly. "That's how the fashion world works."

"I don't give a shit! I don't want anything to do with you or your fucking parties ever again! Are you hearing me?"

"That's not going to be possible," he says.

"That's not going to be possible??" Laura repeats, incredulous. "I'm telling you it's certainly going to be possible. Don't ever call me again or I'll call the police!" she yells, slamming the phone down.

For a long minute she looks at the phone, her breathing ragged, afraid it will ring again. But it remains silent.

Her heart is racing and it takes her a long time to calm herself. When her breathing finally returns to normal, she opens her laptop to finish the science project she's going to present at the end of the week but instead sees that she's received a new email from the agency.

Again her heart begins to race. Even though she's tempted to simply delete the message without looking at it, she gives in to her curiosity and opens it. *What harm can it do just to look at it?* she thinks. Maybe the photographer has thought better of it and written to apologize and give her all the explanations she deserves.

But neither of these is true.

The only thing the email contains is an address, the time at which she needs to be at the next party, and the sentence *If you don't want everyone to see this.*

Laura understands that the cryptic message refers to the attached Zip files. With a trembling hand, she clicks on the keys to unzip the files and is met with a series of short, untitled videos. Opening the first of these, she almost falls out of her chair.

The video's been filmed with a handheld camera and isn't the best quality, but it's still possible to see clearly five middle-aged men, completely naked except for their masks, standing around a bed on which lies a young girl, also naked and obviously drugged.

It takes Laura's brain a few seconds to recognize that the bed in the video is the one she woke up in that terrible morning and the naked girl is herself. The dissociation of the images from what she remembers is absolute. It's as if she's looking at another person. One part of her mind refuses to believe that what she's seeing is real, but then she realizes it's useless to deceive herself, especially when the men begin to run their eager hairy hands over her skin, to stick their fingers into her mouth and her vagina, to masturbate while they await their turn as the first of them flips her over like a doll and, panting like a pig, begins to penetrate her from behind.

47

Nuria has barely left the Ministry of the Interior when her phone rings. Looking at the screen, she sees it's an unknown number. "Yes?" she answers.

"Officer Badal?"

"This is she. With whom am I speaking?"

"This is Eugenia, from Human Resources at the Teknon Clinic. We spoke yesterday."

"Oh, yes. What's up?"

"I'm calling you because after you left I wrote the College of Gynecology to ask about Dr. Martínez. They told me she'd ended her membership in the association in January of 2008."

"Okay," Nuria answers once she realizes nothing else is coming. "And that's important because . . ."

"I don't know," the admin says. "But if she quit the association that means she was intending to stop practicing as a gynecologist or she was moving somewhere else."

"Apparently," Nuria explains, "she moved out of her home in Barcelona. So it's likely she went to some other city."

"Yes, that's what I thought. But the weird thing is that I've checked all the other professional medical colleges in the country and she's not a member of any of them. Without belonging to a professional college," she clarifies, "you can't practice medicine, at least not in Spain."

"I see. What about abroad?"

"I have no information about that, Officer. If she validated her medical license, she could work in almost any other country in the world."

"I understand," Nuria says. "Thanks so much for your collaboration, Eugenia. You've been a great help."

"Happy to have been able to help, Officer. Good day," she says before ending the call. Thoughtful, Nuria sits for a moment, gazing at the black screen on the phone. The fact that María Martínez would leave her apartment and the painful memories attached to every nook and cranny of the place seems logical to Nuria; surely she would have done the same thing. But to abandon a profession that had taken so many years of study, internships, residencies . . . that makes less sense.

Nuria dismisses the possibility that María had also taken her own life. To do that, she wouldn't have needed to go to the trouble of officially canceling her membership in a professional association or erasing any trace of herself on the Internet. The other option, she reasons, aside from changing jobs, is that she might have moved to another country, in which case it will be impossible to track her down.

In summary, one way or another, Dr. Martínez has vanished like one's sense of shame at a karaoke club at three a.m.

A flutter in her belly tells Nuria that this woman is the key to the whole business—but she's arrived at yet another dead-end street and she's out of options. She highly doubts the minister will help her with something that might reflect badly on his political career—even if he himself may be next on the murderer's list. No, it's much more likely that her spur-of-the-moment interrogation of him in the men's bathroom of the ministry will only hasten her dismissal from the Mossos.

Nuria has nothing, not even an incriminating recording with which to pressure him if it comes to that. She's devoted the last week to digging her own professional grave, and she's just handed the shovel to the minister so he can begin to cover her with dirt.

"How brilliant can you get?" she says to herself with a wry grin.

Wandering down Diputación Street, the smell of Asian food wafts past her nostrils, and she pauses in front of a hot pot restaurant. But she doesn't feel like cooking her own food so, in spite of being ravenous, she keeps walking in search of a place that offers good, cheap—and already cooked—food.

She reaches the Gracia intersection without having found a single reasonably priced restaurant and realizes that the best decision she can make is to take the metro home and forget about all of it: eating out, pursuing the case further, her career . . . Her future is darker than the black clouds threatening the city. For a moment she stops and watches the people walking by her on the wide sidewalk, each one engrossed in his or her own problems but still walking with the air of confidence and firm step belonging to those who know where they're going and why.

With some surprise, she realizes she was one of them only days ago. What the hell happened? How could things get so majorly fucked up in such a short time?

For a moment she's tempted to call Grandpa Pepe and confess everything to him so he can give her advice. She even considers, for an even briefer moment, calling her mother. She feels terribly alone, in need of someone to tell her everything's going to turn out fine, no matter how flagrant a lie that is. But no. She can't put this on her family. Neither can she unload on Susi or any of her friends, not that there are that many of them to begin with.

Buying a plane ticket to the Canary Islands or anywhere else with sun and beaches, turning off her phone, and staying away until she's summoned to Egara to testify in her own defense, seems like a stupendous idea right now. Countries like Brazil and Thailand that don't have extradition treaties with Spain seem like even better destinations, given what could happen.

For once in her life she'd thought she'd found the right path. But of course, Nuria wouldn't be Nuria without that inborn habit of fucking everything up, twisting and manhandling everything until it broke. For the last thirty years she's been repeating the same pattern in her relationships, her studies, and her jobs. Nuria Badal couldn't possibly let any opportunity that came along to turn everything she touched into shit go by, oh no.

And here she is now, leaning against the wall next to the ostentatious shop window of a Louis Vuitton outlet, surrounded by strangers with artificially bolstered self-confidence and without a clue about what to do next.

Instinctively, she takes out her phone, as if it can somehow help her in her dilemma. After vacillating for a moment, she clicks on her contact list, searching for someone she can call, like a shipwreck victim searching for a life preserver in the middle of the ocean. Her eyes scan the list and then alight on a name that immediately catches all her attention: Ismael Flores.

For a second she rubs her thumb over the name of the ex-cop, wondering whether to call him or not—but then she has a better idea.

Forty minutes later, Nuria is standing in front of an intercom next to the door of a hundred-year-old building on Rambla del Poble Nou.

The metallic-sounding voice of the man comes through the device. "Yes?"

"Good afternoon, Mr. Flores. It's Nuria Badal."

His answer takes a few seconds to come through. "The officer from the Mossos?" he asks incredulously.

"One and the same."

"What are you doing here? What do you want?"

"To talk."

"To talk?" he repeats. "I already told you everything I had to tell you. Leave me alone."

"I can't," Nuria presses him. "Laura Gómez's father died and her mother vanished. I've gone to see the Minister for Home Affairs and I don't think he's going to help me either. I have no one left to talk to except for you."

The intercom remains silent for so long that Nuria's beginning to fear Ismael Flores has hung up. Finally he speaks. "You talked to the minister?"

"I was just there."

Another pause, a little shorter than the previous one. Then the buzzer sounds, indicating that the door is open. "Come up," he says.

When Ismael Flores opens his door to her on the fifth floor, there's no protocol. He invites her into the entrance hall and repeats his question point-blank as soon as he closes the door. "You seriously went to see the minister?"

Despite the fact that it's already afternoon, the ex-cop looks disheveled and unshaven. *At least he's not still wearing his pajamas,* Nuria thinks when she sees him.

"I was out of options," she says with a shrug. "He was the superintendent in 2006 and I thought he could help me with that report, but the only thing I achieved was to make him angry."

"What did you expect? Jordi Soler stopped being a cop a long time ago, if he ever really was one. He's a politician now and, as such, is only interested in himself."

"Yeah, well. I had to try."

Ismael lets out a noisy exhale. "Anyway," he mutters, shaking his head. "Do you want a coffee?"

"Yes, please. Thank you."

Ismael goes into the kitchen and turns on the electric coffeemaker. "Black or with milk?"

"Black, with just a little sugar."

Nuria's stomach grumbles loudly and Ismael turns toward her. "Something to go with your coffee?" he asks, raising an eyebrow. "Some cookies or madeleines?"

Nuria smiles timidly. "That would be great, thanks," she answers, blushing.

A few minutes later, seated in front of the coffee table in the living room with a steaming cup of coffee in her hands, Nuria looks around surreptitiously. The apartment is small and a bit dark, decorated in an antiquated style, and none too clean or neat. Ismael follows her eyes and apologizes. "I wasn't expecting company."

Nuria looks at the newspaper clippings that are tacked to the walls like pictures. Some of them, yellowed by time, are about cases involving the police from decades earlier. Others are more recent. "Are these all your cases?" Nuria asks, waving a hand to encompass them all.

Ismael gives a quick nod. "Some," he answers. "The oldest ones."

"And the others?"

"I'm a cop who took early retirement and I have no hobbies," he explains, shrugging his shoulders. "Following some cases keeps me entertained."

"Once a cop always a cop, huh?"

"Something like that." Ismael takes a sip of his coffee and gazes at her. "What exactly do you want?"

"Answers," Nuria replies.

"I don't have them, I've already told you."

"I need to understand what's happening."

"And I need a new TV."

"Please, Ismael . . . I need you to try to remember. There's a lot at stake here."

"Are you talking about your job? You're still suspended, right?"

Nuria's left speechless for a moment. Finally she asks, "How long have you known?"

"Since five minutes after I talked to you the first time. I've still got contacts in Egara."

"Did you talk to Sánchez?" Nuria inquires, suddenly worried. "Did you say something about—"

"I haven't said anything to anyone," he reassures her. "I just wanted to know who you were."

"And now you know?"

"I know you're a rookie who's gotten herself into deep shit because of insisting on doing things her way. Ignoring police procedure, the chain of command, and even the law."

"Yes, well, that's one way to put it," Nuria agrees. "But what I'm wondering is, if you already knew all that, why did you ask me up to your apartment?"

"Because I want answers too," he replies. "Beginning with why you would risk your job in an effort to resolve a case that's almost twenty years old."

"I'm convinced there's a link between that case and the murderer who's skinning people alive every two or three days."

"You haven't answered my question," Ismael insists. "Why are *you* in particular so interested in this case?"

"I . . . I don't know," Nuria confesses. "I suppose I want to do what's right. Catch him before he keeps on killing."

"Ignoring usual police procedure isn't exactly doing the right thing, is it?"

"I know," she admits. "But I thought it was worth taking a risk for."

Ismael leans back in his chair, crossing his arms. "And was it?"

This time Nuria's the one to shrug. "I don't know yet," she says. "It depends on whether you're going to help me solve the case."

A small laugh escapes Ismael. "You are certainly . . . persistent."

"Pigheaded is the right word. According to my mother."

"It's true," Ismael says with a smile, "I've never met anyone on the police force that would put solving a case ahead of their own career."

"Yeah, well. If we're going to be honest . . . I wasn't really expecting to be suspended. I thought if I could single-handedly catch the murderer I would get a promotion, even a medal."

"And do you still believe that?" says Ismael.

"Well, the way things have played out, I'll be satisfied if I don't get kicked out of the Mossos."

Ismael fixes his gaze on her for several minutes before saying, "And even so, you still insist on solving the case."

"Now that I've come this far," Nuria answers, opening her hands, "what else can I do? I can't simply turn around and forget everything. I have to . . . at least try."

"To do the right thing."

Nuria nods, closes her eyes and then opens them again.

"Will you help me?"

<h1 style="text-align:center">48</h1>

Nuria sets her phone on the table and shows Ismael the image of a woman of around sixty, hair drawn back into a severe bun, mouth in a straight line unmarked by smile wrinkles at the corners, and black eyes that seem to hand down sentences at first sight.

"This is Judge Martina Mas Serret," she says to the ex-cop, zooming in on the photo. "She was murdered only a few hours ago," she goes on, giving him a sidelong glance to see his reaction. "Tell me this wasn't the judge who dismissed Laura's case."

"How . . . When did they—"

Nuria cuts him off. "I don't know the details. But it seems as if the murder was similar to the previous ones. It's her, right?"

"It's possible."

"It's *possible*?" Nuria shoots back, raising her voice unconsciously. "Don't fuck with me, Ismael! Someone is murdering everyone who was involved with the case. First the ones who apparently sexually abused the girl, and now the ones who didn't do everything possible to judge those who were guilty."

"That's a big assumption on your part."

"I know I'm right."

"You know?" Ismael interrupts. "You don't know shit, little miss. You're just speculating and coming up with assumptions that fit your theory."

Nuria straightens up in her chair with annoyance, tapping the screen of her mobile. "I'm right," she insists with a frown, "and you know it. I saw your face when you looked at the photo of the judge. You recognized her. Why are you denying it?"

Ismael Flores pauses for several long moments, almost as long as he has previously. He leans over the table, studying first the photo of the judge and then Nuria. "Why do you ask me if you already have the answer?"

Nuria ignores the question. Like him, she leans forward over the table, interlacing her fingers. "I need you to help me, Ismael."

"How?"

"If the murderer continues to follow this pattern, there aren't many people left on his blacklist. And one of them is you."

Ismael jumps in surprise. "Do you think he's coming for me?" he asks her, incredulous.

"You were the officer in charge of the case until it was deep-sixed, right?"

"I did everything I could until it was taken away from me," he protests. "You already know that."

"The important thing isn't what I know but what the murderer knows. If he thinks you're responsible for the case being buried . . ."

"Well," Ismael snorts, apparently unworried at the prospect. "I guess we'll find out sooner rather than later."

"I can help you," Nuria offers. "We can help each other, Ismael."

"What do you mean? Do you want to be my bodyguard?"

"Better than that. If he comes after you, we could set a trap for him."

"With me as bait, right? Do I have *S* for *stupid* tattooed across my forehead?" he says, turning his face toward her.

"Do you have a better idea?" Nuria says challengingly, crossing her arms over her chest.

"You mean, apart from sitting in my apartment and waiting to be killed? I'm sure I can come up with something. Don't you have any suspects?"

"Yes. Well . . . I don't know. Maybe."

"Yes-well-I-don't-know-maybe?"

"I think the murderer might actually be a woman."

"A woman?" Ismael asks, surprised.

"María Martínez, Laura's mother. She was a gynecologist."

"And?"

"She vanished back in 2007 and erased every trace of herself online," Nuria explains. "She has medical knowledge, she knows how to use a scalpel, and she might possibly have access to the paralyzing drugs that have been used in the murders."

Ismael's expression vacillates between incredulous and amused. "Do you seriously believe the mother of the girl is a serial killer?"

"After her daughter committed suicide, her husband did too, so there's no lack of motive for her to have flipped out and decided to take revenge on everybody."

"Seventeen years later?" Ismael protests, shaking his head. "It seems unlikely to me that someone would wait that long to take revenge, especially a revenge as brutal and bloody as these murders have been."

"On the contrary!" Nuria says. "Think about it. How could a normal, everyday woman manage to kill half a dozen people over a period of ten days in the methodical way they've been killed without leaving a single shred of evidence and with all the police clueless?"

Ismael takes a few seconds to consider his answer, then says, "With a lot of preparation."

"Exactly. María Martínez has had seventeen years to plan these murders down to the last detail. That's why it's been impossible to catch her, because she's got years of advantage on us. She's been leading us down the garden path with fake prints and red-herring clues from the beginning, just so we'll look in the wrong place. She's made us believe it's all about some satanic sect or a maniac with a knife on the loose."

Ismael turns this over in his mind. "It's crazy," he says finally.

"But it makes sense. Revenge is a dish that's best served cold, right?"

"Yes, but this is an exaggeration. Seventeen years is a lot of years."

"Actually," Nuria points out, lifting her index finger, "if my theory is correct, the first murder happened long before, in 2010. The photographer that took pictures of Laura to post online was knifed to death and his wife, who collaborated in his work, was accused of the murder, though she insists she's innocent."

"They all say they're innocent," Ismael reminds her. "Even when you catch them with the smoking gun in their hand."

"Yes, that's what my inspector said too," Nuria agrees. "But Luisa Domínguez alleges that she doesn't remember anything and that she was drugged with something like scopolamine—which is exactly what they used on the girls so they wouldn't resist."

"Pfft . . . It's a bit convoluted, isn't it?"

"Everything about this case is convoluted," Nuria reasons. "But it's the only way all the pieces fit."

"Are you suggesting that María Martínez murdered the photographer first and then decided she liked it?"

"Maybe at first she only wanted to kill him, but it's possible that before he died he may have given her the names of his accomplices and she decided to take justice into her own hands and do what the cops and the judges hadn't."

"And all that business about the *666* painted in blood at the crime scenes?"

"I don't know," Nuria admits. "She might have done that to throw us off, or maybe it has some meaning we haven't been able to figure ou—" Nuria goes silent all at once, her eyes widening as if she's just seen a ghost. "It can't be," she murmurs incredulously. "Holy shit . . . It's not possible."

"What is it?"

Nuria turns her gaze on the ex-cop. "The date of Laura's suicide. The exact date. Do you remember it?"

Ismael shakes his head. "It was in 2006. I think June, if I remember right? But the exact day . . ."

"The news about the suicide appeared in the press on June 7," Nuria recalls. "So it could possibly have happened the day before, no?"

"I guess so, and?"

"June 6, 2006," Nuria says slowly, waiting for a reaction from Ismael that's slow in coming. "06/06/06."

"Fuck me!" Ismael exclaims. "It's a date!"

"That clinches it. There can be no doubt," Nuria states. "The cases are related."

This time Ismael's pause is much longer. He stares at the ceiling like a mathematician trying to resolve an especially complex equation in the air. Nuria waits expectantly in silence. It's the first time she's spoken her theory aloud. If she's made a mistake in her deductions, now will be the time for it to show up.

Ismael takes a deep breath, exhaling slowly as he lowers his gaze. "I think you're right," he affirms, still staring into space.

Nuria bites her lip to keep from heaving a sigh of relief. "Of course I am," she says, pretending a confidence she doesn't feel. "That's why I need you to help me."

"I'm not going to be the bait," he warns her, looking her full in the face now.

"It would be the best way to—"

"I've got a better idea," he interrupts. "Maybe . . . let the bait be someone else. For example, the minister. If the murderer's going to come for me, it's more likely she'll go after him since he was my boss and the one who authorized me being taken off the case."

Nuria shakes her head. "He's not going to want to cooperate," she warns. "Besides, he's got his own security team, and they're never going to expose him to a situation where he could be running even the smallest risk just on the say-so of a suspended officer and a retired cop."

"Well, in that case, it would be best not to tell him."

"Are you suggesting we protect him without him realizing we're doing it?"

"Can you think of a better way to set a trap?" Ismael leans over the table toward her, a wolfish smile on his face. "Using someone as bait who doesn't know he's being used as bait?"

49

From a corner on the other side of the street, about fifty meters away, Nuria squints through binoculars, keeping her eyes fixed on the main entrance to the Pedralbes building where the Minister for Home Affairs for Catalonia has his luxurious apartment.

"Not a soul on the street," she murmurs without lowering the binoculars.

"It's still early," Ismael says from the front passenger seat where he's seated. "I doubt if the minister gets up before seven."

They've been there almost twelve hours, from six p.m. of the day before, monitoring the home of the "very honorable" minister Jordi Soler i Casas, waiting for María Martínez or whoever's acting in her name to make an appearance.

It's been twelve hours of cold, tedium, and gas-station sandwiches. Directly in front of the lobby door, a Mossos patrol cruiser has also stood guard all night, but with the motor running so the officer can keep the heater on. Nuria looks at the patrol car with a certain envy, seeing as they haven't been able to allow themselves the luxury of calling attention to themselves. Besides, if they'd kept the heater going all night using just the battery, the only way they would get out of there would be pushing the car.

"I'm going to take a piss," Ismael announces, opening the car door.

"I have to go too," Nuria says, lowering the binoculars. "But it's harder for us girls."

"It'll only be a few minutes until they open the café down there," Ismael says, jerking his head in the other direction. "Can you wait?"

"I guess I'll have to," Nuria says with a sigh, raising the binoculars to her eyes again.

The ex-cop closes the door as silently as possible and walks down the street in search of a bush or two. Nuria's left alone in the car. She recalls the first time she kept watch like this; she'd still been a cadet and the objective had been a petty drug dealer on Montjuic mountain. On that occasion, the stake-out had seemed exciting to her, like being in a detective movie, ready to leap out of the car at any moment, gun in hand, and take off after a fleeing suspect. This time all she feels is the urge to pee, take a hot shower, lower the blinds in her bedroom, and climb into bed after taking a strong sleeping pill.

Turning away from the door of the building for a moment, Nuria pours the remainder of the coffee from her thermos into a disposable plastic cup. It's cold and bitter, but at least it helps wash away the pasty feeling she has in her mouth.

Ismael returns, climbing back into the passenger seat. "Well . . ." he says, rubbing his hands against his thighs to get his circulation going again, "I think we should call it a night. I don't think anything's going to happen at this hour."

Nuria's about to say they should wait until the team that protects the minister by day arrives, but instead she nods wearily. "I agree," she says, turning the key in the ignition. "Shall I drop you at home?"

"No need. The metro's running and there's a stop really close to my place. I'd like to stretch my legs a little."

"Okay, sounds good. Shall I come by for you this afternoon at the same time?"

"Sure. Will you bring coffee?"

"And some diapers," Nuria says half seriously, making a wry face.

The impatient sound of her alarm clock awakens her in her bed almost ten hours later. She reaches out and stops the insidious noise. In the end she hadn't needed a sleeping pill nor had she had the energy to take her longed-for hot shower. After feeding Melón, she'd left a trail of her clothes on the way to her bedroom, lowered the shades, and curled up underneath her down comforter, drifting off seconds later. As she awakens now, she feels an incipient headache pressing on the nape of her neck, as if she'd used a brick for a pillow.

Reluctantly, she pushes the bedclothes aside, stands up and, feeling her way in the darkness, enters the bathroom, emerging twenty minutes later wrapped in a towel with her bladder emptied.

She wanders around the apartment picking up the pieces of clothing she'd left scattered around the living room and the hallway. Returning to the bedroom, she raises the blinds on the window that overlooks the street. As she opens the curtains, her eyes widen as she stares at the narrow street several floors below her window. "Wow!!" she cries, as excited as a little girl who's just been given a puppy. "Look, Melón! It's snowing!"

A cloud of ethereal flakes is drifting down in front of her window, blurring the sharp lines of the buildings around hers, muffling the street noise, and blanketing the street and the sidewalks with a snowy mantle disturbed only by the tires of the few cars that are driving down Verdi Street at a snail's pace.

Ecstatic over this sight that's so rarely seen in Barcelona, Nuria remains at the window until Melón, considerably less excited by the snow, rubs against her leg and gives her a demanding meow.

"I know, just a moment," Nuria says, reluctant to tear her eyes away from the scene outside the window.

"Meooooowwww."

"All right. For Pete's sake!" Nuria gives up and pulls the curtains closed again. "You're so tiresome."

As she walks to the kitchen to take care of the feline issue, Melón's meows increase in volume and insistence, reaching their climax when she opens the can of food and dumps the whole thing into his bowl. "Enjoy," she says, but the cat is already devouring his meal, ignoring everything else but the gelatinous mass of chicken that he's wolfing down in huge bites. "You're going to get a tummy ache if you eat so fast," Nuria warns him with a shake of her head. Her own stomach growls, reminding her she hasn't eaten since the day before. Opening the fridge to see what she can find, she realizes all there is is a few eggs, a wilted head of lettuce, half a lime, and a couple of beers. "Shit," she mutters.

Checking her watch, she figures that all the restaurants are going to be closed at that hour, so she can forget about having a nice pad thai or an order of Singapore noodles. Luckily, there's a hamburger stand a couple of blocks away that she knows is open, so after dressing as if she's setting out on an expedition to the Antarctic, she pulls on a white wool hat with a bobble on it and goes out the door after casting a last look at Melón, who's settled on the sofa now to digest his breakfast.

Nuria takes the stairs two by two. When she opens the street door and sees the sidewalk covered with snow, a happy smile appears on her face. Taking care not to slip, she heads for the hamburger stand, enjoying the crunch of the snow beneath her feet. The multicolored Christmas lights above her head are reflected in the ice crystals, multiplying their various hues. Kids and older people alike are playing in the snow while parents film their young ones. A couple of young girls film an improvised dance for TikTok against the snowy background. Some people are walking with their arms out, surveying everything with wide eyes, while others stroll with their disconcerted dogs dressed in colorful sweaters. A good number simply look up toward the sky, sticking their tongues out to see what snow tastes like. The city looks completely unfamiliar and its inhabitants seem to have been turned into playful children, neither hurried nor embarrassed about their actions. It's like everyone has agreed that anything goes today as long as everyone is happy.

Just then, Nuria's phone rings and her smile falters when she sees the name on the screen. She answers. "Hi, Mom."

"Hi, Nurieta, how are you?"

"Fine. I'm out walking, going to get something to eat. Have you seen the snow?"

"Yes, everything's so beautiful! No doubt it's a gift from the Lord for this special day."

"Special? Why?"

"What do you mean, why? It's Christmas Eve, Nuria!"

"Really??" Nuria pulls the phone away from her ear and sees on the screen that it is indeed December 24th. "Fuck me," she murmurs, then puts the phone to her ear again. "I'd totally missed that."

"You work too much."

Nuria swallows and bites her lower lip. "Um . . . Yeah, that must be it."

"What time will you be here?" her mother continues. "You're not going to do what you did last year, are you? When you came right before dinner and then ran out right after we'd finished eating."

A couple of neurons connect in Nuria's brain, producing a small spark. That's when she remembers her promise to have dinner at her mom's house on Christmas Eve. "Uh . . . Yes, of course. I'll try to be there before."

"At what time?"

"Um, I'm not sure. Let me speak to my inspector and see what he says."

"All right. But tell him for me that this is not a day when people should be working. Even the criminals are at home with their families."

"Mom, you know I don't have a nine-to-five desk job. Criminals don't take days off, not even at Christmas."

There's a moment of silence at the other end of the line. "But you are coming, aren't you?" her mother asks at last in a piteous tone.

Nuria hates to lie and especially to her mother, but she doesn't have the energy to tell her the truth, which will result either in an argument or in tears on her mother's part. "I'll do everything I can to be there," she says finally. "But I can't promise you anything, Mom."

She hears a deep sigh of disappointment and realizes that if she stays on the phone the conversation is only going to deteriorate. "I have to let you go," she adds before her mother's sigh can be followed by a reproach. "I'll call you later, Mom," she says, clicking the call off.

Shit, she thinks, sticking her phone back in her pocket. *How can it already be Christmas? Though maybe the Christmas lights should have tipped me off.*

Pushing her feelings of guilt to the side, she focuses on reaching the hamburger joint while thinking that Ismael hadn't mentioned that tonight was Christmas Eve either. Though she barely knows him she's fairly sure he has no one to celebrate with either.

Could this be the fate of police officers who are dedicated to their jobs? Loneliness and lack of understanding on the part of family and friends? Was it really worth it to give so much in return for so little?

She opens the door to the hamburger place and finds all the tables full of families with children, young lovers, and adolescents flirting with each other.

"It seems like the snow makes people happy, doesn't it?"

Nuria turns toward the voice and finds herself looking into the black eyes of a handsome Indian waiter who's standing on the other side of the counter, wearing a Santa Claus cap and a dazzling smile.

"Yes, it does seem that way." Nuria returns his smile. She casts her gaze around the restaurant again and feels deep inside her the need to protect them all from the darkness of the real world.

Doing what she does is worth the sacrifice, she realizes. Even if she wanted to, she couldn't be any other way than how she is.

50

On her way to pick up Ismael Nuria sees several streets that have been blocked off by demonstrations. It appears that neither the snow nor the imminent festivities have dissuaded the Reborn from coming out in droves with their torches, their crosses, and their colorful posters decrying abortion, homosexuality, and euthanasia. In spite of being at different poles ideologically, Nuria has to admit that the fact they've been able to get several thousands of demonstrators to come out on a day like this is impressive.

It's just shy of five p.m. when she and Ismael find a parking space very close to where they'd been the night before. From their position, they can see the main entrance to the building, the patrol car keeping watch in front of the door and, five floors up, the warm lighting of the exclusive penthouse belonging to the minister. The drawn curtains prevent them from seeing what's going on inside, but silhouettes of adults and children are projected onto them as in a shadow play. It's easy for Nuria to imagine that they're busy preparing for the family dinner.

"I've brought a couple of blankets," Ismael says, opening the duffel bag he has on his lap. "Looks like it's going to be colder than yesterday."

Nuria glances at the half-open bag. "And I brought a thermos of coffee and a package of cookies."

"Lovely Christmas dinner, huh?" Ismael remarks, making a face. "That asshole there stuffing his face in front of the fireplace with his family and us here shivering and having coffee and cookies for dinner.

"They're chocolate chip," Nuria informs him.

"Oh, I see. You should have said that before. That changes everything."

Nuria and Ismael exchange a complicit glance and a resigned smile. *It's what it is,* their looks say, with no need for words.

Just then, a black official vehicle with tinted glass pulls up in front of the entrance to the building and a burly man wearing a dark suit gets out and surveys the surroundings with a professional air. Once he's satisfied, he circles the vehicle and opens the passenger door from which alights Minister Jordi Soler i Casas.

Holding his briefcase over his head to protect him from the snow, the minister crosses the sidewalk, followed by his bodyguard who escorts him inside the building, exiting again only once he knows the minister is safe, like a young man walking his girlfriend home in a dangerous neighborhood. He climbs into the official vehicle, which starts up again and drives down the street, disappearing into the snowfall.

"Well, we've got the worm on the hook again," Ismael murmurs.

Nuria turns to him, raising an eyebrow. "Could the worm have some ulterior motive?"

"At least one. When he was superintendent he was a cretin and a brownnoser, and I would say he probably hasn't improved with time."

"But there must be a reason they've made him Minister for Home Affairs, don't you think?"

Ismael Flores makes a sour face. "Knowing him, the most likely explanation is that he got there by elbowing people out of the way and stabbing them in the back."

Nuria rubs her chin pensively. "I'm beginning to get the feeling you don't like him much."

"Very perceptive of you," Ismael says dryly. "You know, you should be a cop."

"Did something happen between the two of you?" Nuria asks.

"I doubt if he even remembers my existence," Ismael says, shaking his head. "We only spoke a handful of times while he was superintendent and none of those times was to congratulate me for my work. He didn't even say goodbye to me the day I retired."

"Now that you mention it, why did you take early retirement?" Nuria asks.

Ismael shrugs and heaves a heavy sigh. "I was burned out. Too many years looking at, smelling, and stepping in shit."

"But . . . I saw your flat," Nuria protests. "You've got clippings about cases pinned up all over your walls."

"I'm not talking about the police work," he clarifies, turning to look at her. "Though that takes its toll as well. I'm referring to all the rest: the funny business some people were always up to, the stupidity of others, the politics and the infighting, the—"

"The closing of a case and the burying of the file," Nuria puts in.

Ismael nods. "That's one example," he agrees. "Or, like in your case, that they suspend you because you want to do your job right."

"Yeah, well . . . though I think I also fucked things up royally."

"That doesn't matter," he objects. "I mean, not entirely. The line of investigation you wanted to follow was the correct one, and instead of supporting you in it they suspended you. Meanwhile, they don't have the faintest idea of what to do and the murderer's roaming the city, free."

Nuria raises her eyebrows and expels a lengthy exhale. "It still remains to be seen if I'm right," she cautions. "Right now you and I are just here, watching a lobby in the snow instead of celebrating Christmas Eve with our families."

"Well, I don't know about you," Ismael says, making a face, "but I almost prefer to be here. My family consists of a brother who's an imbecile, an ex-wife who got fed up with me, and a daughter who hasn't spoken to me in years." He pauses before adding, "What about you? Do you have family to be with at Christmas?"

"My mother and my grandfather."

"And why aren't you with them? I could be doing this on my own."

"Here is where I need to be," Nuria explains. "It's my duty."

"Not anymore. You're suspended, remember?"

"And you're retired," she replies. "Whatever the reason, I'm still a cop, and this may be the last chance we have to trap him."

Ismael sits silently, contemplating the snowflakes as they drift down onto the windshield. "Neither of us has to be here, in reality," he mutters after a while.

"Yet here we are."

"Here we are," Ismael repeats resignedly. Laying his hand on the thermos he asks, "Coffee?"

"I still don't—" Nuria begins, breaking off when she sees the patrol car turn on its roof lights. "What's going on?"

Before Ismael can answer, the vehicle pulls away from the curb and disappears down the street, its lights flashing silent reflections onto the snow.

"What the fuck?" murmurs the ex-cop with a frown.

"Why is he leaving?"

"Who knows?" he responds. "I imagine that since it's Christmas Eve they're short of personnel, and maybe they needed them for something more urgent."

"So they're leaving the minister unprotected?"

Ismael glances at her, a wolfish smile on his face. "Maybe I'm not the only one who isn't a big fan of the minister," he suggests. "Though most likely, someone else will be here to take their place before too long."

"I hope so."

"Don't worry. We're here, after all, no?"

"Yeah, I guess. I would prefer to have a couple of armed officers close by, though."

Ismael sticks his hand inside his coat and withdraws a black gun from the inner pocket. "Heckler and Koch P30, nine millimeter," he says, showing the gun to Nuria.

"I didn't know you were armed," she says.

"You didn't ask," Ismael retorts, putting the gun back into his pocket. "Where's yours?"

"In my locker in Egara."

"Fantastic," he comments ironically. "That's really going to be useful to us."

"I didn't think I would need it."

Ismael gives her a sidelong glance. "A weapon is like a condom. It's better to have it and not need it than need it and not have it."

Nuria snorts. "Such wisdom compressed in a single sentence."

"Go ahead and laugh. But I feel calmer if I've got Porsiaca with me."

"Porsiaca?" Nuria repeats in surprise. "You named your gun? Don't tell me you're one of those guys who refers to his penis as 'Little Isma'."

The ex-cop raises an eyebrow and looks at her again from the corner of his eye. "No, but if I were, I assure you the word 'little' wouldn't be part of the name."

And then, at the precise instant Nuria's opening her mouth to issue a retort, the streetlights, the Christmas decorations, and the lights inside the minister's building blink out all at once, leaving their surroundings shrouded in complete darkness.

51

In spite of the fact that it makes her want to vomit, Laura watches all the videos the agency has sent her. They're all short clips of what must be much longer videos, lasting hours, perhaps, but it doesn't take much imagination to visualize what had happened during the rest of that night.

Laura buries her face in her hands and weeps disconsolately, for herself, for the girl in the video, and for the way she's lost control of her life. Filled with rage, she thinks of calling the police and reporting what's happened, of taking back control. But as she watches herself in the videos she's aware that no one would call her the victim of a manipulation. She looks completely submissive, a willing participant, never resisting any of the degrading acts those five men perpetrate on her, either separately or as a group, while a sixth films them—possibly the same photographer.

The phone rings again and the man himself asks her, "Did you watch them?"

"You're a fucking son of a bitch," Laura answers through gritted teeth.

"I'll take that as a yes."

"I'm going to report you," Laura warns. "You and all the rest of those pigs. You're all going to end up rotting in jail."

She hears a guffaw at the other end of the line.

"No, little girl. That's not going to happen."

"The fuck it's not. I'm going to—"

He interrupts. "You're not going to do anything. No one will believe you when they see that video. Anyone who sees it will swear you're having the time of your life."

"You drugged me."

"Scopolamine disappears from the body after a few hours, so for the police all you'll be is a young girl who wanted to make a little extra cash by selling herself and then trying to blackmail me to make more. You won't be able to prove anything."

"But that's a lie!!"

The man heaves a weary sigh as if he shouldn't be expected to have to explain these things. "Grow up, Laura," he says as if he's doing her a favor. "In this day and age truth and lies don't mean anything. The only thing that matters is what people think—and they'll think what we want them to think."

"But justice—"

This time his laugh is real. "Justice," he repeats, amusement evident in his voice. "Who do you think it's going to protect? A young girl who had nude photos taken and then showed up at a party full of adult men that she had sex with? Or honest, decent businessmen who are also respected family men?"

"What nude photos?" Laura suspects the answer even as she asks the question.

"Do you still believe that photo session was to create a portfolio for you?" the man asks, sincerely surprised. "Why do you think I never showed them to you?"

It takes Laura a few moments to process all this. She feels like an idiot, and what's worse, ashamed of being so stupid. She was duped like a little girl who's been offered a piece of candy, and she never even suspected a thing until it was too late.

Because, unlike what the Hollywood movies show, not every problem has a solution, the truth doesn't always win out, and in her case it's too late to do anything. She's been fucked, literally and metaphorically, and she sees no way to solve the problem. Laura understands that Félix, though he's a terrible person, is right. Neither the police nor the judicial system are going to condemn any of those men. On the contrary, public opinion will race to label her a whore, a drug addict, a nymphomaniac. The video will reach millions of men who will masturbate while watching how she's being used and it will stay on the Internet forever.

It's not uncommon that when the media publishes news of a rape, part of the public brutally judges the victim, accusing her of inviting the attentions of the rapist by wearing a skimpy skirt or going out alone at night. What will these same people say about her after seeing her not even putting up a fight on this video?

One day, years or decades down the line, she might have a partner who will see the video, a daughter who will see the video, a boss or colleague who will see it . . . and her explanations won't mean a thing. Perhaps they'll act horrified and agree with her, but in their hearts the doubt will always linger. In the hearts of the faceless public but also her father, her mother, her teachers, her friends at school . . .

From the day that video goes public Laura's life will be over, no matter what she says or does, no matter what a judge rules. She doesn't want to go through that . . . but neither does she want to be a blow-up doll again in the hands of depraved men.

Even before she hangs up the phone Laura realizes there's no way out.

52

"Shit," Nuria remarks, seeing the lights go out all up and down the block. "I don't like this one bit, Ismael."

"I don't either. What should we do?"

"I don't know but I don't think we should stay in the car."

"I think we should go take a look," Ismael suggests, taking the gun from his breast pocket.

Nuria agrees. Pulling on her wool hat, she gets out of the car. The frigid night bites at her face like a living being and a cloud of vapor forms in front of her mouth when she breathes. The snow crunches beneath their feet, breaking the phantasmagoric silence that holds court over the night. There's not a soul in the street, not a single car on the road, just the snow falling silently like a lazy rain of tiny white feathers.

Stealthily, they approach the lobby of the building, looking all around them as they walk. When they reach it, though, they find the door locked. The faint yellow glow of an emergency light is the only light that illuminates the entrance into the building. The lights on the intercom are also out and though Nuria presses the button next to *Penthouse Suite,* there's no answering bell nor voice.

"Let's look around the back," suggests Ismael in a low voice, taking a small flashlight from his pocket. Nuria follows in his footsteps, circling the manicured garden by the cobblestone path that runs along the edge of the building.

"There's the service entrance," Nuria says, pointing to a simple metal door partially hidden by shrubbery.

Ismael shines his flashlight at the lock and Nuria realizes something has happened. Something bad. "Fuck, it's open!" she exclaims.

"Worse," says Ismael, squatting and running his hand over the edge of the lock. "Look, it's been forced."

"She's here already," Nuria concludes, throwing a quick glance toward the interior through the partially open door.

"We have to go up," Ismael says resolutely, pulling back the bolt on his H&K to load a bullet into the chamber. "Now."

"Let's go," Nuria agrees, grabbing the doorknob and pushing the door wide open. Ismael steps over the threshold, shining the flashlight he holds over his gun in all directions.

The rear entrance consists of a small anteroom, a service elevator, and a narrow staircase that leads upward, losing itself in the darkness of the upper floors. Nuria uses the flashlight on her mobile to look behind her and into the small nook under the stairway. "No one here," she mutters in a low voice. "Let's go up."

"Follow me," says Ismael. He begins to climb the stairs, aiming his gun and the flashlight in front of him.

The two of them are like a bubble of light in the dark, gloomy service stairway. There are no emergency lights to cast even the faintest illumination.

Nuria feels her head begin to sweat under the woolen cap. With the sleeve of her coat, she wipes away the drops of perspiration that begin to slide down her forehead as she maintains maximum alertness, shining the light on her phone behind her and into every dark corner on the landings.

Very slowly and in absolute silence they ascend one floor after another. Voices of adults and children, the sound of footfalls, and the scraping of chairs against the floor emerge from the doors of the floors as they continue to climb, families preparing their Christmas dinners by candlelight, unaware of what's happening scant meters from their homes.

Nuria jumps when she hears a scream issue from one of the apartments; a young woman, to judge by the voice. It's not until a burst of laughter follows the scream that her breathing returns to normal and her heart begins to beat again.

Ismael continues up the stairs at an unhurried but constant pace, his back to the wall and his flashlight illuminating as much of the space before him as possible. Nuria, focused on covering their backs, almost runs into him when the ex-cop suddenly stops on a landing. "What's up?" she whispers.

Ismael lifts his index finger to point out the golden plaque set into the wall above his head. *PENTHOUSE,* it reads in capital letters. Unlike the lower floors, there's only one door opening off this landing. Ismael sets his hand on the solid wood door and gives it a slight push. "It's locked," he informs her.

Nuria approaches and puts her ear to the door. She can hear people's voices talking calmly. "I think we got here in time," she says. A moment later, she raps on the door with her knuckles.

There's a sudden silence and they can hear footfalls on the other side of the door. "Yes?" a woman's voice says. "Who is it?"

"Police!" Nuria exclaims, perhaps a little too loudly given the circumstances. "We need to speak with the minister," she says, lowering her voice.

"He's having dinner right now."

"It must be the housekeeper," Ismael whispers.

"Tell him I'm Officer Nuria Badal," she presses. "I need to speak to him urgently. It's a matter of life and death."

The woman seems to think this over for a moment, then says, "Just a moment, please."

Ismael's the one who's keeping watch over the stairway now, sweeping it with his flashlight while Nuria waits.

"Hello?" Jordi Soler i Casas's voice comes through the door, which remains closed.

"Minister," Nuria says. "It's Nuria Badal. I need to speak with you."

"You again?" the politician says in an unbelieving tone. "I don't know who you think you are, but coming to my house to disturb me is absolutely unacc—"

"Minister!" she interrupts. "Listen to me. You are in danger."

"What? What are you talking about?"

"The Satanic Assassin," she says. "We believe he's coming for you."

"The Satanic . . . ? Have you lost your mind?"

"No, Jordi," Ismael puts in. "Believe her. You're in danger."

The door finally opens and the face of the minister appears, dazzled by their lights. Behind him is the soft glow of several candelabras, and the voices of a couple of children sound. "Officer Flores?" he asks, disconcerted. "Is that you?"

Wow, he does remember him after all, Nuria thinks.

"I haven't been an officer for a long time," Ismael says. "Almost as many years as you haven't been a superintendent."

"And you two are here together?" he inquires. "What in the name of God is going on here? Can't you see I'm having Christmas dinner with my family?"

"Sir," Nuria says. "You're not safe here. You and your family need to go to a safe place."

"A safe place? Are you joking? This door is reinforced steel and I have a patrol on duty outside the building."

"The patrol is no longer there," Nuria informs him. "And the service door has been forced. We believe the murderer may already be in the building."

"Well, that's even more reason not to go out!"

Nuria shakes her head vehemently. "If there's anything we know about this murderer, it's that he—or she—is terribly methodical and always has everything calculated in advance. He's killed several people in their homes."

"If he's coming for you," Ismael confirms, "It's because he already has a plan to get in . . . In the same way that he planned a way to get rid of the Mossos patrol car and cause a power outage on this street."

"What's going on, darling?" asks a female voice from inside the apartment. "Clotilde is serving dinner."

The minister turns toward the voice. "Just a moment," he says.

"We've got to go," Ismael urges him. "Every second you delay here increases the danger you're in."

"But I can't just leave!" the minister says, waving a hand toward the candlelight behind him. "It's Christmas Eve! My family . . ."

"If you want to protect your family, the best thing you can do is come with us."

"No," he replies. "I'll call Egara and have them send out another patrol."

"It's Christmas and it's snowing, Minister," Ismael says. "They're short of personnel and no doubt the traffic's in such a snarl out there because of the snow"—he points toward the street—"you'll be lucky if someone's free in an hour."

Ignoring the warning of the ex-cop, the minister takes his phone from his pants pocket and, after quickly scrolling through his contacts, chooses a name and presses on it to make the call. Bringing the phone to his ear, he says, "There's no signal." He looks at the screen, confused. "Why is there no signal?"

"They may be using a jammer," ventures Ismael, "to keep you from calling to ask for help."

Nuria takes out her phone and rapidly checks it. "It's true. There's no signal," she confirms worriedly. "We've got to go."

Fear begins to show in the face of the minister, usually so haughty and sure of himself. "But . . . But . . ."

Ismael cuts him off. "There's no time for buts. We've got to go now."

"My family," protests the minister, visibly upset now. "I can't leave them here."

"Do you have a car?"

"A car?" he repeats. "Yes, of course."

"Nuria," Ismael says, taking her by the arm, "you take his family in his car and I'll take the minister to the Plaza España police station in yours."

"Uh . . . yes, of course," Nuria responds to Ismael's unexpected request.

"Just a moment," the minister puts in. "Why are you separating us? I would prefer—"

Without letting him finish his sentence, Ismael interrupts. "It's the safest way for everyone. If the murderer decides to pursue us, do you want your wife and children with you? It will be better for them to spend tonight in a hotel or the house of another family member."

Jordi Soler i Casas's face is a mask of confusion. "I . . . I don't know . . ."

"I do," Ismael says, stepping close to the minister and laying a hand on his shoulder. "Tell your family to come immediately, Minister. We've wasted too much time already."

53

Two minutes later, Nuria's leaving the underground parking lot of the building, driving a white Volvo XC90 belonging to Elisenda Masferrer, the minister's wife who right at this moment is sitting at Nuria's side wearing a low-cut evening dress, more confused than she's ever been in her life.

From the corner of her eye, Nuria observes her regal bearing and impeccable grooming. Not a hair is out of place in spite of having been hurried from her house with no time to get ready. If it had been her in this situation, Nuria thinks fleetingly, her hair would have been wild and uncombed and she'd be wearing worn-out pajamas and pink plush bedroom slippers. The wife of the minister must be ten or fifteen years younger than her husband, she calculates; the typical upper-class elitist woman from a good Barcelona family, brought up to produce upper-class, elitist children with hyphenated names for political climbers and businessmen without a pedigree.

In the back seat, a boy and a girl, eight and ten years of age respectively, dressed as inappropriately as their mother, are keeping a stony silence, unhappy about having missed their Christmas dinner and the opening of the gifts waiting piled up under the Christmas tree.

"Where are we going?" asks the girl crossly.

"I've already told you, to Grandma's house," her mother responds calmly.

"I don't want to go to Grandma's house!" protests her younger brother, crossing his arms over his chest. "And who's she?" he adds, referring to Nuria with calculated disdain.

"She's a police officer, Aleix," Elisenda Masferrer explains, though the sidelong glance she throws Nuria seems to put that assertion into some doubt.

"And where did Papa go?" asks the girl again. "Why isn't he coming with us?"

"Papa had to go resolve an urgent issue, Mireia," her mother responds, turning to look at her daughter. "Tomorrow morning he'll come by to pick us up so we can go home and open the presents."

"But I want to open them now!" Aleix demands. "Grandma is old and boring!"

"Quiet, both of you," Elisenda says in a no-nonsense tone without raising her voice. "If either of you opens his mouth again, you're not getting any Christmas presents at all. Is that clear?"

"Yes, Mama," the two children reply submissively, looking at the floor. Nuria glances at them out of the corner of her eye, surprised at their docility. At that age, she remembers, she would have driven her parents crazy until they gave in and gave her what she wanted.

Driving through the semi-deserted streets blanketed by an ever-thicker layer of snow, Nuria takes Calatrava toward Bonanova Boulevard. Of course the maternal grandmother's house turns out to be in the Sarriá neighborhood, just a few minutes' drive from the minister's apartment. It was only a couple of minutes ago that Nuria had watched Ismael and his passenger depart on their way to police headquarters in Plaza de España, the largest department in the city, where the minister would be able to spend the night safe and protected.

Instinctively Nuria glances in the rearview mirror, making sure no vehicle is following them. The fact that there's practically no one out and about on a night like this is an advantage since it would be almost impossible for someone to follow them without being seen. She'd been afraid during their descent in darkness from the penthouse suite with the whole family in tow—including the housekeeper, who had gone to her own house—that the murderer might have chosen that moment to attack them. The five floors they'd gone down had seemed like an eternity to her, terrified as she was of running into a screaming, knife-wielding psychopath on each landing.

Luckily, none of that had happened. There had been a few stumbles in the darkness but they'd arrived at the underground parking garage without incident. From there, Nuria had emerged onto the avenue, keeping a vigilant eye on both sides of the street like a character in a zombie movie.

If everything goes as planned, she thinks now as she guides the luxury SUV toward Sarriá, *the minister and Ismael will be arriving at the Plaza de España police headquarters within ten minutes and it will all be over.* Her bosses would see that she was right, that the death of Laura seventeen years before and the way that case had been buried had provided the motive and the source of the current rash of killings. *You reap what you sow,* as Grandpa Pepe would say. With a bit of luck the minister would even intercede in her favor and she would be reinstated in her position, maybe even given a promotion in gratitude for her shrewdness in solving the case. Nuria suddenly feels an overwhelming need to call her grandfather and tell him that everything's going to turn out fine for her.

Ten minutes, she tells herself. *Ten minutes and all this will be over.*

Reaching Bonanova Boulevard, Nuria turns onto it. At her side, Elisenda Masferrer says, "We're almost there. Make a left at the third stoplight."

"Okay," Nuria answers.

The woman leans toward her and whispers in her ear. "Everything's going to be okay, right?" Her expensive perfume and haughty expression contrast sharply with the contained anxiety Nuria can hear in her voice.

"Sure, of course," she replies, bolstering her own enthusiasm for the other woman's benefit. "Ismael is a competent officer. They'll be arriving at police headquarters any minute now."

"Can I call my husband now?" Elisenda asks her, holding up the iPhone in her hand.

"Yes, of course," Nuria says. "Call him. Relax."

Elisenda immediately turns on her phone, finds her husband's number in the address book, and quickly presses it. "It's ringing," she confirms, raising the phone to her ear. Nuria can hear the ring tone but there's no answer at the other end of the line. "Come on, Jordi . . . pick up," Elisenda murmurs but a few seconds later the unanswered call ends. The minister's wife turns to Nuria with a frown. "Why isn't he answering?" she asks in a worried tone.

"Did he take his phone with him?" asks Nuria.

"I put it into his pocket myself."

"Maybe it's on silent."

"His smartwatch would notify him, though," persists Elisenda.

"I don't know . . . maybe they're in the General Mitre tunnel and there's no reception," Nuria ventures. "Don't worry, everything will be all right." She takes out her own phone and taps on Ismael Flores's name on the screen. His phone also rings but there's no answer.

Seeing that Nuria hasn't gotten through either, Elisenda shoots her a worried look.

Nuria soothes her. "There could be a thousand reasons they're not answering. Seriously, stop worrying. They're going to be fine."

"We need to call the police," the other woman says and then, realizing the senselessness of what she's just said, adds, "I mean, more police, with weapons, sirens . . . You know what I mean."

"I understand," Nuria says. "As soon as you're safely deposited at your mother's house, I'll take care of it."

Elisenda hesitates for a couple of seconds, then nods and points out a three-story house a hundred meters further down the street. A gray-haired woman wrapped in a mink coat is waiting in the doorway. "There it is," she says. "You can drop us at the door. We'll be fine."

"Great. Could I ask you a favor?" Nuria says.

"What favor?"

"I need your car to get to Plaza de España headquarters so I can pick mine up. I can give your husband the keys."

This time the response is immediate. "Sure, take it. And when you see Jordi, tell him to call me right away."

"No worries," Nuria responds, pulling the Volvo to the curb in front of the family house. "I'll call headquarters right this minute to see if they've arrived yet."

Meanwhile, the two children have jumped out of the car and rushed into the house without stopping to greet their grandmother. Their mother pauses a moment at the open door of the car, looking at Nuria as if unsure whether to thank her or curse her out for turning their Christmas Eve into a nightmare. "Find my husband," she says at last. Slamming the door, she turns, picks her way through the snow covering the sidewalk, and embraces the gray-haired woman under the cover of the recessed doorway.

"You're welcome," Nuria says to the empty passenger seat. She takes out her phone and calls Ismael again. No answer. "What the fuck, Ismael? What's going on?" She realizes she's forgotten to ask Elisenda for her husband's number so she can't make contact with either of them.

Starting the car, she heads for the Plaza de España police headquarters while punching in Susana's number with her free hand. Her friend picks up instantly, sounding tipsy. "Hi Nurieta! Merry Christmas!"

"Susi," Nuria says, her voice tense. "Are you at headquarters?"

"What? No, of course not. What's up?"

"I need an urgent favor from you."

"A favor?" Susi repeats. "Sure, no problem, but . . . what's up? Are you all right?"

Nuria cuts her off. "I'll explain later. Right now I need you to call police headquarters at the Plaza de España and find out if the Minister for Home Affairs has arrived with an ex-cop named Ismael Flores."

There's silence at the other end of the line for a few seconds and then Susana answers. "Are you drunk, Nuria?" she queries. "If this is some kind of joke, I'll tell you right now that—"

"It's not a joke!" Nuria interrupts again. "It's a matter of life or death. Can you call for me?"

"Um . . . sure. But why can't you just call directly?"

"I can't waste time giving explanations to whatever officer answers. Insist that it's urgent and that they should let me know as soon as they arrive, if they haven't already."

"Okay. I'll do it. But you owe me a very detailed explanation of—"

"Tomorrow. Please, call now. And let me know what you find out." Without waiting for a response, Nuria ends the call and focuses on her driving as she crosses the snowy Pedralbes neighborhood as fast as she dares.

Not two minutes later, her phone rings and Susi's name appears on the screen. "What did they say?" Nuria asks, running the red light on the Diagonal and careening onto the avenue without braking.

"They haven't shown up at the Plaza de España headquarters," Susana informs her. "I asked them to call you as soon as they do."

"Thanks."

"Do you need anything else? A Valium, perhaps?"

"No. I need you to call the rest of the headquarters in Barcelona in case they went to a different one."

"Nuria, I'm in the middle of Christmas Eve dinner with my family."

"It's super important, Susana," Nuria begs. "Please."

She hears her friend heave a sigh at the other end of the line. "All right," she says in a resigned tone. "But you owe—"

"Yes, I know," Nuria says. "I owe you yet another favor. But please, make those calls."

"I will."

"Thanks, Susi," she says, punching the end button.

What the fuck is going on here? Nuria thinks as she races past the giant Christmas tree in front of the large department store *El Corte Inglés.* The tree is covered in snow and blinking, multicolored lights. "Where the hell have you gone, Ismael?" she asks aloud. Her brain is spinning in circles.

That's when Nuria remembers that her iPad is in her bag in the back seat of her car. She'd brought it along in case she got bored while they were keeping watch. She pulls the Volvo up onto the sidewalk and slams on the brakes, then opens the *Find My* app on her phone. She asks it to find her Apple tablet and show its location on the map.

In less than a second the map zooms in on a point in the city Nuria can't identify. She has to zoom out to understand that her car is parked in the last place she could ever have imagined.

Right in front of the Tibidabo temple.

Instinctively, Nuria's eyes go to her left and, raising her gaze, she contemplates the ostentatious basilica perched on the summit of Mount Tibidabo. Brightly illuminated by the many lights covering it, it gives the illusion of floating in the air like an immense apparition suspended five hundred meters above the city spread out at its feet.

54

Dismissing the possibility that Ismael and the minister felt a sudden urge to go and say their prayers at the Temple of the Sacred Heart of Jesus, which is the official name of the Tibidabo church, the only thing that occurs to Nuria is either that they might have had to flee there or that someone might have forced them to go to the summit of the mountain. Not being able to contact Ismael or the minister only heightens her suspicions that something has gone catastrophically wrong.

Anguished by the possibility that everything is going to shit, Nuria understands she has no choice other than to make the phone call she really doesn't want to make.

After several rings, a grumpy male voice answers. Nuria swallows and says, "Hello, Inspector."

"Officer Badal?" Sánchez asks incredulously. "Is that you?"

"Yes, it's me. Forgive me for calling your private line."

"I'm right in the middle of my Christmas dinner," he barks at her.

"Yes . . . I'm sorry. But I have to talk to you, it's extremely urgent."

"What's happened?"

"The Satanic Assassin is going after the Minister for Home Affairs," Nuria blurts out. "We got him out of his house in time and I've deposited his family in a safe place, but he was supposed to be going to headquarters at the Plaza de España and instead I've localized the car at the Tibidabo. You need to send reinforcements right away," she adds. "I think something terrible is happening."

After rushing out this brief account of the situation Nuria goes quiet, waiting for Sánchez's response, but all she hears at the other end of the line is his breathing. Finally he says, "Are you on drugs, Officer?"

"What? No, for fuck's sake!" she explodes. "I'm not drunk or high! Listen to me, Inspecto—"

He cuts her off. "No, you listen to me, Officer Badal! My patience with you has reached its limit. Yesterday the minister called the department to let us know that a tall blond officer with green eyes, currently suspended from CID, had interrogated him on the basis of an absurd conspiracy theory."

"What the hell? What a sonofabitch," Nuria mutters, shaking her head, then addresses the inspector again. "I didn't interrogate him, Inspector. I asked for his help on a twenty-year-old case that I believe to be related to the current case. And if I'm correct"—she raises her voice—"right now, he's in grave danger of—"

"That's enough, Officer!" Sánchez interrupts her again. "Go sleep it off or do whatever the fuck you want, but forget about the minister and whatever you think is happening if you don't want to end up in a psychiatric hearing."

"Accuse me of whatever you want, Inspector," Nuria begs, "but please send reinforcements right now to the Tibidabo temple."

"I'm not sending anyone anywhere, Officer Badal," the inspector replies coldly. "I want you at Egara first thing Monday morning, ready to turn in your badge and your sidearm. Understood?"

"But Inspector—"

"I won't say it again, Officer. Good night and . . . merry Christmas." The line goes dead.

"Shit!" Nuria swears, flinging the phone into the passenger seat with all her might. Desperate, she brings her hands to her face, pressing her palms against her eyes. "Fuck!" she yells at the top of her lungs, banging the steering wheel with her fists. "Fuck, fuck, fuck!!" She looks around as if the solution to the problem might be found somewhere in the interior of the Volvo, but all she sees is pale gray leather and walnut paneling, nothing that might be helpful.

Just in case it wasn't clear to her before, she's now received conclusive proof that she's alone. No one and nothing is going to help her. She doesn't even have the faith her mother has to be able to ask her god or some patron saint for help. It's just her.

Nuria tries to calm herself by taking slow deep breaths. *One. Two. Three.* She's almost out of options. Very few remain to her, in fact.

In reality, she realizes at last, there's only one thing she can do.

Putting the car in drive again and bumping brusquely down off the sidewalk, Nuria whips a U-turn. Going against traffic, zigzagging across every lane of the Diagonal at unreasonable speed, she peels onto General Mitre going north, her gaze fixed on the spectral illuminated temple that sits on the summit of Mount Tibidabo.

In spite of the snow that's accumulated on the Collserola range, the sparse traffic and the fact that the SUV she's driving has four-wheel drive allow her to drive at top speed up the winding road that leads to the Tibidabo summit. In barely twenty minutes, she's almost reached the point where her phone localized her iPad.

Glimpsing through the thick snowfall the majestic, illuminated temple on the summit, Nuria lifts her foot from the accelerator. Here, the snow is falling much more heavily and several inches have accumulated on the ground.

There's not a soul in sight, which isn't surprising. Who in their right mind would want to be out there on Christmas Eve with all the snow that's falling? *Not me,* Nuria tells herself with a grimace of resignation.

Slowly, she inches forward on the narrow road until, around a hundred meters ahead, she makes out on the shoulder a vague red blur under a streetlight.

Her car.

She stops the Volvo and turns off the lights, then remains inside the vehicle for a few minutes with the lights off, allowing her eyes to adjust to the darkness, alert for any movement. But there's nothing moving inside or around her second-hand Ford Fiesta.

There's no one there.

She has no gun, not even the extendible nightstick she usually carries in her purse, not even a small container of pepper spray. Truth be told, she wouldn't get very far as a secret agent.

Alighting from the vehicle, she opens the trunk and pokes around a bit, finally finding a tire iron next to the spare tire. It's not the weapon she would have chosen to confront a serial killer but at any rate, she thinks, hefting its weight in her hand, at least it's a metal rod that weighs more than a kilo. With that, a soup spoon, and a comb, John Wick finished off the entire Sinaloa cartel in a half hour.

Holding the tire iron firmly in her hand and crouching low as she creeps along the side of the road, Nuria stealthily makes her way to her car. Actually, with the copious snowfall, they'd have to strain to see her even if she were turning cartwheels, but better safe than sorry.

When she reaches the vehicle, she peeks through the back window and sees that the car is empty. The keys have been left in the ignition.

For a second she's tempted to climb in, turn on the ignition, and drive away, but summoning all the courage she has, she tells herself she hasn't come this far just to wimp out now.

Opening the driver's door to take the keys, she realizes there are no signs of a struggle, no blood or any other indication that something violent has taken place in the interior. This fact calms her and she tries to convince herself that maybe nothing's happened, that for some reason, instead of going to the police station, Ismael and the minister preferred to take refuge from the snow inside the temple just in front of her.

That theory doesn't make much sense, she recognizes. But what has in the last few weeks?

Despite the abundant snowfall, Nuria can make out footprints leading from the Ford Fiesta toward the basilica. As these leave no doubt as to which direction they went in, Nuria wraps her overcoat more tightly around her and follows the trail to the imposing staircase that winds from the base of the building up to the main entrance, twenty meters above her.

Step by step, she ascends the stairs. Halfway up, she stops for a moment and looks around. Squinting her eyes, she can make out the vague silhouette of the Ferris wheel and the roller coaster in the nearby amusement park. Right now it's closed, all the attractions shuttered like everything else around the temple. The faraway lights of Barcelona twinkle five hundred meters below her but everything surrounding them is a sea of darkness over which the Templo Expiatorio del Sagrado Corazón de Jesús looms, its forest of sharp spires scratching the sky.

Lifting her gaze, Nuria contemplates the open-armed Christ figure that crowns the sanctuary's highest spire. "I know I'm not your most faithful client," she murmurs, "but if you could lend me a hand today I'd be seriously grateful."

Following this unorthodox prayer, she continues up the interminable staircase. It's a full minute later that she reaches the level area that extends outward from the main door of the church.

The footprints continue into the building. Following them from the top of the stairs with the help of the yellowish light that reflects off the white stone walls, Nuria arrives at the giant wooden door. It's slightly ajar.

To keep from making the slightest noise, Nuria doesn't touch the door but rather, tiptoes through the aperture into the interior of the basilica. Her eyes take a few seconds to adjust to the gloom mitigated only by a few lit candles at the other end of the nave, next to the altar. In the dim candlelight, she sees Ismael and the minister.

When Nuria finally understands what's happening, her legs buckle under her and she has to lean against the wall to keep from crumpling to the floor.

55

Naked and gagged, his hands and feet bound, the Minister for Home Affairs lies faceup on the black marble altar. He appears to be dead or at least unconscious. Wearing latex gloves and holding a syringe in his hand, Ismael Flores bends over him like a surgeon about to operate.

Nuria feels as dizzy as if she's just gotten off a roller coaster. Confused and disoriented, she tries to make the scene before her fit in some way with what she knew or thought she knew.

The murderer is Ismael? An ex-cop she'd spent the night before with in her car? How can it be possible? Nuria's neurons try to come up with new connections. The only thing that occurs to her is that, for some reason, Ismael Flores is closing the case that had been dismissed by judges and his superior officers seventeen years before in his own way. It makes no sense, but that matters less than everything else right now.

As she watches from the shadows, Ismael thrusts the hypodermic needle into Jordi Soler i Casas's neck and, pressing down on the piston of the syringe, empties the yellowish liquid into the minister's blood stream.

She can't waste time trying to understand what's happening. That will have to wait for later. The only thing she can and must do now is to keep Ismael from committing a new crime.

Tightening her grip on the tire iron, Nuria crouches down behind the wooden pews and begins to make her slow way up the left side of the nave. Ismael has his back to her, totally concentrated on the inert body of the minister.

For a moment Nuria wonders if she should call for backup, claiming some urgent need, but that would mean she'd have to exit the temple again, risking discovery. Besides, no matter how fast they arrived, it would be too late. Jordi Soler i Casas's life is running out quickly . . . that is, if he's even still alive.

Whatever she does, she's on her own.

From where she is, Nuria can see the bulge of Ismael's gun protruding from the back of his pants. If he discovers her approaching at a crouch, it's quite likely things will end badly.

Nuria wedges the tire iron between her teeth to free her hands and begins to crawl in Ismael's direction as stealthily as she can. She only hopes the ex-cop won't turn around just then and see her in that ridiculous posture. If she's going to be shot, she would prefer not to be on all fours with an iron bar in her mouth.

In this fashion she approaches cautiously, coming around the row of wooden pews until she's three meters behind Ismael's back. The bad thing is that there's a sort of railing surrounding the altar, about half a meter high, that she'll have to negotiate to reach him.

At this distance, the light from the candles surrounding the altar illuminates her perfectly. She no longer has darkness to cloak her approach, so she'll have to depend on stealth if she's going to surprise Ismael.

With extreme caution, Nuria rises to her feet, takes the steel bar in her right hand and, approaching the railing, slowly lifts her left foot over it. Just as she's lifting the right one, the sole of her left boot squeaks against the marble floor. For an instant that seems eternal to Nuria, Ismael freezes, as still as a statue. Holding her breath, her right leg still in the air, Nuria stares at the nape of the ex-cop's neck, waiting for his reaction.

Ismael leans over the body of the minister again. For a second she thinks he's going to continue with whatever he was doing but then, unexpectedly, his right hand goes to the butt of his gun and he whirls around at the same time he pulls it from the waistband of his pants.

Luckily, Nuria's good reflexes compensate for the years of experience she lacks, and the second she sees Ismael move she takes two steps forward, closing the distance between them. By the time he's turned around, Nuria's right in front of him, holding the tire iron high above her head.

Ismael's eyes register a flash of surprise and confusion as he recognizes her. Nuria brings the stainless steel bar down against his temple with all the force she can muster. A horrible sound of bones crunching follows the impact and the man crumples to the ground before her like a marionette whose strings have just been cut.

With a long exhale Nuria releases the breath she's been holding. Resting her hands on her knees as if she's just finished running a marathon, she attempts to catch her breath and steady her heart rate.

Ismael lies at her feet, unmoving. She hopes she hasn't killed him. She squats down to take his pulse, putting a couple of fingers against his carotid artery. Luckily, a slow but regular beat pulses against them, reassuring her that he's alive, though he's going to have a mother of a headache.

Nuria takes his gun and sticks it into the pocket of her coat. Then she turns toward the altar, where Jordi Soler i Casas is still lying faceup, apparently unconscious. Removing the gag from his mouth, she unties his hands and feet and slaps his cheek a couple of times to see if he reacts but nothing happens. Not even the tiniest response.

Concerned, Nuria takes his pulse as well, heaving a sigh of relief when she realizes that his heart is still beating, though the rhythm is slow and weak. No doubt what she'd seen Ismael inject into his neck had been some sort of sedative.

For a moment Nuria stands contemplating the scene: Ismael stretched out on the floor, the minister naked on the altar, and a crucified Christ hanging on the wall of the apse serving as an uncomfortable witness.

Outside, the falling snow intensifies its impetus and the wind howls furiously against the stained-glass windows of the temple. Meanwhile, inside the nave, darkness reigns, illuminated only by the flickering flames of the candles around the altar that create a small bubble of yellowish light.

Shaking off the sensation of unreality, Nuria pulls out her phone to dial the emergency number for backup but again, the call fails.

What the hell? She stares at the screen of her phone, disconcerted. Then, glancing at Ismael, Nuria realizes he must have the jammer. That explains why her calls went through when they'd separated and why they don't now that she's close to him again.

Kneeling beside him again, Nuria begins to go through his pockets. A jammer can be the size of a mobile phone, so she knows he could perfectly well be carrying it on him but she finds nothing. Looking around, her gaze falls on the small leather case where Ismael carried the syringes he injected the minister with. But there's nothing there either.

"Where the hell have you hidden it?" she asks the unconscious ex-cop while she searches around the altar for the device. "Shit," she swears after a while, giving up.

For a moment she considers putting the minister into a fireman's carry, taking him to her car, and driving him to the nearest hospital, but a rapid glance at the man is enough to tell her he must weigh a minimum of ninety kilos, most of those no doubt accumulated at opulent dinners he's financed on the taxpayer's dime. Nuria realizes she wouldn't even make it to the door.

The most logical action to take, she concludes, is to get far enough away from the source of the interference that she can make her call. But before she does that, there are a couple of pressing issues she must attend to.

She covers the minister with the altar cloth first. Having narrowly escaped being murdered, it would be a shame for him to die of hypothermia. Next, she uses the same cords Ismael had tied Jordi up with to immobilize the ex-cop. He doesn't look like he'll be waking up anytime soon, but it's best not to take any chances.

Once she's satisfied with the tangle of knots with which she's secured Ismael's wrists and ankles, Nuria prepares to brave the snow once again.

It's then she realizes she's not alone. A solitary silhouette is outlined against the gloom of the main entrance.

"Hello, Nuria," the person greets her regretfully. "I was hoping not to find you here."

56

During the last few weeks, Laura's managed to hide the marks and bruises, both physical and psychological, that she'd sustained that night by wearing pants and long-sleeved tops. So far no one at home or school has noticed them. She hasn't wanted to give explanations to anyone, not even Paula.

But after the photographer's last call her spirits have sunk drastically and she hasn't been able to keep her mother from giving her looks of concern. "Is something wrong, Laura?" she asks now.

Laura simply shakes her head. "No."

"Are you sure?"

"I'm fine," she answers in a tone of voice that clearly belies her words.

"Sure there's nothing you'd like to talk about?"

"No, Mama," she says, internally hoping her mother will keep insisting to the point that she will have no choice but to break down and share her unbearable burden.

"Something's not right with you," her mother says with a sigh, "but I can't help you if you don't tell me what it is."

Laura says nothing this time. The tears are stinging her green eyes, trying desperately to escape, while her sobs rise to her throat like a geyser ready to explode.

I was raped, Mama. The sentence takes shape in her mind and begins to move to her lips just as her mother's cell phone rings.

Pulling it from her pocket, she answers it. "Hello? . . . Are you sure no one else can go?" she asks after a few seconds. "No . . . yes, of course," she says after hearing the answer to her question. "I'll be there in a half hour." She ends the call.

Laura's witnessed this scene with the first syllable of her confession on her partially open lips, but she closes them when her mother sticks her phone back in her pocket.

"I've got to go," she says. "But let's talk more later, okay? You know you can tell me anything."

Laura nods. "Sure, of course."

Her mother plants a kiss on her cheek and sets her hands on Laura's shoulders. "You know . . . you're almost a woman, Laura. Whatever the problem is, I'm sure you'll find a way to resolve it."

Laura nods again but this time says nothing. Her mother's gaze rests on her for a few more moments as if she's about to add something more. Finally she says, "Your father will be home at nine." She glances quickly at her watch. "There are eggs and cheese in the fridge in case I don't make it home in time for dinner."

Laura is mute. The pain has gripped her throat so hard she's incapable of making a single sound. Her mother, however, interprets her silence as acceptance of her words. Turning on her heel, she walks away down the hall.

A few seconds later the door of the apartment opens and closes again with a sharp click and Laura is left alone in the house. She feels as if a dagger has cleaved her chest and it's difficult even to breathe.

A wave of nausea hits her and she runs to the bathroom. No sooner has she lifted the lid of the toilet than the vomit rushes up her throat without any warning. Lowering her head into the toilet, she vomits up the entire contents of her stomach.

When there's nothing left to bring up, Laura sits back on the bathroom floor, exhausted and empty. Empty of life, empty of hope. As empty as if someone had driven a hand down her throat and ripped out her heart by the roots. Empty and with the numbing certainty that she can never go back to who she was before, that the unbearable pain that floods her will never go away.

Her future, her dreams, her hopes have all drowned in the sea of suffering and shame inside her and can never be recovered. Her life is over, plain and simple, and all that's left to her is to accept a future of sorrow and disgrace.

Her eyes alight on the disposable razor that sits forgotten on the edge of the sink. It's something that has never in her life occurred to her but right now it seems like the best solution to her problems. A quick, easy solution that will free her from this terrible pain forever.

Weakened by the convulsions of her recent vomiting, Laura pushes herself up from the floor by holding on to the toilet and picks up the blue razor. It's an easy matter to break the plastic and extract the sharp steel blade. It lies glinting in the palm of her hand.

"To hell with it all," she says, reaching out and turning on the hot water tap in the bathtub.

For the first time in the last several weeks, Laura feels relieved and at peace with herself, convinced that for once in her life she's making the best decision.

Nuria recognizes the raspy voice but it's not until the woman walks down the central aisle of the nave toward her and the light of the candles illuminates her face that she realizes her ears haven't deceived her.

She greets the other woman effusively. "Antonia!" She's confused but at the same time overjoyed to see the chief forensic officer of the CID. "I'm so happy to see you! Did Sánchez ask you to come?"

It's not until Antonia comes a few steps nearer that Nuria sees the gun in her hand. A gun that's aimed directly at her. "What . . . what are you doing?" she asks.

"You shouldn't be here," the forensic officer says, shaking her head sadly.

"I . . . I don't understand, Antonia. Why are you aiming your gun at me? Do you think I—" She turns toward the unconscious minister and realizes the possible misunderstanding. "Oh no, fuck no," she says, pointing at Ismael. "*He's* the one who was about to kill the minister. He's the murderer! I've got nothing to do with it. I came here to stop him!"

"I know," Antonia agrees with a bitter smile. "But he's not the murderer either."

"What? He certainly is! I saw myself how he—"

"I'm the murderer, Nuria." Antonia falls silent, allowing the words to take their full impact in the silence of the nave.

Nuria blinks a half dozen times before she's able to speak. "What . . . what are you talking about?"

"You remind me so much of Laura," adds Antonia, walking to the other side of the altar without taking the gun off Nuria. "If she were still alive, she would look a lot like you."

"Did you . . . know her?"

Antonia gives her a sad smile. "From the day she was born."

The pieces suddenly fall into place in Nuria's dazed brain. "María?" she asks incredulously, taking a step back. "You were . . . her mother?"

"María Martínez died seventeen years ago," Antonia says flatly. "When monsters like him—" she adds, looking at the naked man in front of her covered by the altar cloth, "decided that Laura's life wasn't as important as their perversions or their political careers."

"You . . . ?" Nuria's having trouble putting her thoughts in order. "You killed them?"

Antonia shrugs wearily. "I did what I had to do."

"But you're a cop, Antonia," Nuria says, shaking her head in incredulity. "That's not how we do things. You could have tried to get a new investigation opened. You could have—"

"*You're* going to lecture me about how we should do things by the book?"

Nuria can't deny the irony of Antonia's words. She's right, but even so . . . "There had to be another way," she protests, her tone not entirely convinced. "Another way to resolve it."

Antonia cuts her off. "Who are you trying to kid? You know perfectly well how it went down and how those scumbags cover for each other. There was no other way to exact justice for what they did."

"By skinning and torturing them?"

"They had to know what real pain is. Mine, my husband's, Laura's, the pain of all the other girls whose lives they destroyed . . . I couldn't just kill them, Nuria." She pauses before adding solemnly, "They had to suffer."

"But that's not justice. That's just revenge."

Antonia Grau sets the barrel of her gun against the minister's temple. "Call it what you want," she snorts. "But the fact is that today there are five perverts, one corrupt judge and one venal politician less for us to worry about. The world will be just a little bit better starting now."

Nuria shakes her head. "This isn't the way," she insists. "If everyone ignored the law whenever it suited them, it would be chaos."

"The law?" Antonia's expression is suddenly twisted by rage. "The same law that let five rapists go free just because they had money and influence? I thought that by now you'd know how to distinguish between justice and the law, Nuria."

"You call this exacting justice?" Nuria challenges her, pointing to the man on the altar. "Doesn't this make you even worse than them?"

"I know what I've done and what I've become," the other woman admits. "There's no way back for me and maybe not for him either." She waves a hand at Ismael, who's still unconscious. "But I've been planning this for seventeen years, Nuria. I left my former life behind, my friends, my career, even my name . . . I sacrificed it all to do what others didn't want to do. If this rat hadn't sold himself in exchange for support for his political career, he wouldn't have bribed the judge and the men who raped my daughter would be rotting in jail."

Nuria suddenly understands. "That's why you became a forensic scientist."

"It was the best way to carry out my plan without anyone trying to stop me. After I killed the photographer, after I'd gotten all the information I needed from him, I realized that in the future I needed to be more careful."

"By having access to the evidence and falsifying it," Nuria says, understanding. "That's why nothing made sense."

"It took me a long time and a lot of work to prepare everything." Antonia glances at the minister and adds, "But in the end, it was all so easy I was afraid someone would suspect me."

"Holy fuck. Of course! You were the one who emailed me about Monells and the Sons of Lucifer so I would go and search his basement," Nuria reasons with a frown.

"You were the most logical choice. I needed someone to poke the hornets' nest, and a young, smart officer who was dying to show what she was worth was the best option."

"You manipulated me. You used me," Nuria says.

"Not just you, honey," Antonia says, waving her hand. "All of you."

"You falsified the evidence your team collected," Nuria went on. The pieces were finally all falling into place.

"I had years to collect the DNA and the fingerprints I needed," Antonia admits calmly. "Later, when I became the head of forensics, it was child's play to swap them out during the investigation."

"But . . . how could you get so close? Why weren't the victims wary after the first ones were killed? Didn't they all know each other?"

"That was the ironic part of the affair," Antonia says with a malicious smile. "Since they all wore masks so the victims wouldn't recognize them, they didn't recognize each other either. So they didn't feel threatened because they didn't relate the murders to their own rapes of minors. Getting close to them in the circumstances we needed without making them suspicious was the most complicated part of it all," she admits. "But police credentials can be quite useful for that."

"You made sure to do it in places where there were no cameras or witnesses," Nuria says slowly, "and later you painted the *666* to make us believe that the criminals belonged to a demonic sect."

"The date when Laura died," Antonia explains. "That was quite a convenient coincidence but even so, you realized the truth. Though it sounds odd to say it under these circumstances," she adds, "I'm proud of you."

"And him?" Nuria jerks her head toward the ex-cop on the floor. "Did you manipulate him too?"

"It wasn't necessary. Actually, he was the one who told me what was happening with my case and how unjust it was. He helped me to create Antonia Grau and to succeed all these years. Ismael is a good man."

"A good man who's a party to seven murders."

"I've just told you he didn't kill anyone," Antonia corrects her. "And yes, the right thing to do is to get rid of this vermin so they can't continue to rape little girls and corrupt judges and cops. Do you have any idea how many other girls have been subjected to the same treatment as Laura? Dozens! With their contacts in the exalted circles of society, they were able to get away with whatever they wanted, scot-free. If I hadn't stopped them," she says, "no one else would have done it."

Nuria closes her eyes and takes a deep breath. "You may be right," she admits. Looking at the minister, she adds, "But I can't allow you to kill him." With a rapid movement, she puts her right hand behind her back, pulls Ismael's gun from her waistband, and aims it at the forensic scientist. "It's over, Antonia."

The other woman shakes her head in disappointment. "What are you going to do? Are you willing to shoot me to protect this worm? Do you know that after you went to see him he told Sánchez he wanted you kicked out of the department?"

"Drop the gun, Antonia," Nuria says without answering.

"It's too late for that. If I've come this far, I'm not going to stop now. Minister Jordi Soler i Casas is the last one on my list."

"And I can't just stand by with my arms folded while you kill him. He has a wife and children."

"I'll be doing them a favor," Antonia replies immediately. "And I can tell you, they won't be going hungry."

"Please . . . Antonia. This is insanity. Do you believe . . . do you think Laura or your husband would have wanted you to do this?"

"Don't give me that cheap psychology. You're smarter than that."

Nuria realizes she's not going to win an argument that's been going on for years inside Antonia's head. She has to change her strategy. "And later?" she asks her. "What will happen after you kill him? Will you kill me too and just continue your work in the CID as if nothing's happened?"

"I'll turn myself in," the other woman says to Nuria's surprise. "I'll let you arrest me yourself. I also have sins to expiate."

"What??"

"You heard me. Let me finish this and I'll confess to it all. You'll be a hero."

"I don't want to be a fucking hero. I want you to drop the gun."

Antonia shakes her head sadly. "That's not going to happen, Nuria. It's up to you. Either shoot me now . . . or leave."

"Leave?"

"Go out the door. Come back in a half hour and it will all be over. I'll say you didn't arrive in time."

"Are you kidding? I'm not going to be an accomplice to a murder!"

Antonia Grau shakes her head from one side to the other. "Well . . . in a way, you already are. After all, who showed up tonight at the minister's house and practically dragged him from his home?"

"Fuck!" Nuria exclaims, realizing the trap she's fallen into. "You two made it look like I was helping you!"

Antonia nods. "We didn't plan it that way, but when you showed up at Ismael's house after talking to the minister . . . Well, let's say we simply took advantage of the opportunity. Don't take it personally."

"Fuck you," Nuria says, adding after a second, "And that *is* personal. Drop the gun, Antonia." She steadies the butt of the weapon with the palm of her left hand to improve her aim.

To her surprise, the forensic scientist obeys, leaving her gun on the altar. But then she takes the scalpel from Ismael's kit and, squatting next to him, she begins to cut his bonds.

"Stop!" Nuria orders her. "What are you doing?"

Ignoring her, Antonia Grau pulls the cords off Ismael's wrists and ankles. She pulls his eyelid open to check on how dilated his pupils are. "Ismael, are you okay?" she asks the ex-cop. He opens his eyes just a little.

"Antonia?" he mutters, attempting to sit up. "What . . . what happened?"

"Don't try to get up," Antonia says. "You got a good crack on the head." She runs her hand over his forehead and caresses his cheeks and Nuria sees in the gesture something that goes beyond friendship.

"But . . . what the fuck?" Ismael asks, putting a hand to his temple and bringing it away bloodstained.

"Our dear Nuria has turned out to be more obstinate than we thought she would be," Antonia explains.

Ismael turns and looks at Nuria who is standing in front of them, training her gun on them. On her face is a frown that suggests either determination or doubt. "Jesus fucking Christ, you hit me hard," he protests, holding out his bloodied hand for her to see. "How . . . did you find me?"

"I have superpowers," Nuria says, then continues in a reproachful tone. "You deceived me, Ismael."

"Not well enough, it would appear."

"Have you decided whose side you're on?" Antonia asks Nuria as she gets to her feet. "His"—she throws a sidelong glance at the minister—"or what's right?"

Nuria's breath is agitated and the gun trembles in her hand. "There has to be another way."

"No, there isn't," Antonia answers firmly. "Either he dies . . . or you'll have to shoot both of us."

"Killing him won't bring your daughter back."

"Leaving him alive won't either," she replies. "But at least this way I can be sure that her death and my husband's won't have helped further his political career. Did you know that he was planning to be the next president of the Generalitat?" Seeing Nuria's surprise, she adds, "Do you want someone like that governing eight million people?" She reaches out and takes a glinting scalpel from the leather kit bag.

"Don't do it," Nuria says to her, almost begging.

The CID forensic scientist ignores her and brings the sharp steel blade close to the minister's jugular.

"Drop the scalpel. Please, María . . . I don't want to shoot you."

"You'll have to if you want to stop me." Antonia makes a small incision in the unconscious man's neck. A rivulet of blood begins to flow from the cut.

Tears of desperation gather at the corners of Nuria's eyes. Her heart is pounding in her chest and her knees are weak. Her hands are trembling and the gun they hold weighs a ton. She knows that what she has to do must be done immediately or it will be too late. The bad thing is, she can only do one thing.

Her vision clouded by tears, she squeezes the trigger. She hears a cry. Maybe it's coming from Ismael, maybe Antonia, maybe even herself.

A cry that's drowned out by the noise of the gunshot that echoes through the nave of the temple.

The Funeral

Outside the Sant Gervasi funeral home a wintry sun shines from a cobalt-blue sky, painting the city in vivid, dazzling hues. The gray skies are gone, taking with them the snow accumulated during the abundant snowfall of Christmas Eve, of which only traces survive in the most shadowy streets.

Two days have elapsed since that night, two days that have seemed like two weeks to Nuria. The consequences of that night's events have multiplied like an echo in a deep valley and will continue to do so for a long time, perhaps the rest of her life.

At her side, people unknown to her file past, all of them dressed in black or their Mossos uniforms. Lots of dark glasses are in evidence, murmured words of consolation and gestures expressing sorrow—but not for her. Many questions whispered under people's breath to which no one has the answers.

Scraps of other people's conversations reach Nuria's ears: *how was it possible . . . someone should have realized . . . a tragedy for all concerned.* But Nuria's already disconnected herself from everything going on around her and fortunately, no one approaches her to engage her in a conversation she doesn't want to have. Not even with herself.

All she wants is for the funeral to be over as quickly as possible, for the body to be incinerated so she can go home and be with her cat. To close this chapter of her life so completely she'll never have to think of it again.

Some of the mourners look at her from the corners of their eyes and murmur imperceptibly or not so imperceptibly. She hears a few people say under their breath, *yes, that's her,* but she acts as if she hasn't heard them.

Yes, it's me, she would say to them. *The suspended police officer who ignored all the warnings her superiors gave her and paid no attention to the chain of command or proper protocol. The real reason you're all here today to see a body about to be incinerated in a pine box.*

"Good morning, Officer."

She turns around at the familiar voice to find herself face to face with Sánchez, who's attired in his full-dress uniform with a black ribbon bow in his buttonhole.

"Good morning, Inspector."

"How are you doing?" he inquires, his tone paternal.

"How do you think I'm doing?" she replies curtly, though at this point it doesn't really matter any more.

"I saw that you asked for a transfer to Organized Crime."

"I thought it best."

"No . . . it's not necessary. Your suspension has been lifted and after what you did, Internal Affairs isn't going to touch you."

"Yes, I know. But I still want to go."

Visibly ill at ease, Sánchez runs his tongue over his lips, then lowers his gaze and mutters, "I, uh . . . haven't had the opportunity to tell you before but I'm sorry I didn't pay more attention to your . . . line of investigation."

Nuria fixes her eyes on him for a moment, her expression clearly communicating *it's about time,* but in the end she nods.

"No problem," she lies. "I was the rookie, I disobeyed the rules, and you did what you had to do."

"Yes, of course," he mutters, relieved at having gotten this exchange out of the way. Raising his gaze to the white building from which people continue to stream, faces lowered, he adds, "Who would have thought it, eh? It seems incredible that Antonia managed to fool us all for so long. Christ, seventeen years planning her revenge. Now that's crazy."

"She's a woman who lost everything and nobody paid her any attention. It's not surprising to me that she ended up that way."

Sánchez casts her a curious look. "Are you justifying her?"

"No, but I understand her."

"The system has its defects, like everything else. But to go from that to murdering all those people . . ."

Nuria shrugs. "I suppose."

Just then Superintendent Moncada walks by them, escorted by a small cohort of officers and asslickers of differing standings. Nuria and Sánchez stand at attention and give him a martial salute, raising their hands to the visor of their caps. He makes a lukewarm gesture of recognition as he approaches with a firm stride. "At ease," he murmurs. Looking back at the white building of concrete and glass he's just exited, he adds, "Well, looks like it's all over."

"That's right, Superintendent," Sánchez agrees.

"Though too much time and too many lives were sacrificed in the process."

"We did all we could with what we had to work with."

"Some more than others," Moncada specifies, throwing Nuria a sidelong glance.

Sánchez clears his throat uncomfortably. Weeks ago, Nuria would have said something in defense of her superior officer, downplaying her own merits and transferring them to the CID inspector in a show of modesty. Today, though, she remains silent, her eyes fixed on the superintendent.

"All the counts against you have been dropped," he says to her, "except the charge of kidnapping the minister. But I don't think that will go to trial; all of us were deceived. That said," he adds, fixing a steely gaze on her face, "I want it understood that you are not to take this as an approbation of the methods you used. In future, if you diverge even a millimeter from official police-department standards of behavior, you won't escape the consequences even if you find Kennedy's killer. Is that clear?"

"Absolutely clear," she answers, a hint of insolence in her voice. For a moment Moncada seems to be pondering whether he should say more but in the end, with a brief nod of farewell, he turns around without further comment and continues walking toward his official vehicle.

As Nuria follows him with her gaze she sees among the throng, close to the exit, her friend Susana's coppery mop of hair. "Excuse me, Inspector," she says to Sánchez. "I have to talk to someone."

Without waiting for a response from him she crosses the terrace, pushing her way through the people still streaming out of the building. When Susana sees her coming she puts her hands on her hips and shoots her friend a humorless grin.

"Man, did you ever fuck up big time, Nurieta," she says in her usual dry tone.

"You know me. I like to be the center of attention."

"How are you?" Susi asks, fondly running a hand over her back.

"Oh, just fabulous."

"That bad? Fuck, Nuria. You should be proud. You did what no one else was able to do."

"Yeah, well." Nuria makes a wry face. "The way most people are looking at me it doesn't exactly seem as if they're proud of me."

Susana waves a hand dismissively. "Oh, just ignore them, Nuria. Half of them are idiots and the other half are jealous."

Nuria smiles in spite of herself. The way Susana can make her smile is one of the things she likes best about her friend from the academy. "Should we get out of here?" she suggests. "I'll buy you a couple of beers."

"That's the most sensible thing I've heard you say in a long time." Now Susana's the one to smile at her. "I know a bar five minutes from here where the firemen usually go for breakfast," she says, pointing to a spot in the city laid out at their feet. "It's almost as good as a Chippendales show."

"Well, what are we waiting for?" Nuria jerks her head toward the exit. "If I stay here one second more I'm going to throw up."

Arm in arm like the old friends they are, they cross the terrace toward the parking lot. As they pass the door leading into the funeral home, Susana gives her arm a comforting squeeze, murmuring soberly, "You did what you could. Don't blame yourself for getting there a few minutes too late."

As Nuria turns to look at Susi her eyes fall on the announcement posted next to the entryway: *Funeral service in memory of the Honorable Minister Jordi Soler i Casas.*

"Oh, I don't," she says to her friend.

AUTHOR'S NOTE

Thank you for making it all the way to this page. I hope you enjoyed the book. If you'd like to read another adventure featuring Nuria (if you haven't already, of course), I invite you to read *Redemption.* I'm sure you'll enjoy it as well.

I would also be enormously grateful if you could write a review of *Skin* for Amazon, even a short one. Reviews help so much to encourage other readers to buy the book and make it possible for me to continue publishing new novels. Also, to show my appreciation, if you'll drop me a line at gamboaescritor@gmail.com to let me know you've written a review, I'll email you an extra chapter entitled "Consequences."

I want to stress that this extra chapter isn't necessary to the enjoyment or understanding of my novel, which ends with Nuria's last sentence you just read. "Consequences" is a sort of epilogue in which I outline a possibility of what could have happened that final night in the basilica on Tibidabo mountain. I must emphasize, though, it's just one possible explanation among many of what could have happened. You, as the reader, must decide how this story ends.

That's all for now. Nuria will be back with new cases to solve in the future but for now, if you enjoyed *Skin,* I'm sure you'll like the rest of my novels. If you feel like immersing yourself in a new adventure, you can find all my books at www.gamboabooks.com.

I send you a heartfelt embrace. Thank you for reading my books and I hope to see you again very soon!

@gamboaescritor

ACKNOWLEDGEMENTS

Before I bid you farewell, I'd like to thank my parents, Fernando and Candy, my sister Eva, and all those who helped me and put up with me while I was writing this book. I'd especially like to thank my alpha readers for their insightful suggestions. I'm grateful to Andriy Liventsev for teaching me to fly, to Carlos Manich, Albert Mirabet, and my friends from the Aeroclub Empordá for giving me such a warm welcome, to Montse Pámies for throwing me a life preserver just in time, to Rosina Iglesias for her judicious corrections, and to Ana M. for polishing up the cover design. Above all, I'm thankful to Marta Tonda for her love, efforts, good ideas, and infinite patience with this stubborn, scatterbrained writer.

Without the support of all my friends, the old and the new, the young and the not-so-young, those with their feet on the ground and those with their heads in the clouds, those I know in person and those I know through social media, the left-wing ones, the right-wing ones, the ones I see often and the ones I don't see as often as I'd like, those who live close by and those who live far away, those who buy my books and allow me to continue living my dream as a writer . . . Without all of you, neither this book nor any of my other books would have been possible.

For this I thank you all from the bottom of my heart. Without your affection and generosity none of this would be happening.

I love you all.

Fernando Gamboa